OLD
TESTAMENT
PARALLELS

Praise for *Old Testament Parallels: Laws and Stories from the Ancient Near East*

"...definitely 'user friendly.' With its modest price and decent illustrations, it should be of good service to the current generation of students."
—J. Andrew Dearman, *Biblical Archaeologist*

"...for the undergraduate student and for those engaged in private study this is strongly recommended as an excellent introduction to the mysteries of ancient accounts of creation, law codes, Ugaritic epics, and the like."
—Richard Coggins, *Theological Book Review*

"...accessible to the lay person because the texts are not literal renderings or reproductions of the originals, but rather paraphrases of the ancient documents." —*Biblical Archaeologist*

"...the best asset of this book, in my opinion, is the wide variety of texts collected in it. From creation stories to legal codes, from treaties to historical annals, from instructions to hymns, from love songs to visions, *Old Testament Parallels* offers a comparison to virtually every major type of literature found in the Bible. Moreover, this book has included a number of texts which are not readily found elsewhere. In comparison to the two-volume paperback set of Pritchard's *Ancient Near Eastern Texts*—the standard anthology, and the predominant alternative to *Old Testament Parallels*—it contains the following additional texts: the Atrahasis Story, the Hymn to Atum, the Treaty of Ramesses II and Hattusilis III, the Story of Balaam, the Yavne-Yam Inscription, the Story of Kirta, the Lament of Ur, the Mari Prophecies, the Sufferer and the Soul, and the Farmer and the Courts. These are all very important texts and shed substantial light on the interpretation of the Hebrew Bible. Their inclusion in *Old Testament Parallels* increases the value of this book." —Ronald A. Simkins, Creighton University

"...this collection should serve students well in basic courses who often find more text-oriented translations formidable and the price of other available collections excessive." —W. Lee Humphreys, *Religious Studies Review*

"...important, convenient, essential." —*Library Journal*

"...Matthews and Benjamin have done a fine job in sorting through what's accessible, picking out the best, modernizing the translations and explaining their relevance to Scripture.... there may be more scholarly apparatuses on the market, but for preparing a sermon or adult Bible there's little comparable." —*Religious Book Club News*

More praise for *Old Testament Parallels: Laws and Stories from the Ancient Near East* at the end of this book

OLD TESTAMENT PARALLELS

LAWS AND STORIES FROM THE ANCIENT NEAR EAST

Fully Revised and Expanded Third Edition

VICTOR H. MATTHEWS
and
DON C. BENJAMIN

Paulist Press
New York/Mahwah, New Jersey

Cover design by Lynn Else
Cover art is taken from a fresco in one of the thirty-nine large rock-cut tombs at Beni-Hasan, about fifteen miles south of el-Minya, Egypt, on the east bank of the Nile. It depicts thirty-seven members of the household of Absha arriving from Syria-Palestine in the sixteenth nome or province of southern Egypt during the reign of Pharaoh Senworsret II (1897–1878 BCE). See P. E. Newberry, Beni Hasan (London, 1893): 1: pls 28, 30-31; D. Kessler, *Studien zur altagyptische Kultur* 14 (1987), 147–66.

Library of Congress Cataloging-in-Publication Data

Matthews, Victor Harold.
    Old Testament parallels : laws and stories from the ancient Near East / Victor H. Matthews and Don C. Benjamin.—Fully rev. and expanded 3rd ed.
        p. cm.
    Includes bibliographical references and index.
    ISBN 0-8091-4435-2 (alk. paper)
    1. Bible. O.T.—Extra-canonical parallels. 2. Middle Eastern literature—Relation to the Old Testament. 3. Law, Ancient—Sources. 4. Law—MiddleEast—Sources. 5. Bible. O.T.—History of contemporary events—Sources. 6. Bible. O.T.—Antiquities. 7. Middle Eastern literature—Translations into English. 8. Middle East—History—To 622—Sources. I. Benjamin, Don C. II. Title.
    BS1180.M42 2006
    221.9'5—dc22

                                                                    2006004233

Published by Paulist Press
997 Macarthur Boulevard
Mahwah, New Jersey 07430

www.paulistpress.com

Printed and bound in the
United States of America

For our parents

E. Harold and Lillie Mae Matthews
Don C. and Edith B. Benjamin

Whose love gave us life

CONTENTS

Leviticus, Numbers, Deuteronomy

Joshua, Judges

Ruth

Samuel, Kings

Chronicles, Ezra, Nehemiah

Job, Ecclesiastes

Psalms, Lamentations

Proverbs, Sirach, Wisdom

Song of Songs

Isaiah, Jeremiah, Ezekiel, Daniel, Hosea, Amos

FOREWORD

The Bible belongs to a wonderful family of traditions from Mesopotamia, Asia Minor, Syria-Palestine and Egypt. *Old Testament Parallels: Laws and Stories from the Ancient Near East* offers an exciting guide to this larger world of law-making and storytelling. Introductions, illustrations, and a variety of reference tools clearly explain the relationship between each ancient Near Eastern tradition and the Bible.

James Henry Breasted (1865–1935) pioneered the art of introducing the Bible in its ancient literary context. By 1907 he had published five volumes of *Ancient Texts*, including translations of virtually every document recovered to that time. In 1919, he founded the Oriental Institute at the University of Chicago, whose museum today houses an impressive collection of ancient Near Eastern artifacts.

Ancient Near Eastern Texts Relating to the Old Testament (1950–1969) by James B. Pritchard (1909–1997) became the standard critical edition of parallels to the Bible. Pritchard's book provides scholarly and rigorously text-oriented translations of ancient Near Eastern traditions.

In 1990, Simon B. Parker (Boston University) launched the *Writings from the Ancient World*. The series offers new, scholarly, critical editions of ancient Near Eastern texts that date from the beginning of Sumerian civilization to the age of Alexander. Fourteen separate volumes had been published by 2006.

In 2003 William W. Hallo (Yale University) and K. Lawson Younger, Jr. (Trinity International University–Divinity School) published *The Context of Scripture* in three volumes. This work also offers new scholarly, critical editions of Ancient Near Eastern texts.

Translations in critical editions like *Ancient Near Eastern Texts Relating to the Old Testament* that often sacrifice clarity to create word-pictures in English of ancient language texts have now given way to a more readable English in critical editions like *Writings from the Ancient World* and *The Context of Scripture*. Nonetheless, all three remain reference works for the library; they are too large and too expensive for the classroom.

From time to time, small and less expensive anthologies have ap-
peared. There is a two-volume paperback set of *Ancient Near Eastern
Texts Relating to the Old Testament* called *The Ancient Near East: An Anthology of Texts and Pictures* (1965), for example, as well as D. Winton
Thomas's *Documents from Old Testament Times* (1958), Michael David
Coogan's *Stories from Ancient Canaan* (1978), Klaas A. D. Smelik's *Writings from Ancient Israel* (1991), and Bill T. Arnold and Bryan E. Beyer's
Readings from the Ancient Near East (2002). Not all these resources are
still in print and some are too selective.

Students and teachers in that important first course in biblical
studies today need a readable, affordable, and portable anthology of
ancient Near Eastern laws and stories. Therefore, in 1991, we published
Old Testament Parallels: Laws and Stories from the Ancient Near East. We were
delighted with how well this first edition served so many students and
teachers. As a continuing service to them, and with an interest in further increasing the use of Old Testament parallels in introductory
courses, we prepared a revised and enlarged edition in 1997. Now, this
third edition has been completely revised in light of the ongoing and
exciting discoveries of more and more ancient Near Eastern texts. It in-
cludes selections that have not yet appeared in *Writings from the Ancient
World* and which were not included in *COS.* Many of the parallels from
the first two editions have been expanded to provide more coverage of
larger texts like the "Stories of Gilgamesh" and the "Code of Hammurabi." New parallels have been added, enlarging the anthology to
sixty-three selections.

A. Leo Oppenheim, who died in 1974, was an outstanding philolo-
gist and Assyriologist, whose major contribution to scholarship was
made in his work as editor of the *Chicago Assyrian Dictionary.* He, however, described himself as a cultural anthropologist. By expanding his
interest from text to society, Oppenheim did much to make
Mesopotamian texts as understandable in the modern world as those of
Greece and Rome. In the introduction to *Ancient Mesopotamia: Portrait
of a Dead Civilization* (1977:3), to which Oppenheim devoted more than
twenty years of his life, he wrote:

> ... translated texts tend to speak more of the translator than of
> their original message. It is not too difficult to render texts
> written in a dead language as literally as possible and to sug-
> gest to the outsider, through the use of quaint and stilted lo-
> cutions, the alleged awkwardness and archaism of a remote
> period. Those who know the original language retranslate
> anyhow, consciously or unconsciously, in order to understand
> it. It is nearly impossible to render any but the simplest Akka-

dian text in a modern language with a satisfactory approxima-
tion to the original in content, style, or connotation. A step
nearer to the realization of the legitimate desire to make the
texts "speak for themselves" would bring us, perhaps, an anthology of Akkadian texts, with a critical discussion of the literary, stylistic, and emotional setting of each translated piece.

In preparing *Old Testament Parallels* we tried to meet Oppenheim's
challenge. Our readings are not literal or visual text-oriented translations, but responsible, reader-oriented paraphrases. The English vocabulary and idiom emphasizes the relationship between the ancient Near
Eastern tradition and the Bible. *Old Testament Parallels* imitates com-
monly used patterns of speech today. It avoids awkwardness and ar-
chaism. It avoids as much sexism and racism as possible. There was
certainly sexism and racism in the world of the Bible, and where it
clearly appears in a tradition, we have left it in our readings. Where the
traditions are indifferent to questions of gender and race, we have tried
not to introduce it. Hopefully, *Old Testament Parallels* offers teachers and
students readings that are dynamically equivalent to the way in which
they were heard, felt, and understood in their own worlds.

Clearly, *Old Testament Parallels* reflects our scholarship in recon-
structing the world from which these traditions come, and our own understanding of the style and meaning of each ancient Near Eastern
tradition. Nonetheless, we have tried to keep our reconstructions con-
sistent with scholarly work currently in progress, and to avoid as much
eccentricity as possible, by making our readings reflect the consensus of
scholars working in the field.

Ancient Near Eastern texts are artifacts recovered by archaeologists.
Some, like those from the Dead Sea Valley between Jordan and Israel
today and the city of Ebla in Syria, dramatically change the way we reconstruct the world of the Bible. Establishing the correct connection between
related biblical and non-biblical traditions is never easy. Simple solutions
are generally misleading solutions. The ancient Near Eastern traditions we
have selected are a limited, not an exhaustive, window on both their own
culture and the cultures of their neighbors. We want to take advantage of
all that these traditions have to offer to understand Israel and its culture,
but not to blur the distinction between all the cultures in the world of the
Bible, or to imply that the cultures of Mesopotamia, Asia Minor, Syria-
Palestine, and Egypt have value only insofar as they relate to the Bible. We
also do not wish to destroy the distinctiveness of the Bible by overstating
its similarity with the traditions of surrounding cultures.

Parallels between ancient Near Eastern traditions and the Bible can
be based on their similarities as well as their contrasts. Some biblical and

non-biblical traditions are parallels because they belong to the same genre. The Enuma Elish stories and the stories of the heavens and the earth (Gen 1:1—2:4a), for example, both belong to the genre of creation story. Other biblical and non-biblical traditions are parallel because they deal with the same topic. The Annals of Mesha and the Annals of Joram (2 Kgs 3:1–27), for example, both deal with a war between Israel and Moab that took place around 830 BCE. Some of the most important parallels come from the Middle Bronze period (2000–1550 BCE) and the Late Bronze period (1550–1200 BCE). For the books of Genesis, Psalms, and Daniel, there are parallels from Ugarit in Syria, whose liturgical traditions reflect Late Bronze period ritual and worship. For the books of Exodus, Leviticus, Numbers, and Deuteronomy, there are parallels from Babylon in Iraq, whose legal library from the Middle Bronze period illustrates judicial systems like the gate-court as well as a wide variety of legal precedents. For the books of Joshua and Judges, there are parallels from el-Amarna in Egypt, whose diplomatic communiqués document the unstable social and political conditions in Syria-Palestine during the Late Bronze period. For the books of Samuel-Kings and the prophetic traditions in the Bible, there are parallels from Mari in Syria, whose government and diplomatic traditions illustrate social institutions like covenant, judge, and prophet during the Middle Bronze period.

We offer our readers four tools for using parallels in the classroom. First, the table of contents and the body of the book itself arrange parallels according to the canonical order of the Old Testament found in most English translations of the Bible. Within each of these chapters, the parallels are arranged chronologically. Second, some of the most significant biblical parallels are identified in the introductions to our readings, and we have placed biblical references on the same line of text where they apply. Third, a chart at the end of the book identifies six ways in which laws and stories from the ancient Near East can parallel the Bible. There are genre parallels, vocabulary parallels, motif parallels, social institution parallels, plot parallels, and parallels in historical events. Fourth, a subject index allows readers to identify personal names, place names, and general topics that they may wish to examine in the volume.

Introductions to each parallel describe the physical appearance of the text, the language in which it was written, where it was recovered, and where it is preserved today. There is also a summary of its contents. Short explanations of those portions of parallels that we have not included are given to provide continuity, and to encourage students to read the entire text on their own. To that end, a selective bibliography directs readers to both the original, critical editions of the parallels as well as to the most recent scholarship on these texts. There are also out-lines of the history of Mesopotamia, Egypt, and Israel, which we hope will be helpful.

Spellings for the names of rulers of Egypt and Mesopotamia and the dates of their reigns follow John Baines and Jaromir Malek, *Atlas of Ancient Egypt* (Facts on File Publications) and Michael Roaf, *Cultural Atlas of Mesopotamia and the Ancient Near East* (Facts on File Publications). Dates for archaeological periods follow Amihai Mazar, *Archaeology of the Land of the Bible, 10,000–586 B.C.E.* (Doubleday). Spelling for the names of rulers of Israel and Judah and the dates of their reigns follow John H. Hayes and J. Maxwell Miller, eds., *Israelite and Judaean History* (Westminster/John Knox).

Colleagues who took time from their own work to help us with ours are a blessing. We have been helped repeatedly by fellow scholars who looked at drafts of *Old Testament Parallels* and made valuable suggestions in their reviews of the previous editions. We want to thank them all, especially Robert J. Miller (Juniata College), Robert Gnuse (Loyola University, New Orleans), J. Andrew Dearman (Austin Presbyterian Theological Seminary), Ronald A. Simkins (Creighton University), Bernard F. Batto (DePauw University), Diedre Dempsey (Marquette University), and Thomas M. Bolin (St Norbert College).

Frank S. Frick (Albion College) paid us a truly gracious compliment by his use of our *Old Testament Parallels* in *A Journey through the Hebrew Scriptures* (Wadsworth). Here, and in our own introductions to the Old Testament—Victor H. Matthews and James C. Moyer's *The Old Testament: Text and Context* (Hendrickson) and Don C. Benjamin's *The Old Testament Story: An Introduction* (Fortress)—teachers will find creative models of how to teach comparative material in an introductory course.

In addition, we would like to thank Lawrence Boadt and the other members of the editorial staff at Paulist Press for their good work on this third revised and enlarged edition.

Victor H. Matthews, Ph.D.
Don C. Benjamin, Ph.D.

GENESIS

HYMN TO PTAH

The origins of a hymn to Ptah date to the Nineteenth Dynasty (1307–1196 BCE) at Memphis. One version, copied on a slab of black granite known as the Shabaka Stela, was recovered by British archaeologists in Egypt in the 1830s. It is written in an archaic style similar to the Pyramid Texts and is preserved today in the British Museum in London (BM 498).

The Hymn to Ptah contrasts how the divine patron of Memphis creates with the way Atum, the divine patron of Heliopolis, creates. The people of Heliopolis imagined Atum to be an artist who physically worked creation into existence. The people of Memphis imagined Ptah to be a judge who pondered and then simply called creation into existence.

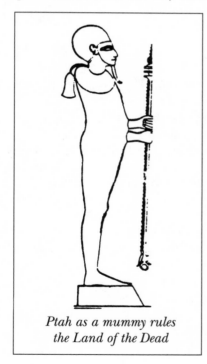

Ptah as a mummy rules the Land of the Dead

When the Hymn to Ptah opens, the Ennead, which is a divine assembly of the nine most important divine patrons of Egypt, is ratifying the unification of northern and southern Egypt as a single state. Horus, the divine patron of northern Egypt, assumes the responsibilities of Seth, the divine patron of southern Egypt, and becomes the absolute ruler of Egypt. The hymn goes on to tell how Horus also assumes

Anubis (left) and Horus (right) touch a priest with the Ankh *symbol to raise him from the dead*

the responsibilities of Ptah to become the absolute ruler of the Ennead.

The dramatic quality of the Hymn to Ptah parallels the stories of the creation of the heavens and the earth (Gen 1:1—2:4). The hymn also authorizes the existing political order of Egypt in which Ptah is the ruler of the Ennead and Memphis is Egypt's sacred center and the capital of a newly united state.

Geb the earth commanded the Ennead to assemble.
    Geb ended war by dividing Egypt between Horus and Seth.

Horus would rule over Lower Egypt in the north;
    Seth would rule over Upper Egypt in the south.

Geb gave the Land of Horus rule over the Land of Seth,
    Horus united Upper and Lower Egypt.

Osiris marched through the Gates of Death,
    Horus conquered the Land of the Living.

Isis proposed an end to wars
    Nephthys decreed that Horus and Seth become brothers.

The *ka*-souls of all the living were created in the image of Ptah.
    All formed in his heart and by his tongue.   (Gen 1:3)

Horus was created from the thoughts of Ptah's heart.
    Thoth was formed by the words of Ptah's tongue.

Ptah's heart guides the Ennead,
    Ptah's tongue directs humans.

Ptah creates the Ennead with only teeth and lips,
    Atum must create with hands and semen.

Atum had to masturbate to bring forth the Ennead.
    Ptah had only to speak, and the Ennead came forth.

Ptah called the names of Shu and Tefnut,
    The wind and the rain gave birth to the Ennead.

Sight, hearing, and smell all report to the heart,
    the heart is the source of all knowledge.

The tongue speaks only what the heart thinks.
    Atum thinks only the thoughts of Ptah.

The Ennead speaks only the words of Ptah....

Ptah's heart grants the gift of life,
    Ptah's tongue organizes life's abundance.

Ptah's heart grants life to the steady heart,
    Ptah's tongue orders death for fools.   (Prov 20:9; 22:11)

Ptah is the creator of all crafts and trades.
    Ptah is the ruler of the Ennead.

Ptah gave birth to the Ennead and all things.
    Ptah is the ruler of the Ennead.

Having done all these things,
    Ptah rested and was content with his work.   (Gen 1:31—2:1)

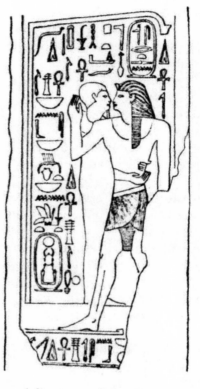

A limestone relief at Karnak
depicts Senworset I (1971–1926 BCE)
honoring Ptah

HYMN TO ATUM

A hymn to Atum was recovered by British archaeologists in 1865 and is preserved today in the British Museum in London (Papyrus Bremner-Rhind, BM 10188). The hymn is written in hieroglyphics on sheets of papyrus. Although the origins of the hymn date to the Old Kingdom (2575–2134 BCE) at Heliopolis in the Cairo of today, this is a version as it was sung after 400 BCE at Thebes in Luxor, which is some three hundred miles south of Cairo.

Egyptians honored Atum as the creator and ruler who accompanied them, their pharaoh, and their land from birth to death to rebirth. Heliopolis, Hermopolis, and Edfu were the most important sanctuaries of Atum. Each day Atum sailed his boat along the clear blue body of Nut, the sky, toward the sunset horizon that was her mouth. At dusk, Nut consumed the sun.

Shu (the wind) supports the body of Nut (the sky) over the body of Geb (the earth)

Throughout the night, Atum navigated his boat through Nut's body, where the serpent Apophis waited to destroy him at the opening of her womb on the sunrise horizon. Like midwives, priests chanted a hymn to Atum as they waited for their creator to be reborn. Having completed the voyage, the reborn Atum would re-create Egypt, thus allowing a new day to dawn and the pharaoh to continue to rule the land in peace. The sun, or its glyph, which was a circle with a dot in the center, the cone-shaped benben stone, the pyramid, the obelisk, the sun temple, and the scarab beetle were among the artistic and architectural symbols connected with Atum. Beetles lay their eggs in balls of manure and roll them from place to place while the eggs gestate. Egyptians described Atum as a beetle rolling the sun from dusk to dawn. Every living thing emerged from the sun, just as the newly hatched beetles emerged from the ball of manure.

Parallels to the Hymn to Atum appear in the stories of the creation of the heavens and the earth (Gen 1:1—2:4).

Columns xxvi:21–xxvii:5

At the moment of creation, Atum spoke:
    I alone am the creator.   (Exod 3:13–14)
When I came into being, all life began to develop.
    When the almighty speaks, all else comes to life.
There were no heavens and no earth,   (Gen 1:2)
    There was no dry land and there were no reptiles in the land....

When I first began to create,
    When I alone was planning and designing many creatures,
I had not sneezed Shu the wind,
    I had not spat Tefnut the rain,
    There was not a single living creature.
I planned many living creatures;
    All were in my heart, and their children and their grandchildren.

xxvii:1–15

Then I copulated with my own fist.
    I masturbated with my own hand.   (Gen 2:6–7)
    I ejaculated into my own mouth.

I sneezed to create Shu the wind,
    I spat to create Tefnut the rain.
Old Man Nun the sea reared them;
    Eye the Overseer looked after them....

In the beginning, I was alone,
    Then, there were three more.
I dawned over the land of Egypt.
    Shu the wind and Tefnut the rain played on Nun the sea....

With tears from my Eye, I wept and human beings appeared....
    I created the reptiles and their companions.
Shu and Tefnut gave birth to Geb the earth and Nut the sky.
    Geb and Nut gave birth to Osiris and Isis, to Seth and Nephthys.
Osiris and Isis gave birth to Horus.
    One was born right after another.
    These nine [Greek: *ennead*] gave birth to all the multitude of the land.

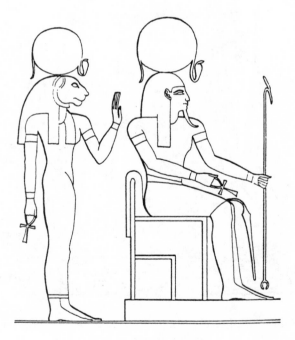

Tefnut standing behind Atum

A Babylonian seal depicting Marduk harnessing the Mushashu dragon and the waters of chaos

ENUMA ELISH STORIES

In 1849, Austin Henry Layard, a collector of artifacts for the British Museum, recovered a copy of the Enuma Elish Stories from Ashur at Koujunjik, Iraq. Ashurbanipal (668–627 BCE) had the copy made for his library at Nineveh. It was written on baked clay tablets about thirty inches high in the Akkadian language using cuneiform script. A duplicate copy of Tablet V was recovered from Harran on the Euphrates River in Turkey.

Hammurabi (1792–1750 BCE) made Babylon the most important city in Mesopotamia and enthroned Marduk, Babylon's divine patron, as head of the divine assembly. Thus the previously minor city-state of Babylon would grow in importance in both historical and epic terms for the next twelve hundred years. Around 1100 BCE the Enuma Elish Stories were compiled from different Sumerian and Amorite stories to celebrate the military and political accomplishments of Babylon and its rulers.

Parallels to the Enuma Elish Stories appear in the book of Genesis as well as in the books of Exodus and Psalms (Pss 8, 19, 50, 104). Originally, the Hebrews celebrated Yahweh as the Divine Warrior whose armies, commanded by Moses, armed with a staff and the east wind, confront the armies of Egypt commanded by Pharaoh (Exod 15:1–10). However, once the Hebrews began to understand Yahweh as both the deliverer who liberates the Hebrews from slavery and the creator who calls the cosmos from chaos, the cosmological language common in ancient Near Eastern creation stories began to appear in the Bible.

I:1–9

The crisis episode in the Enuma Elish Stories describes the birth of the divine assembly in Mesopotamia out of a chaos of water *and darkness through the merging of Apsu, divine patron of fresh water, with Tiamat, divine patron of salt water. The divine assembly in the Enuma Elish Stories is composed of the* **annunaki**, *who are the divine elders, and the* **iggigi**, *who are the divine warriors. Its membership is comparable to that of the village assembly or the city assembly on the human plane that is made up of the "old men," who are elders, and the "young men," who are warriors.*

When on high, no heaven had been named,
    When no earth had been called,
    When there were no divine elders...
When there was nothing...   (Gen 1:1–2)
    Nothing but...
Godfather Apsu and Mummu-Tiamat, Godmother of All Living,
    Two bodies of water becoming one,
When no reed hut was erected,
    When no marsh land was drained,
When there were no divine warriors,
    When no names had been called,
    When no tasks had been assigned.

I:10–19

Then, from these two waters, Lahmu and Lahamu were created,
    Their names were called.
Before they increased in wisdom and stature,
    Anshar and Kishar were created, surpassing their ancestors.
Before they increased in wisdom and in stature,
    Anu was created.
Anu, who was Kishar's heir, rivaling his ancestors,
    Anu, who was Anshar's first born, equaling his ancestors.
Anu made Nudimmud-Ea in his image;
    Surpassing his ancestors,
Ea, increasing in wisdom,
    Increasing in understanding, increasing in strength.

I:20

Ea, greater than Anshar, his ancestor,
    Unmatched among the divine warriors, his ancestors....

⬚ *Eventually, the increasing noise of the divine warriors disturbs Apsu and he makes plans to destroy them. Apsu is prevented from carrying out his plans by Ea, who kills his father and takes his crown. After the assassination of Apsu, another generation of divine creatures is born. The pride of this new generation is Marduk.*

I:79–103

Then, in the Palace of Fates,
    Then, in the Temple of Destinies,
The most ingenious divine warrior was created,
    The ablest and the wisest of the divine warriors...
Then, in the Heart of Apsu,
    Then, in the sacred Heart of Apsu,
    Marduk was created.
Ea was his father,
    Damkina, his mother.
Divine the breasts from which he nursed,
    Nurtured with care and endowed with glory.
Marduk's posture was erect,
    His glance inspiring.
Marduk's stride was commanding,
    His stature venerable.
His grandfather Anu's face beamed,
    His heart filled with pride.
He declared Marduk flawless,
    His father endowed him with a double share of divinity.
Marduk surpassed all of his ancestors....

His head was incredible,
    It was incomprehensible, inconceivable in power.
No sight escaped his eyes,
    No sound evaded his ears.
Marduk's voice was strong,
    His words blazed like fire.
Marduk's hearing was acute,
    His eyesight sharp.
Marduk's body was unsurpassed.
    His physique was powerful.
Marduk's arms and legs were huge,
    His height dwarfed all others.

"My son," Anu sang,
    "My beloved son.
My son, who is the sun.
    He is the sun in the sky."
Clothed with the powers of ten members of the divine assembly,
    Marduk excelled them all....

≋❨ *To become the ruler of the divine assembly, Ea had murdered Apsu. Tiamat then marries Kingu, who encourages her to revolt against the divine assembly for having allowed Ea to kill her first husband. To help her overthrow the divine assembly, Tiamat creates a team of ferocious and monstrous creatures.*

I:132–40

Tiamat, the mother of all,
    Gave birth to peerless and hideous monsters.
Serpents with fangs for teeth,
    Snakes with venom for blood.
Terrifying dragons,
    Filled with divine power.
To see them was to die,
    Once prepared to strike, they were invincible.

≋❨ *Ea and the divine assembly are afraid to face Tiamat and these monsters. At this point, Marduk, divine patron of the storm and divine patron of Babylon, steps forward to serve as the divine warrior for the assembly. For his service, however, he exacts a price.*

III:116–22

"If I agree to serve as your deliverer,
    If I am successful in defeating Tiamat,
    If I save your lives,
You must proclaim me the ruler of the divine assembly.
    My word, not yours, must determine all things.
What I create must not change,
    What I command must not be revoked or altered."

≋ *Rejoicing that it has found a warrior to challenge Tiamat, the divine assembly agrees.*

IV:3–32, 35–41

"You will be the most honored member of this divine assembly...
    Your word shall not be challenged,
    Your word shall speak for all.
Your decree shall not be altered.
    Your word shall build up and tear down.   (Eccl 3:3; Jer 1:10)
Your word shall be the law,
    Your command shall be obeyed.
No member of this assembly shall surpass you . . . .

With joy the divine assembly shouted,
    "Marduk is Lord!"
They endowed him with scepter, throne, and staff.
    They presented him with invincible weapons.
The divine assembly proclaimed,
    "We swear allegiance to you as our Lord . . . .
Go and destroy Tiamat,
    Scatter her blood to the winds!" . . .

Marduk builds himself a bow,
    Designs it to his special needs.
He feathers the arrows,
    Ties the string.
Marduk raises his war club,
    Grasps it in his right hand.
Bow and quiver hang at Marduk's side,
    Lightning he carries as a shield.
Marduk dons a blazing aura of fire as his armor;
    He weaves a net big enough to trap Tiamat.

≋ *Tiamat, disguised as a sea serpent (Ps 74:13-14), taunts Marduk as he comes to the field of battle. Taunting before battle was a common part of military strategy in the ancient Near East (2 Sam 5:6-8; 1 Kgs 20:1-11; 2 Kgs 18:19-37). Marduk responds to her taunt with a retort.*

Assyrian (right) watches Marduk (left) battle a winged monster

IV:77–86

"Why do you raise your hand
    against the divine assembly,   (1 Sam 17:8–10)
  Acting like its ruler? You deceive yourself;
  You cannot disown your own children.
You cannot designate Kingu to be its divine warrior;
  You cannot give Kingu the power of Anu, who rules the sky.
You rebel against Anshar, who commands the dusk;
  You are in revolt against the divine assembly.
Of your armor, I am not afraid,
  Of these monsters, I am not frightened.
I challenge you to come forward alone.   (2 Sam 2:18–23)
  I dare you to duel with me, one on one."

🕮 *When Tiamat hears the retort of Marduk, she is infuriated. Out of her mind with anger, she rushes away from the other monsters and attacks Marduk by herself. As she opens her mouth to roar, Marduk inflates her with storm winds to incapacitate her. Then, he pierces her with an arrow of lightning (Isa 41:2). After his victory, Marduk processes triumphantly to the sacred mountain to*

*be proclaimed ruler of the divine assembly. Here he builds his
temple on the grave of Apsu, and names the temple for his slain
ancestor. Marduk transforms Tiamat's monsters into statues,
which he erects outside the gate of the temple to remind all who
enter of his victory (Tablet V Sultantepe).*

V:71–76

Marduk rounded up the monsters of Tiamat;
    He brought them as trophies before the divine assembly.
Marduk trapped the eleven of Tiamat in his net.
    He shattered their weapons, and shackled their feet.
Marduk transformed these serpents into statues.
    He mounted them at the gate of his temple, the Apsu.
"Let these statues be a memorial," he proclaimed,
    "So that this revolt may never be forgotten."

*Having remodeled his temple with the spoils of war, Marduk
then uses Tiamat's body to build a new world. He crushes her
skull with his war club and scatters her blood into the wind. He
splits her body in two. He uses half to make the heavens, and
half to make the earth. The body of Tiamat seals out the
primeval waters at the mountains on the horizons (Gen 1:6-7).
Marduk assigns the members of the divine assembly as constellations to mark each season of the year. He assigns the moon to
guard the night and to mark the month with its phases (Gen
1:15-16). Finally, Marduk and Ea discuss a plan to create humans.*

VI:5–8, 23–42

I will knead blood and bone into a savage,   (Gen 2:7)
    "Aborigine" will be its name.
These aborigines will do the divine assembly's work.   (Gen 1:26–27)
    These savages will set the divine assembly free.

*Ea suggests that Marduk sacrifice one of Tiamat's allies to create
the savage. So, Marduk convenes the divine assembly to discuss
Ea's proposal.*

Who planned Tiamat's uprising?
      Who advised her to rebel?
Hand over the instigator of this revolt,
      Punish the conspirator for his crimes, and live in peace.
The divine assembly testified: "Kingu planned the uprising.
      Kingu advised Tiamat to rebel."

> So the divine assembly binds Kingu and Ea slits his throat. They use his blood to fashion the aborigines, whom Ea assigns to do the divine assembly's work in the new world.

Marduk arrested Kingu, his rival,
      Ea arraigned him.
Marduk convicted him of conspiracy;
      Ea executed him by cutting his throat.
Ea formed the aborigines from Kingu's blood,   (Gen 2:7–15)
      Marduk set the aborigines to work.
Ea emancipated the divine assembly,
      The wise created the aborigines.
Marduk put the aborigines to work;
      He set the divine assembly free.
      What an incredible accomplishment!
Nudimmud-Ea created.
      Marduk masterfully designed.
Ea the wise created the aborigines,
      Marduk ordered them to work for the divine assembly.

A Sumerian seal depicting Marduk battling a winged dragon

What an incomprehensible task,
   What a work of art.
The aborigine designed by Marduk,
   The savage executed by Nudimmud.
Marduk the king split the divine elders into groups,
   Appointed Anu their supervisor.
Marduk stationed three hundred elders in the heavens above,
   Three hundred more on the earth below.

 *To celebrate Marduk's coronation, the divine assembly builds the Esagila, a great ziggurat in the city of Babylon. The culmination of the cosmology of creation occurs when the divine assembly transfers their divine titles to Marduk and establishes the Babylonian celebration of the* akitu *New Year, when the Enuma Elish Stories were to be retold in honor of Marduk, the divine warrior who delivered Babylon from its enemies.*

VI:48–75, 95–114

The divine elders spoke to Marduk their Lord:

"You have freed us,
   Therefore, we must glorify you.
We will construct a House for Marduk known throughout the land
   Its precincts will be our place of comfort and rest."

Ziggurat of Ur

Pleased with these words, Marduk glowed with pleasure.
  He instructed the divine assembly:

"Build my House in Babylon!
  Lay its bricks,
  Make it a sacred place."

For a year the divine elders labored,
  And in the second year they completed the Esagila,
A ziggurat higher than the House of Ea,
  A House of Marduk to rival the House of Ea...   (1 Kgs 8:12–13)

Enthroned within his House, Marduk convened the divine assembly,
  The divine elders and warriors were all seated at his banquet table.
Marduk proclaimed, "This, too, is your House.
  Take your seats and enjoy its pleasures!"

The divine assembly bowed down and affirmed Marduk's power.
  They uttered a sacred oath of allegiance, cursing all violators.

They solemnized their vow touching water and oil to their throats.
  They officially crowned Marduk as "Ruler of the Divine Assembly."
Anshar the Ancient spoke for all, saying,
  "When Marduk speaks, the divine assembly will take heed and
      obey.
  His word shall be the law in the heavens and on the earth....
      He shall rule unrivalled.
  He shall shepherd the Black-Headed People,
      His own creation shall retell the story of his triumph to all gen-
      erations.

Marduk shall ensure that the divine assembly receives due offerings,
      That their sanctuaries are maintained,
      And that the sweet smell of incense fills their sacred chambers.

He shall order the earth to be a mirror of what transpires in heaven,
  Its people serving him and caring for the needs of the divine
      assembly.

STORIES OF GILGAMESH

In 1872, George E. Smith announced that during 1848-49 Austin
Henry Layard had recovered baked clay tablets about six inches
high from Nineveh in Iraq. They contained a version of the Stories of Gilgamesh, the origins of which date to the Early Bronze
period (3300-2300 BCE). This version was popular during the reign
of Ashurbanipal (668-627 BCE), Great King of Assyria. The stories
were written in Akkadian cuneiform, with about three hundred
lines covering ten to twelve tablets, which are preserved today in
the British Museum. Because the tablets from Nineveh are damaged and incomplete, portions of the stories below have been
taken from an older Babylonian version from the Middle Bronze
period (2000-1550 BCE).

   The stories of Adam and Eve (Gen 2:4—4:2) and the flood stories (Gen 6:1—11:26) are parallel to the Stories of Gilgamesh.
Enkidu is parallel to Adam, Utnapishtim to Noah, and Dilmun,
the land at the mouth of the rivers, to Eden.

HARIMTU SHAMHAT AND ENKIDU

When the Stories of Gilgamesh open, Gilgamesh rules Uruk as a
tyrant, so the divine assembly creates Enkidu to be his companion. The assembly hopes that Enkidu will take Gilgamesh on dar-
ing adventures and keep him from using his energy to oppress
the people of Uruk. At first Enkidu has little interest in Gilgamesh and prefers to run with wild animals. Therefore, the divine assembly dispatches the Wise Woman [Akkadian: harimtu
shamhat] who teaches Enkidu how to be human.

A Sumerian seal depicting Gilgamesh (left) with other heroes and beasts

Tablet I, col. iii:49–51

The hunter and the Wise Woman took up positions,
    For two days they waited by the watering hole.
Finally, the wild beasts came to drink,
    The animals came to splash in the water.

col iv:2–7

Enkidu, like a creature from the hills, came with them,
    Grazing with the gazelles,
Watering with the wild beasts,
    Splashing in the water with the animals.
The Wise Woman saw this creature primeval,
    This savage from deep within the treeless plains.

col iv:15–21

The Wise Woman bared her breasts,
    Enkidu took hold of her body.
She was not bashful,
    She welcomed his passion.
She spread her clothes on the ground,
    Enkidu had intercourse with her on them.
She treated this savage like a man.
    Enkidu made love with her.
For six days and seven nights Enkidu took her,
    Every day and every night he had intercourse with the woman.

col iv:22–29, 33–45

Having satisfied himself with the Wise Woman,
    Enkidu turned to rejoin the animals.
Seeing him, the gazelles ran off,
    The beasts of the steppe shied away from him.
Enkidu felt weak, his body was paralyzed,
    His knees locked when the beasts began to run.
Enkidu became weak, unable to run as before,
    But his mind was filled with a new wisdom....   (Gen 3:5)

Finally, the Wise Woman said: "Now you are wise, Enkidu,
    Now you have become like us.
Why do you run with the wild animals?
    Why do you run through the plains?
Let me lead you to Uruk, the city of great markets,
    Come with me to the sanctuary of Anu and Ishtar
    To the place where Gilgamesh rules."

OB Version Tablet II, col ii:31–35

She took some of her own clothes and dressed Enkidu,   (Gen 3:7, 21)
    Then she dressed herself.
The wise woman took his hand and led him like a child.
    They walked to the corral, where the herders gathered to stare.

*A Babylonian seal depicting Gilgamesh (left) wrestling with Enkidu
while their divine patron (right) watches*

col iii:1–25

Enkidu knew only how to nurse . . .
　　To breast-feed like a wild animal.
When they placed beer and bread before him,
　　He turned away, he sniffed, and he stared.
Enkidu did not know how to eat bread.
　　No one had taught him how to drink beer.
Then the woman said: "Eat the bread, Enkidu; it is the staff of life.
　　Drink the beer; it is the gift of the land."

Enkidu ate bread until he was full.
　　He drank beer from seven jars.
He became cheerful and playful.
　　His heart rejoiced and his face glowed.
He bathed and oiled his body,
　　He combed his hair.
Enkidu became human.

GILGAMESH AND DEATH

⧉ *Following a wrestling match in the streets of Uruk, Gilgamesh and Enkidu become fast friends. For adventure, they plan to kill the Guardian Humbaba and cut down a sacred cedar. However, Enkidu begins to consider the danger in which they are placing themselves and talks with Gilgamesh about the possibility of dying.*

Tablet III, col iii: 96–115

One day Gilgamesh said to Enkidu,

"Fierce Humbaba lives in the Cedar Forest.
　　Let us kill him and thus deliver our land from evil . . . ."

Enkidu said to Gilgamesh:

"When I ran with animals, I learned that the Cedar Forest has no end.
　　No one goes there.
Humbaba's roar is like a flood,
　　His mouth is fire, and his breath is death.
Why do you want to do this?
　　No one can kill Humbaba the destroyer."

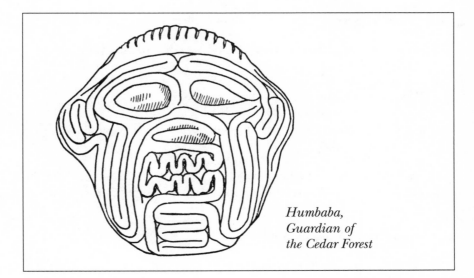

Humbaba,
Guardian of
the Cedar Forest

OB Version: Tablet III, col. iv:138–48

Nonetheless, Gilgamesh insisted:

"Who can climb to heaven and become immortal?
    Only the members of the divine assembly live forever.
The days of humans are numbered;   (Job 14:5)
    Human deeds are like a breath of wind.   (Job 7:16)
Here you stand afraid of death.
    What about your mighty arm? I will stand in front of you.
Encourage me, saying: 'Fear nothing!'
    If I die, I will at least have made a name for myself."

The divine assembly sentences Enkidu to death for killing Humbaba and cutting down a sacred cedar. The prolonged death of Enkidu sets Gilgamesh on a quest for immortality.

GILGAMESH AND SIDURI THE BREWER

Along the way to Dilmun, the land at the mouth of the rivers, Gilgamesh encounters Siduri, a woman who brews beer, with whom he discusses his quest for immortality.

Tablet X, col. ii:1–14

Gilgamesh told Siduri, a woman who brews beer, his story:

"My friend . . . Enkidu . . .
    Was overtaken by the fate of all mortals.
For six days and seven nights I wept for him
    Until maggots crawled out of his nose.   (Job 24:20; Isa 51:8)
Then I became afraid.
    Fearing death, I roamed the steppe . . . .
The friend I loved has become clay. . . .   (Job 34:15; Ps 22:29)
    Shall I not also lie down like him, never to rise again?"

OB Version: Tablet X, col. iii:6–13

⌔ *At first, Siduri tells Gilgamesh that the members of the divine assembly keep immortality for themselves. She tries to convince Gilgamesh to forget his quest and go home to enjoy life as a mortal.*

Siduri gave Gilgamesh this advice:

"Let your belly be full,
    Make merry day and night.
Turn each day into a feast of rejoicing,   (Eccl 3:12–13)
    Dance and play day and night.
Put on fresh garments,
    Wash your hair and body in water.
Play with your children,
    Take pleasure in your wife."

Assyrian Version: Tablet X, col. ii:21–31

⌔ *But Gilgamesh remains adamant about continuing his quest, so Siduri teaches Gilgamesh how to cross the Sea of Death and reach Dilmun safely.*

Siduri went on:

"From the beginning of time, no one has crossed the Sea of Death,
    No one, but Shamash, the divine patron of the sun . . . .
Even if you, Gilgamesh, do cross the sea
    What will you do when you come to the Sea of Death?

If it is possible, cross with Urshanabi the boatman,
    Who has the Stone Charms.
If not, then return home."

GILGAMESH AND UTNAPISHTIM

*Gilgamesh follows Siduri's instructions to find Urshanabi. Inad-
vertently Gilgamesh destroys the Stone Charms that the boatman
uses to navigate, so he cuts sixty poles to steer the boat across the
Sea of Death. At Dilmun, Gilgamesh asks Utnapishtim how he
and his wife became immortal. The story that Utnapishtim tells
describes how the divine assembly tried to destroy all mortals
with a flood. When Utnapishtim and his wife survive in an ark,
the divine assembly changes them into immortals and lets them
live in Dilmun, so that its decree ordering the destruction of all
mortals could, at least technically, be fulfilled.*

Tablet XI, col. i:7–40

"Tell me, Utnapishtim, how did you and your wife become immortal,
    How did you join the divine assembly?"

"Well, Gilgamesh, let me tell you the story of a divine conspiracy,
    Of a divine plot to exterminate humanity. . . .
Godfather Anu, Enlil, and Ninurta convened the divine assembly,
    Which decided to flood the earth. . . .
Ea, divine patron of fresh water, opposed Enlil.
    Ea repeated Enlil's plan aloud outside the reed walls of my house.

"'Listen to me, wall,' Ea whispered,
    'You reed mat, pay attention to me.
Inhabitant of Shuruppak, son of Ubar-Tutu,
    Pull down your house! Build a barge!
Abandon all your possessions,
    Save your life.
Take specimens of every living thing on board.   (Gen 6:19—7:9)
    Make the ark square with a roof like the dome of the heavens.'"

"I told Ea that I would obey,
    But I asked: 'What shall I tell the people of Shuruppak?'

Say: 'Enlil, the divine patron of Shuruppak, is angry with me.
   I can not remain in the land of Enlil,
   So I must move to the coast where Ea is lord....'"

col. ii:58–94

"I built the hulls of the ark one-hundred seventy-five feet high,
   And the decks one-hundred seventy-five feet wide.
I constructed a top deck and six lower decks;
   I used nine bulkheads to separate the hull
      into compartments.   (Gen 6:15–16)
Then I caulked the ark with bitumen
   And asphalt thinned with oil.   (Gen 6:14)
I fed my workers with bulls, sheep, beer, oil and wine,
   As if it were festival time.
So the ark was completed in seven days....
I loaded all my gold and silver up the gangplanks into the ark,
   I boarded my household, my animals, wild beasts, and craftspeople.
Finally, at the precise moment set by Shamash, I boarded the ark,
   I battened down the hatch as the storm came in sight,
      and I turned the ark over to Puzur-Amurri the boatman."

col. iii:96–144

"At dawn...the horizons turned black with clouds,
   Adad, divine patron of thunder, roared.
Shullat and Hanish, the divine messengers, flew before the wind....

"Nergal, divine patron of the dead, unlocked the fountain of the deep.
   Ninurta, son of Enlil, opened the dikes.   (Gen 7:11–12)
The divine assembly strafed the earth with lightning,   (Isa 30:14)
   Adad turned the day into night; the land was smashed like a pot.
One person could not see the other,
   The downpour hid one from another.
The flood ran the divine elders into the heavens,
   It frightened the divine assembly like stray dogs against city walls.
Ishtar, divine patron of love and war, shrieked,
   She cried out like a woman in labor....   (Isa 42:14; Mic 4:9)
'How could I kill my own people?
   How could I conspire against those to whom I gave birth?
Their bodies float on the sea, swollen like schools of dead fish.'
   The divine elders sat humbled and wept...."

For six days and seven nights the winds blew.
    On the seventh day, the storm subsided and the sea grew quiet.
I felt the stillness.
    All humanity had become clay....   (Gen 7:23–24)

"I opened the hatch, sunlight fell on my face.
    I bowed my face to the deck and wept....
The ark ran aground on Mt. Nisir....   (Gen 8:3–4)
    It remained grounded for six days."

col. iv:145–98

"On day seven, I released a dove which flew away, but returned.
    There was no place for it to rest.
I released a swallow, which flew away, but it also returned.
    There was no place for it to rest.
I released a raven, which saw that the flood had subsided.
        It ate, circled, and flew away.   (Gen 8:6–12)

"Then, I released all the creatures,   (Gen 8:17–19)
    Which scattered to the four winds.
I prepared an altar there on the mountaintop.   (Gen 8:20)
    I set out my sacred vessels;
    I kindled a sacred fire of reed, cedar, and myrtle.
The divine assembly smelled the aroma,   (Gen 8:21–22)
    They swarmed like flies around the sacrifice.
Ishtar arrived and removed her necklace of lapis-lazuli, saying:
    'By my necklace, I swear, I shall never forget these days.
Let every member of the divine assembly enjoy this meal,
    But let Enlil eat no sacrifice which mortals prepare.
Enlil thoughtlessly created a flood;
    He drowned the mortals who feed the divine assembly.'
But, when Enlil did arrive and saw the ark, he was furious.
    'Have mortals escaped? Every one was to be destroyed!'
Ninurta convened the divine assembly.
    He indicted crafty Ea for revealing Enlil's plan....

"Ea responded: "How could you bring on a flood?
    Is it not better to punish sinners, rather than destroy them?
Instead of a flood to control the population,
    Send a lion, send a wolf, and send a plague..."

"But Ea testified: 'I did not tell Utnapishtim of Enlil's plan,
    I did not warn him of the impending doom.
The Wise One dreamed alone.
    He discovered our divine conspiracy for himself.'

"Enlil boarded the ark, and told me and my wife to kneel.
    He laid his hands on our heads and announced:
'Utnapishtim and his wife have been mortal, now they are immortal.
    They shall live far away at the mouth of the rivers.'
So, the divine assembly settled us at the mouth of the rivers.

"This concludes our story.
    Now how can you convince the assembly to make you immortal?"

GILGAMESH AND THE SNAKE

Tablet XI, col. vi:258–307

As Gilgamesh and Urshanabi prepared to cast off,
    the wife of Utnapishtim said to the Faraway One:
"Gilgamesh has worked and slaved to come here.
    What can you give him to take back to his land?"
When she spoke, Gilgamesh poled his boat back to shore.
    Utnapishtim said to Gilgamesh: "I will tell you a divine secret.
There is a plant like the buckthorn...
    It will prick your hands like a bramble.
If you can find the plant,
    You will find the secret of immortality."

No sooner had Gilgamesh heard the words of Utnapishtim
    Than he poled his boat toward the well cap that fills the sea.
He tied heavy stones to his feet.
    They pulled him down to the bottom where he saw the plant.
Gilgamesh pulled up the plant;
    It pricked his hand;
He cut the heavy stones from his feet,
    And the sea cast him up upon its shore.
Gilgamesh said to Urshanabi: "This is the miraculous plant.
    This is the plant that restores life.
I will take this miraculous plant to Uruk, the city of sheep,
    An old man will eat it to test its properties...."

Gilgamesh holding a cub

He will become: 'Old Man Now Young Again.'
    I will eat it myself, and regain my youth."

After fifty miles Gilgamesh and Urshanabi stopped to eat.
    After seventy-five miles they dropped anchor for the night.
Gilgamesh saw a spring whose water was cool.
    He went to bathe in the water.
A snake smelled the fragrance of the plant.
    It came up from the water,

And carried off the plant.
     As it returned to the water, the snake shed its skin.
Gilgamesh sat down and wept,
     Tears ran down his face.
"...for whom have my hands toiled,
     For whom has my heart pounded?
I have nothing to show for my work.
     I have worked for this snake...

     Let us finish our journey on foot, leave the boat on the shore..."

When Gilgamesh and Urshanabi arrived at Uruk,
     Gilgamesh said: "Let us climb the walls of Uruk.
Let us marvel at their magnificent foundations,
     Let us be grateful for their fired brickwork.
Let us remember the seven sages who founded Uruk.
     Let us enjoy this great city with its orchards and pastures,
     Rich with clay quarries and blessed by the House of Ishtar."

STORIES OF ATRAHASIS

Copies of the Stories of Atrahasis in the Babylonian and Assyrian dialects of Akkadian, written in cuneiform, have been recovered by archaeologists in Mesopotamia and Syria-Palestine. These tablets are preserved today in the British Museum in London, the Archaeological Museum in Istanbul, and the Musee de'Art et d'Histoire in Geneva.

   The Stories of Atrahasis begin in a world populated only by divine warriors [Akkadian: iggigi] and divine elders [Akkadian: anunnaki]. When the divine warriors revolt and refuse to do all the work necessary to keep the world running, Ea-Enki negotiates a settlement with them. Workers [Akkadian: lullu] will be created to take care of the world and dredge its canals. The elders ratify the settlement and assign Nintu-Mami to carry out the

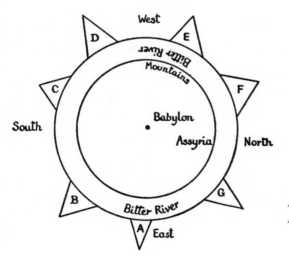

Map of the world of
Babylon, 2000 BCE

project. The workers revolt and refuse to do their work. The divine assembly tries to force them back to work with epidemics and famines. Finally, the decision is made to destroy them all with a flood.

Parallels between the Stories of Atrahasis and the Bible include the stories of the creation of the heavens and the earth (Gen 1:1—2:4) and the flood stories (Gen 6:1—11:26).

I:192–95

"Summon Nintu, the divine midwife!
    Let her create workers to labor for the divine assembly."
So, the divine assembly summoned Nintu-Mami.
    They asked the wise woman, "Will you midwife the *lullu?*"
Create workers to labor for us.
    Let the *lullu* bear the yoke,
Let them work for Enlil,
    Let them labor for the divine assembly."

Three different episodes in the Stories of Atrahasis describe the creation of the lullu. One compares Ea-Enki with a woman who bathes three times during her menstrual cycle: first when the new moon appears, then seven days later, and finally fourteen days later when the moon is full. Intercourse is described as the mixing of the clay of Ea-Enki with the blood of We-ila, another member of the divine assembly. During pregnancy, Nintu-Mami massages Ea-Enki's uterus, just as a potter would shape a vessel, until the lullu are born.

Blessing on a small clay charm of Pazazu worn by women in labor

I:200–230

Nintu said to the divine assembly: "I cannot do Ea-Enki's work.
    Only Ea-Enki has the power to create.
    Let him give me clay to create."
Ea-Enki spoke: "I will bathe to mark my time...
    At the new moon, the seventh day, and the full moon, I will wash.
Let the divine assembly sacrifice We-ila.
    Let them bathe in his blood.
Let Nintu thin my clay with his blood.   (Jer 18:2–6)
    Let Nintu mix clay with blood, human with divine.
Let the drum mark off the days,
    Count down the time.
Let divine blood give these workers life,
    Let the spirit within allow them to live."
The divine assembly agreed.
    The divine elders consented.

At the new moon, the seventh day, the full moon, Ea-Enki bathed.
    The divine assembly sacrificed We-ila the wise....
Nintu thinned the clay with his blood.
    The drum marked off the days... and counted down the time.
We-ila's blood gave the workers life,
    The life in the clay allowed them to live.

➱ *In a second episode, Nintu-Mami creates the* lullu *by thinning
clay with the saliva of the divine elders and the divine warriors.*

I:233–40

The divine assembly gave Nintu-Mami moisture to thin the clay.
    She wet it with saliva from the divine elders and warriors.
Nintu-Mami sang: "Praise to you who gave me this task,
    Praise to you who sacrificed We-ila to help me complete my work.
I have created workers to labor for the divine warriors....
    I have loosened your yoke, I have set you free."
The divine assembly heard the hymn that Nintu-Mami sang.
    The divine assembly kissed her feet.   (Ps 2:12)
"Yesterday, we called you 'Mami.'
    Today, you are 'Mother of the Divine Assembly.'"   (Gen 3:20)

 A third episode describes Ea-Enki having intercourse with Nintu-Mami, while she sings. Nintu-Mami conceives seven sets of fraternal twins: seven males and seven females. Her midwives help Nintu-Mami mount the birth stool and prepare the room for her delivery.

I:250–59; K 3399+3934:8–18

Ea-Enki and Nintu-Mami entered their birthing room,
    She summoned her midwives, he worked her clay.   (Gen 2:7)
She sang the sacred song;
    He prayed a prayer for life.
When Nintu-Mami finished singing,
    She pulled off fourteen pieces of clay.
The clay was laid in parallel rows of seven;
    A birthing stool was placed between them . . . .
The midwives shaped seven males
    Nintu-Mami's seven helpers shaped seven females from the clay.

Leave the birthing stool in place for seven days,   (Exod 1:16)
    Honor Nintu-Mami, the wise, for seven days.
Let the midwife sing for joy in the labor room,   (Gen 35:17; 1 Sam 4:20)
    Let the mother cry out when her child is born . . . .

I:277–302

The midwives helped Nintu-Mami mount the birth stool . . .
    She counted ten months to determine her date.
The tenth month came;
    Nintu-Mami went into labor.
With a face beaming with joy,
    The midwife put on her cap.
    She donned her apron.
    She began to pray.
    She scattered the flour around the birth stool.
On the birth stool, Nintu-Mami sang: "I have created life.
    Let the midwife rejoice when a mother gives birth.
Erect the birth stool for nine days,
    Honor Nintu-Mami and her midwife . . . .
Praise Nintu-Mami,
    Praise her midwife, Kesh.

Let husband and wife lie together in their wedding room.
    Let them do what Ishtar commands...."

🏳 *Soon the quickly growing number of workers begins to disturb
the members of the divine assembly, and Enlil tries to control
them with a plague.*

I:355–60

In less than twelve hundred years...there were more and more workers,
    The workers continued to multiply.
The land bellowed like a bull,
    The uproar disturbed the divine assembly.
When Enlil heard the noise, he complained:
    "I cannot stand this uproar, I cannot sleep....
Send plagues upon the land...."

*Pazazu, divine patron of the winds
of illness and death*

≋ *Atrahasis prays to Ea-Enki for help and Ea-Enki teaches him how to end the plague.*

I:376–83

"Command messengers to proclaim,
    Tell them to shout throughout the land:
'Do not feed the members of the divine assembly,
    Do not pray to their wives.'
Go to the gate of the House of Namtar.
    Place your finest bread on the threshold.
This gift of grain will please Namtar.
    Your gift will shame him into withdrawing his hand."

≋ *Atrahasis persuades the elders to follow Ea-Enki's advice. They renovate the House of Namtar, the divine patron of fate. They place offerings at Namtar's gate and he stops the plague. Over the next six years, Enlil tries other means of controlling the workers with drought and a famine. Each time, Atrahasis appeals to Ea-Enki, who advises the workers to stop feeding the members of the divine assembly. Each time, the strategy works and the workers survive and continue to multiply.*

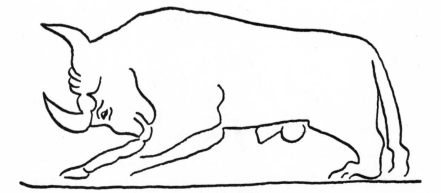

Bull relief at Enink

II.i:7–20

"I cannot stand this human uproar,
      I cannot sleep!
Reduce their food supply.
      Let plants become scarce.
Adad! Withhold the rain!   (1 Kgs 17:1)
      Do not allow springs to rise from the deep.
Winds! Blow the earth dry!
      Clouds! Gather, but do not rain.   (Isa 5:6)
Let harvests be reduced.   (Hos 2:9)
      Let Nisaba, divine patron of grain, reduce their harvests.
Let the joy of the harvest be gone...."

iv:11–14

After three years...every worker's face was drawn with hunger.
      Every worker's face looked like the crust on fermenting beer.
      Every worker lived on the brink of death....

K3399+3934: S.vi:7–12

After five years daughters watch their mothers go into the houses alone;
      ...while their own mothers lock them out of the house.
Daughters stare while their mothers are sold as slaves.
      Mothers stare while their daughters are sold as slaves.
After six years daughters are cooked and eaten.
      Sons are served as food.

◄▤ *Every effort of the divine assembly to control the workers is blocked by Ea-Enki. Therefore, the divine assembly decides that only a flood will get the workers back into line. They order Ea-Enki to take an oath not to advise Atrahasis on how to save the workers. Nonetheless, Atrahasis falls asleep in the House of Ea-Enki, who sits behind his screen woven from reeds, talking to himself about the decision of the divine assembly. Atrahasis thinks the voice of his divine patron is a dream (1 Sam 3:3-4).*

III.i:18–48

"If I were you—my woven lattice,
      —my braided reed screen— I would pay close attention.

I would pull down my house,
    I would build a barge.
I would abandon all my possessions
    ... to save my life....

Place a roof over the barge,
    Cover it as Apsu, the heavens, covers the earth.
Do not let the sun see inside,
    Enclose it completely.
Make the joints strong,
    Caulk the timbers with pitch.   (Gen 6:14)
I will gather flocks of birds for you
    ... and schools of fish."
Then, Ea-Enki filled the water clock,
    Set the time for the flood on the seventh night.   (Gen 7:4–10)

Atrahasis addressed the elders at his gate:
    "My divine patron and yours are angry with one another.
Ea-Enki and Enlil are at odds,
    So I must leave this place.
Since I worship Ea-Enki,
    I am a partner in this conflict.
I can no longer live here,
    I can no longer dwell in the land of Enlil."

> *After explaining his decision, Atrahasis begins to build a barge. When it is finished, he fills it with all sorts of animals, and then hosts a banquet before sending his household on board. As he sits, saddened by the impending flood, it begins to rain.*

ii:48–55

The weather begins to change....

Adad roars within the clouds.
    Atrahasis hears Adad's voice,   (Gen 7:11)
He bolts the door
    And seals it with pitch.   (Gen 6:14)
Adad's roar fills the clouds,
    The winds blow fiercely.

Atrahasis cuts the mooring rope;
    He lets the barge float free.

III.iii:10–20, 23–40, 51–54

The noise in the land ceases,
    Like the silence following the breaking of a pot.   (Isa 30:14)
The flood rushes forward,
    The flood charges the people like an army.
One person cannot see the other;
    In the water no one is recognizable.
The flood bellows like a bull,
    The winds howl like a wild ass braying.
There is no sun,
    Only the darkness of the flood....

The noise of the flood terrifies the divine assembly.

Ea-Enki is furious,
    Seeing his children destroyed.   (Gen 7:21–23)
The lady Nintu is livid;
    She bites her lips in anger.
The divine elders sit without food to eat,
    The mighty have no wine to drink.
The wise Mami weeps at what she sees,
    The divine midwife breaks into tears.
"How could I have agreed with the divine assembly?
    How could I voted to destroy everything?
Enlil's evil decree has gone too far,
    His words are worse than the demon Tiruru.

"Where is Anu, our leader, now?
    Where are the humans to carry out his commands?
Where is he who so thoughtlessly decreed a flood?
    ...who condemned his own people to destruction?"

   *For seven days and seven nights the flood covers the earth. Nintu
and the divine assembly weep. Because their temples are flooded
and the humans are dead, there are no sacrifices for the members
of the divine assembly to eat or drink. The text is broken at this*

point. In the Stories of Gilgamesh, the flood subsides. Atrahasis disembarks and prepares food for the divine assembly.

III.v:34–45

The divine assembly smelled the aroma,   (Gen 8:21)
    They swarmed like flies around his sacrifice.
After the divine assembly had eaten their fill,
    Nintu indicted them all:
"Where is Anu now?
    Why has this aroma not brought Enlil here?
Where is he who so thoughtlessly decreed a flood?
    ...who condemned his own people to destruction?
You decreed complete destruction;
    You darkened every shining face on the earth...."

III.vi:5–10

Enlil the warrior saw the barge and was furious.
    The divine assembly all swore an oath.
How could anyone survive that flood?
    How did this human escape destruction?"

    Anu immediately accuses Ea-Enki of again interfering with the will of the divine assembly. Ea-Enki denies any wrongdoing. Ea-Enki and Nintu finally resolve the crisis by creating women who are infertile, women whose newborns die from crib death, and women who remain celibate. As long as there is infertility, the world will be peaceful.

III.vii: 1–8

Let there be three new kinds of women...
    Let some be fertile, others sterile.   (Exod 23:26; Isa 54:1)
Let the demon prey on the newborn;
    Let Pashittu steal infants from their mothers' laps.   (Job 3:16)
Let there be women who are taboo;
    Let there be priests forbidden to have children.

STORIES OF ADAPA

≋ The Stories of Adapa are written on four clay tablets in the Akkadian language using cuneiform script. German archaeologists recovered one tablet (EA 356 = B) from el-Amarna, the city of Akhenaten (1353-1335 BCE). British archaeologists recovered the other three tablets (A, C, and D) from the library of Ashurbanipal (668-627 BCE) at Nineveh. The tablets are preserved today in the Pergamon Museum in Berlin and the British Museum in London.

Adapa is a priest of Ea in the city of Eridu. He is human, but he inadvertently performs a divine act. Attacked by the south wind while fishing, he cripples the wind with a curse. Although the wind can do no further harm to those who fish on the lake, it also cannot bring rain to those who farm the land. The drought sets off an epidemic. Because Adapa has performed a divine act, Anu, the ruler of the divine assembly, gives Adapa the opportunity to become divine by offering him the bread of life. On the advice of Ea, his divine patron, however, Adapa refuses. He loses the opportunity for immortality, but returns to teach the people of Eridu how to cure human illness and stop the epidemic. People throughout the world of the Bible sang the Stories of Adapa to protect themselves from disease.

The Gospels of Mark (Mark 4:35-41) and Luke (Luke 8:22-25) portray Jesus in the role of Adapa, dueling with a wind on a lake. Similarly, Jonah, like Adapa, prays as he sinks (Jonah 2:1-10). Anu is parallel to the snake in the stories of Adam and Eve. Both talk with humans about immortality. Adapa wisely follows the advice of Ea, his divine patron, and chooses to remain mortal and enjoy the earth, rather than to become immortal and leave it. In contrast, Utnapishtim and his wife in the Stories of Gilgamesh accept the invitation of the divine assembly and become immortal.

A: Lines 4–5, 8, 15–22

Ea created Adapa to be wise,
    He did not create him to be immortal.
When the wise Ea began to create Eridu,
    He made Adapa to be a just man ....
Ea anointed Adapa to be his priest.
    He anointed him to fish for his temple in Eridu.

One day while Ea was asleep,
    Adapa went about his chores at the House of Ea in Eridu.
He boarded his sailboat at the Harbor of the New Moon.
    The wind drove his boat far out into the lake ....

B: Lines 1–13

Suddenly, the south wind attacked the boat of Adapa;
    Waves swamped the boat with water.
As he sank into the water with the fish, Adapa prayed:
    "Give me the strength to break the deadly wing of this wind."
Suddenly, the wing of the south wind was broken,
    For seven days, no south wind blew across the land of Eridu.

The damage to the south wind had grave consequences for the land of Eridu. When the south wind did not blow, there was no rain, which brought drought and disease.

Then Anu, who rules the divine assembly, asked the wise Ilabrat:
    "Why has the wind not blown across the land for seven days?"
So Ilabrat told Anu:
    "Adapa, the priest of Ea, broke the wing of the south wind."
When Anu heard the charge, he stood and ordered:
    "Bring Adapa before this assembly."

B: Lines 14–32

To win the favor of the divine assembly, Ea advised Adapa:
    "Do not comb your hair or wash your clothes ....   (Lev 10:6)

Anu (right) hands living water to Gilgamesh (center);
small objects and animals represent constellations of stars

When you come before the divine assembly at the Gate of Anu,
     Tammuz and Gizzida will ask you:
'For whom are you mourning?
     Why have you not combed your hair or washed your clothes?'
Answer their question with these words:
     'I am mourning for two divine patrons who have left Eridu.'
When they ask: 'Who are missing from Eridu?'
     Tell them: 'Tammuz and Gizzida.'
Tammuz and Gizzida will be flattered.
     They will support your case before Anu.
     The verdict of Anu will be in your favor.

"When Anu offers you bread to eat,
     Do not eat it.
When Anu offers you water to drink,
     Do not drink it.
When Anu offers you a garment and oil for your body,
     Clothe and anoint yourself."

🔊 *Adapa gains the support of Tammuz and Gizzida, and Anu, the*
ruler of the divine assembly, decides that a mortal who has been
given the knowledge to "...break the wing of the south wind" must
join the divine assembly. Therefore he offers Adapa life-giving

Ea (left), two wrestlers, and a fisherman

bread and water. Adapa's refusal ends any chance for humans to become immortal.

B: Lines 66–70

Anu handed down the verdict of the divine assembly;
　　Anu pardoned Adapa for stilling the wind.
"Adapa, come join the divine assembly.
　　Eat our life-giving bread. Drink our life-giving water.
　　You, mortal, will become immortal."　　　　　　　　(Gen 3:22)
But Adapa replied: "Ea, my divine patron, told me:
　　'Do not eat their bread or drink their water.'"　　(Gen 2:16–17)
So, the divine assembly decreed:
　　"Send this mortal back home to earth."　　　　　(Gen 3:23–24)

D: Lines 4–6, 15–17

Then Anu laughed at the actions of Ea,
　　"Has anyone else ever outsmarted the word of Anu?
Whatever ill Adapa has brought upon the people of Eridu,
　　The disease that he brought to their bodies,
Ninkarrak, the divine patron of physicians, will relieve.
　　Let the illness be removed,
　　Let the disease be turned aside!"

NUZI ARCHIVES

⌇ Nuzi [Arabic: Yorghun Tepe] is one-hundred fifty miles north of Baghdad in northeastern Iraq. The city flourished for about one-hundred fifty years during the Late Bronze period (1550-1200 BCE) and was destroyed by the Assyrians. Nuzi was excavated from 1920 to 1930 by R. F. S. Starr. Some thirty-five hundred tablets were collected from the house of the governor [Akkadian: haz-annu], from sanctuaries, from rich and poor neighborhoods, and from outlying villages. They are in a dialect of Akkadian spoken by the Hurrian people of Nuzi. Hurrian culture spread from Nuzi west into Syria-Palestine. The Nuzi Archives are preserved today in the Iraq Museum in Baghdad.

The Nuzi Archives offer illuminating parallels for political, economic, and legal social institutions in the stories of Abraham and Sarah (Gen 11:27—25:18), and the stories of Jacob, Leah, and Rachel (Gen 25:20—37:2).

CERTIFICATE OF ADOPTION

⌇ Technically, in the world of the Bible, a household could not sell its land. Nonetheless, with a certificate of adoption [Akkadian: tuppi mārūti], the father of a household could adopt a member of another household, who then became eligible to inherit his land in return for a "gift." Abraham uses this legal remedy by

Cylinder seal from Nuzi

adopting Eliezer as his heir because he and Sarah have no natural children (Gen 15:2-3).

Also at Nuzi, heirs inherit the statues of the divine patrons of a household. Therefore, when Rachel lays claim to the statues of the divine patrons [Hebrew: teraphim] of her household, she is declaring that her son is the heir to the household of Laban (Gen 31:1-21).

C.J. Gadd xxiii (1929), 49–161, No. 51

Nashwi from the household of Ar-shenni hereby adopts Wullu from the household of Puhi-shenni. In return, Wullu must provide Nashwi with food and clothing for as long as he lives. When Nashwi dies, Wullu shall inherit his land.

If, subsequently, Nashwi has a natural son, Wullu and this son must divide the land of the household equally.

The natural son of Nashwi, however, shall receive the statues of the divine patrons of the household. If, however, Nashwi dies without a natural son, then Wullu shall receive the statues of the divine patrons of the household.

Nashwi hereby gives his daughter, Nuhuya, to Wullu in marriage.

If, subsequently, Wullu divorces Nuhuya, he must return the land and houses of Nashwi, and pay a fine of eighteen ounces [Akkadian: *mina*] of silver and eighteen ounces of gold.

Cylinder seal from Nuzi

▰❙ *A list of witnesses and the name of the official who negotiated this covenant are attached.*

CERTIFICATE OF ADOPTION

▰❙ *Certificates of adoption resolved various crises. If the father of a household adopted a son and subsequently had a natural child, then the status of the adopted son was altered. If the mother of the household was infertile, she could designate a slave to be a surrogate mother. The surrogate's children were adopted by the mother and father of her household. In addition, care was taken to prevent the transfer of the land and children of one household to another in the event that only daughters might be born to the mother and father of that household. In such a case, the daughters would become eligible to inherit, like the daughters of Zelophehad (Num 27:1-11).*

HSS 5.67

Suriha-ilu hereby adopts Sennima, son of Zike, from the household of Akkuya and gives him his land, his houses, and all his possessions.

If Suriha-ilu has a natural son, then this child will inherit twice as much as Sennima. As long as he lives, Sennima will honor Suriha-ilu as father of his household. When Suriha-ilu dies, Sennima will then become father of the household [Akkadian: *ewuru*].

Suriha-ilu hereby gives his daughter Kelim-ninu to Sennima as his wife. If she has children, then Sennima may not take another wife. If Kelim-ninu is infertile, then she is to give Sennima a slave as a surrogate mother for his child. Kelim-ninu will adopt the child born to her slave as her own.... (Gen 16:1–15; 29:31—30:24)

The sons of Kelim-ninu and Sennima will inherit my land, my houses, and all my other possessions. If Kelim-ninu has only daughters, then Kelim-ninu's daughters will inherit my land and houses. (Num 36:1–12)

Suriha-ilu hereby declares that he will not adopt any sons other than Sennima.

Whoever violates this covenant is required to pay a penalty of eighteen ounces [Akkadian: *mina*] of silver and eighteen ounces of gold.

Suriha-ilu hereby gives Yalampa to Kelim-ninu as her slave.

Suriha-ilu hereby appoints his sister, Satim-ninu, to be the legal guardian of Kelim-ninu. As long as she lives, Sennima shall honor Kelim-ninu as his wife. Satim-ninu may not abrogate this marriage covenant [Akkadian: "untie the knot"].

If Kelim-ninu has children, and Sennima marries another wife, then he forfeits his authority over the land and children of Kelim-ninu [Akkadian: "tears the hem off his tunic"]....

No other son of Zike is to inherit the land or houses of Suriha-ilu.

A list of witnesses is attached.

LAST WILL AND TESTAMENT OF ARIPPABNI, SON OF SHILWA-TESUB

≋ In patrilineal cultures like Nuzi and ancient Israel, the land and children of a household were inherited by males related to the father of the household. The "beloved son" or heir [Akkadian: maru rabu] received the largest share. Typically, the oldest son became the heir, received the statues of the divine patrons of the household, and cared for [Akkadian: "showed proper respect for"] the mother of the household, its marriageable women, and all its children. Wills [Akkadian: tuppi simti] from Nuzi, however, show that fathers of the household could designate heirs who were not their oldest sons, divide property as they chose, and make various stipulations about the use of property, the ownership of the statues of the divine patrons of their households, and the responsibilities of their wives and children. The blessing of Isaac (Gen 27:27-29) and the blessing of Jacob (Gen 48:15-20) are wills in which fathers use their own discretion to designate heirs and distribute the land and children of their households.

HSS 19.17

...all my lands, houses, and possessions...are to be divided equally between my three sons: Akibtashenni, Turrishenni, and Palteya.

I also appoint my daughter, Ukkie, as legal guardian of the land, houses, and possessions of my sons. As long as Ukkie lives, my three sons shall honor her as mother of their households....If any of my three sons fails to obey Ukkie, then she may punish him in the same manner that she would her own son.

No other son of mine shall inherit any of my lands, houses, or other possessions.

≋ Witnesses and seal impressions are attached.

CERTIFICATE OF ADOPTION

≋ Twice Abraham called his wife, Sarah, his "sister" (Gen 12:10-19; 20:1-14). In the Nuzi Archives, there are certificates of adoption [Akkadian: tuppi ahatuti] in which the father of the household adopts a woman as a sister and becomes her legal guardian.

AASOR 16.54

I, Kuni-asu, daughter of Hut-tesup, declare before witnesses: "Previously, Akam-musni negotiated a marriage covenant for me and received thirteen ounces [Akkadian: "forty shekels"] of silver as a bride price. Akam-musni and my husband are now dead. Now, Akkiya, son of Hut-tesup, has adopted me [Akkadian: "seized me in the street"] as his sister. As my legal guardian, he shall negotiate a marriage covenant for me and will receive three ounces [Akkadian: "ten shekels"] of silver as a bride price from my husband."

Whoever breaks this covenant shall pay a fine of eighteen ounces [Akkadian: *mina*] of gold.

COVENANT BETWEEN SHILWA-TESHUB AND URHIYA

Households with more livestock than they could herd themselves negotiated covenants with herders to graze and breed the animals for them. Owners negotiated to pay herders either a flat fee or a commission. A herder's fee might be kids, lambs, wool, dairy products, clothing, or grain. Owners expected eighty percent, or about twenty ewes, in each herd of thirty-eight animals to bear. They expected to lose fifteen percent or five to six animals to predators or disease. Some owners paid herders with any newborn over the projected increase or with any animals that survived the projected loss. The Bible characterizes the household of Abraham and Sarah and the household of Jacob, Leah, and Rachel as herders who care for livestock from both their own villages and the villages of others.

Cylinder seal from Nuzi

Nuzi and Other Cities of Mesopotamia

HSS 9.64

Shilwa-teshub, the father of the household, has entrusted two breed
ewes, seven castrated rams, one male lamb, eleven breed nannies, seven
billies, two male kids and one female kid, a total of thirty-one livestock,
to the herder, Urhiya, son of Ikkianni. (Gen 30:27–34)

PROMISSORY NOTE OF HUTIP-APU, SON OF EHLIP-APU

*Promissory notes [Akkadian: muddu] record a herder's commit-
ments to repay the owner for any animals lost because of negli-*

gence. Herders were not responsible for losses caused by a member of the divine assembly [Akkadian: lipit ilim*], and they might be excused from repaying the loss if livestock were killed by another animal, after the hides of the lost animals were studied by the owners. A sheep lost due to negligence cost the herder about three months' salary [Akkadian: "one and one-third shekels"].*

HSS 13.385

The herder, Hutip-apu, son of Ehlip-apu, acknowledges the receipt of ... three breed ewes, five lambs, two castrated rams, four kids, a total of fourteen livestock ....

ANNALS OF
DEDUMOSE II

🏳 *Dedumose II (1655-1647) was pharaoh just before the Hyksos conquered Egypt in 1640 BCE. His annals were a source for a history of Egypt by Manetho (323-245 BCE), an Egyptian priest who wrote for the Greeks who migrated to Egypt after the conquest of Alexander the Great (332-323 BCE). The annals are preserved only as quotations in the works of the Jewish historian Flavius Josephus (37-100 CE) and in the works of some early Christian writers, such as Eusebius (260-339 CE).*

The Annals of Dedumose, like the Annals of Hatshepsut, portray the Hyksos as barbaric and merciless conquerors from the north, who swept through Syria-Palestine and turned a once fertile Egypt into a desert. Although the linguistic structure of Hyksos names clearly indicates they were a federation of more than one ethnic group, they were primarily a Semitic people. The Egyptians nicknamed them "Hyksos," which carried the same animosity as "damn Yankees" or "carpetbaggers" in the American South following the War between the States.

Seal of Ahmose I

Manetho, Aegyptiaca, frag. 42 in Manetho, Against Apion 1.75–92

⊒ *The inscriptions of Hatshepsut (1473-1458 BCE) at Deir el-Bahari have been badly damaged. Therefore, some restoration is based on the parallel inscription of Amenophis III (1391-1353 BCE) at Luxor.*

During the reign of Pharaoh Dedumose [Dd-(msi) in the Turin Canon, Greek: Tutimaeus], the wrath of the divine assembly struck Egypt unexpectedly from the east. These Hyksos fanatics [Greek: *asemoi*] marched confidently to victory against our land. They easily overpowered Pharaoh and his governors. They ruthlessly burned our cities, and razed the temples of Egypt's divine assembly to the ground. They treated the people of Egypt with hostility and cruelty. They massacred our soldiers. They enslaved our women and children. Finally, they appointed Salitis, one of their own, to be pharaoh. From his palace in Memphis, Salitis dispatched Hyksos soldiers and officials to the most strategic locations in the land to collect financial restitution from both southern and northern Egypt.

The first priority of Salitis was to fortify the eastern border of the Delta, in anticipation that the Assyrians, as they grew stronger, would

Pharaoh's chariot

one day covet and attack Egypt. So, in the name of Sais, Salitis restored the ancient city of Avaris situated at a commanding site on the east bank of Bubas, a branch of the Nile. To defend the border, he reconstructed its buildings, surrounded it with a massive wall, and stationed 240,000 of the best Hyksos soldiers there. Salitis would spend summers at Avaris meeting with government officials and military commanders, and conducting military maneuvers designed to paralyze his enemies with fear of the army. Salitis reigned thirteen years. He was succeeded by Beon, who reigned for forty-four years.... The first six Hyksos rulers never stopped making war on the Egyptian people, whom they were committed to exterminate....

Eventually, the native Egyptian rulers of Thebes declared their independence of the Hyksos, and a long and hard-fought revolt quickly spread across the rest of Egypt. Finally... all the Hyksos were driven into a small area around Avaris...fortified with a massive enclosure wall.... An army of 480,000 Egyptian soldiers laid siege to Avaris. Having realized there was no hope, the Hyksos negotiated a treaty that guaranteed them safe conduct out of Egypt.... Some 240,000 Hyksos left Egypt for Syria....

ANNALS OF KAMOSE

From 1640 to 1552 BCE, Hyksos pharaohs in Memphis and Avaris opened the borders and government of Egypt to non-Egyptians like Joseph, whose teachings close the book of Genesis (Gen 41:9—47:12). In 1552, Kamose and Ahmose, who were native Egyptians from the south, drove the Hyksos back into Syria-Palestine and degraded the social standing of all Semites in Egypt. These are the days and the conditions reflected in the opening of the book of Exodus (Exod 1:7—13:16).

The Second Stela of Kamose was discovered by Mohammed Hammad and Labib Habachi, members of the Egyptian Antiquities Department, in 1954 at Karnak in southern Egypt. The limestone stela, 220 cm. high and 110 cm. wide, one of a pair originally set up, had been reused to form part of the foundation of a statue of Ramesses IV (1163-1156 BCE). The Annals of Kamose report that he drove the Hyksos out of Egypt. The stela is now housed in the museum at Luxor, Egypt.

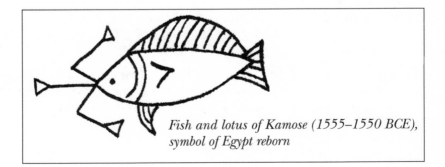

Fish and lotus of Kamose (1555–1550 BCE), symbol of Egypt reborn

≋ *Kamose taunts the Hyksos ruler Apophis (1585-1542 BCE) as his campaign progresses steadily north toward the Hyksos capital at Avaris.*

...My soldiers pursue you.
The wives of Avaris are doomed.
    They are silent as they hear my soldiers' battle-cry.
I moored my fleet at Per-djedken,
    My heart was glad,
I had broken the arms of Apophis, Prince of the Retenu,
    His plans had come to nothing....

As my fleet sailed north
    We plundered the lands of Avaris.
I saw the Retenu women peeking out palace windows,
    They stand unmoving, timid as mice in their burrows,
    They whisper: "An attack is coming."

Behold I have control of Egypt
    My power is uncontested.
As Amun, my divine patron, lives, I will not spare you, Apophis.
    You cannot go to your fields without attack.
O vile Asiatic, I shall drink the wine from your vineyards,   (Jer 5:17)
    Your own people will press it for me.
I will despoil your land,
    I will cut down your trees.   (Deut 20:19–20)
I will take your women
    I will seize your chariots.
I did not leave a plank intact of all your ships,
    I carried off cedar, gold, lapis-lazuli, silver, turquoise, incense.
O vile Asiatic, who said, "I am the lord, I have no peer...,"
    I have stripped your lands of their people.
I have destroyed your cities,
    I have burned them into red mounds
    Reminders of the damage they did to Egypt.

≋ *Kamose prevented Nubia from helping Apophis after he captured a messenger. Kamose, however, died before the end of the war and his successor, Ahmose I, successfully drove the Hyksos out of Egypt.*

Annals of
Hatshepsut

    Hatshepsut (1473-1458 BCE) was the daughter of Tuthmosis I (1504-1492 BCE) and the childless widow of Tuthmosis II (1492-1479 BCE). When Tuthmosis II died, Hatshepsut ruled Egypt initially as co-regent with Tuthmosis III (1479-1425 BCE), who was the son of Tuthmosis II and a secondary wife. Hatshepsut then

Ram-headed Khnum shapes Hatshepsut and her ka-soul at Deir el-Bahari

declared herself pharaoh. Twice before in Egypt, queens had reigned for brief periods, but never had they taken the title "Pharaoh." Hatshepsut, like many rulers in the world of the Bible, was celebrated as the child of a human mother and a divine father. The Annals of Hatshepsut were recovered from Deir el-Bahari, her funeral temple in the Valley of the Pharaohs, by the Egypt Exploration Fund, under the direction of the Swiss archae-ologist Edouard Naville in 1894. Another copy of her annals are inscribed on the architrave of the House of Pakhet that she built at Speos Artemidos [Arabic: Istabl Antar] fifteen miles south of el-Amarna.

After the Annals of Hatshepsut describe intercourse between Amun-Re, her divine father, and Ahmose, her human mother, Khnum shapes Hatshepsut and her ka-soul on a potter's wheel. When Ahmose goes into labor, she is led into a birthing room attended by Bes, divine patron of midwives, and gives birth under the divine protection of Thoth, Khnum, and Heqet, a divine pa-tron of childbearing. The annals describe Hatshepsut as an ideal ruler, protecting Egypt from its enemies and providing food for its people.

The annunciation to the wife of Manoah (Judg 13:1-23), the annunciation to Hannah (1 Sam 1:9-18), and the annunciation to Mary (Luke 1:26-38) parallel the description of the birth of Hat-shepsut. The Annals of Solomon (1 Kgs 3:1-15) parallel the descrip-tion of her care of Egypt. Both Hatshepsut and Solomon describe themselves as rulers with "...an understanding heart."

Deir el-Bahari, north colonnade

The inscriptions of Hatshepsut at Deir el-Bahari are badly dam-aged. Therefore, some restoration is based on the parallel inscrip-tion of Amenophis III (1391-1353 BCE) at Luxor.

"I, Ahmose, dare to speak.
    The queen says to Amun-Re, the powerful,
To Amun-Re, the glorious,
    To Amun-Re, the divine patron of Thebes:

'How great is your power.
    How perfect....
Your heart guides my heart.
    Your breath is in all my limbs.

Khnum shapes Hatshepsut on a potter's wheel under the supervision of Thoth

I am your servant.
    Do with me what you will.'"

"I, Amun-Re, promise Ahmose,
    The divine patron of Thebes says to the queen:
'I have given you a child,
    You will name her Hatshepsut....   (Judg 13:1–23; 1 Sam 1:9–18)
She will reign over the land of Egypt....'"   (Luke 1:26–38)

"I, Amun-Re, now command Khnum,
    The divine patron of Thebes says to the divine potter:
'Go, create this child,
    Give Hatshepsut my *ka*-soul.
Make her a divine child.
    Give the daughter I have begotten life,
Give her strength, and happiness,
    and endow her with the gifts and offerings of Amun-Re forever.'"

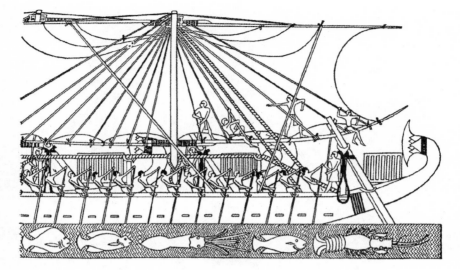

Egyptian ship from the reign of Hatshepsut

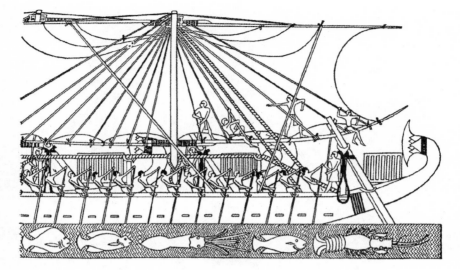 *Khnum affirms that he will do as Amun-Re commands and then proceeds to fashion the child and her* ka-*soul on a potter's wheel. While he works, Khnum repeats the words of Amun-Re.*

"I, Khnum, say to Hatshepsut,
   The divine potter says to the child of Amun-Re: (Isa 64:8)
'I have created you from the divine patron of Karnak.
   I have made you a divine child.
I have given you life,
   I have endowed you with strength and happiness.
You will reign over every land and all peoples.
   I have endowed you with all gifts and offerings....
I will set you above the *ka*-souls of all creatures,
   You will shine over Upper and Lower Egypt,
You will rule both south and north,
   You will govern according to the command of your loving father.'"

The actual birth of the child is represented in a relief depicting the mother sitting enthroned and holding the child while four female members of the divine assembly stand before her as midwives. They extend their arms to receive the child while Meskhenet, the divine patron of birth, gives instructions to the divine midwives. They promise Hatshepsut happiness and a glorious reign.

Speos Artemidos

Between 1640 and 1532 BCE, a Semitic people whom the Egyptians called "Hyksos" ruled Egypt. Hyksos pharaohs adopted Seth as their divine patron and replaced the households that had traditionally ruled Egypt with foreign bureaucrats. Eventually, Ahmose I (1550-1525 BCE) led a successful revolt against the Hyksos and

Asiatic, Ethiopian, and other African prisoners of Ramesses II

founded the New Kingdom (1550–1070 BCE). The Annals of Hatshepsut reveal Egypt's lingering indignation against the Hyksos.

Let all the earth know that I have ruled with an understanding heart (1 Kgs 3:1–15). I have not slept. I have not forgotten to do anything. I have rebuilt all the villages, cities and temples which those herders from Syria-Palestine at Avaris in the north had destroyed or had allowed to fall into ruins and become haunted by criminals and fugitives. These herders from Syria-Palestine ruled without the consent of Amun-Re, and their descendants refused his divine command to acknowledge me as pharaoh.

Now I am established upon the throne of Amun-Re. I was born to be a divine warrior, striking out at my enemies like the uraeus serpent of Horus which rides upon my brow. I have driven the enemies of the divine assembly into exile. Their footprints have vanished in the sand.

I have done everything which Amun-Re, the father of my predecessors, has decreed. No one whom Amun-Re protects shall be harmed. My reign will endure like the mountains. My name will last as long as the sun of Amun-Re shines, and as long as his rays illuminate my royal titles carved throughout the land. Horus the falcon will soar above the obelisks bearing my name for all eternity.

STORIES OF
ANUBIS AND BATA

≋ *Before 1860, French archaeologists had recovered a copy of the Sto-*
ries of Anubis and Bata, as they were being told during the Nine-
teenth Dynasty (1307-1196 BCE). The stories were written on
papyrus, not in hieroglyphic characters but in a hieratic or cur-
sive style of writing. The P. D'Orbiney manuscript is preserved
today in the British Museum (#10183).

Anubis and Bata are brothers who work together successfully
to farm their land, but their rivalry for children leaves them both
infertile. The twin-motif reflects two important convictions.
Twins bless their households with two lives, but curse their house-
holds with sibling rivalry. Twins appear again and again in Egypt's
traditions: Upper Egypt in the Nile Valley and Lower Egypt on the
Nile Delta; the desert of Seth and the farmland of Horus; the grow-
ing season and the flood season; the world of the living to the east
and the world of the dead to the west. Twins, brothers or rivals
like Anubis and Bata, also appear in the stories of Cain and Abel
(Gen 4:3-16) and the stories of Jacob and Esau (Gen 25:19—33:20).
The propositioning of a slave by the master's wife also has a par-
allel in the teachings of Joseph (Gen 39:1-21). The talking animal
who saves the life of its master in the Stories of Anubis and Bata
is parallel to the ass in the stories of Balaam (Num 22:28-30).

Once there were two brothers: Anubis was the older, Bata the younger.
Anubis was a villager, who was married and owned his own house. Bata
was under the care of his brother and lived with him like a son. In return for living in the household of Anubis and wearing the clothes that

Anubis gave him, Bata herded the cattle of Anubis, plowed his fields, tended his crops, and brought in his harvests. Bata was young, but he was righteous and blameless, so the divine assembly of Egypt often let him use divine power.

i:5–10

Every day, after Bata finished grazing the cattle, he headed back to the village loaded down with vegetables, milk and firewood—everything he needed to prepare supper for Anubis and his wife. After supper, Bata went out to the barn to sleep with the cattle.

Every morning, Bata got up, cooked breakfast for Anubis and his wife, and then packed a meal to eat at noon. Then Bata drove the cattle out into the pasture to graze.

As he walked with the cattle, they would tell him: "The grass in this pasture is excellent." Bata would listen to the cattle, and drive them to whatever pasture they wanted to graze. Consequently, Anubis's cattle became prime livestock, calving twice as often as the livestock from any other village. (Gen 30:40–43)

ii:1–5

Now when it was time to plow, Anubis told Bata: "Tomorrow is the first day of plowing. Be sure the oxen are ready to be yoked and the seed is ready to be planted, first thing in the morning."

The younger brother did everything his older brother told him to do. At the break of dawn, Anubis and Bata hurried to the fields with their seed in order to start plowing. They were delighted with how well the work was going.

Some days later, they ran short of seed. So Anubis sent his younger brother to the village to get more. When Bata got to the house, the wife

Plowing with oxen at Beni Hasan

Harvesting flax at Beni Hasan

of Anubis was sitting there combing her hair. Bata said to her: "I need seed for the field; my older brother is waiting for me. Hurry up!"

iii:1–5

Then she said to him: "Go and open the bin and take what you want. I am not finished combing my hair."

Bata went to the barn, took a large jar and filled it with barley and emmer seed, and hoisted the jar on his shoulders.

When the wife of Anubis saw Bata, she said seductively: "How much seed are you carrying?"

Bata naively answered: "Three measures of emmer, two measures of barley: five in all."

But the wife of Anubis continued: "You are certainly strong. Every day I notice your bulging muscles." To convince Bata to make love to her, the wife of Anubis jumped up and threw her arms around him. "Sleep with me just this once, and I will sew some new clothes for you," she pleaded. (Gen 39:7–12)

Bata became furious as a leopard at the very thought of sleeping with his brother's wife. His anger terrified her. He shouted at her. "You and your husband are like a mother and father to me. Because he was older than I, he reared me. How can you possibly suggest I commit a crime like this against him? Nonetheless, if you promise never to proposition me again like this, I won't tell anyone what you said."

iv:1–5

Bata lifted the jar of seed to his shoulders and left for the field. He rejoined his brother, and they worked hard all day together. At sunset Anubis left for home. Bata stayed behind to round up the cattle and

Leading cattle to the barn at Beni Hasan

pick up all the equipment. Then he drove the cattle home so that they could sleep in their own barn in the village.

Meanwhile, the wife of Anubis was afraid of getting into trouble for what she had done. So she drank grease to make herself sick.... She neither trimmed, nor lit, the lamps when it got dark. She did not bring Anubis any water to wash his hands when he got home. She just lay there vomiting....

v:1–5

As Anubis entered the house, his wife told him: "...When your brother came back for some seed, I was here alone. He propositioned me: 'Let your hair down and sleep with me just this once!' I would not pay any attention to him. 'Aren't I like a mother to you?' I pleaded. 'Isn't your older brother like a father to you?' But he panicked and beat me so that I would not tell you. Now, if you let him live, I will kill myself...." (Gen 39:17–19)

Anubis became as furious as a leopard. He fetched his spear, sharpened it, and stood behind the barn door to wait for Bata to return with the cattle later that evening.

...when the first cow went into the barn, she warned Bata: "Your older brother is waiting to kill you with his spear. Run!" (Num 22:28–30)

vi:5–10

...as soon as Bata looked under the door of the barn and saw his older brother's feet...he dropped the tools he was carrying and ran. His older brother chased him with his spear.

Bata began to pray: "Re-Harakhti, you are my divine patron . . . only you can judge between the just and the unjust." (Ps 7:10–11)

The moment Re heard his prayer he created a lake full of croco-diles to protect Bata and to separate him from his older brother. . . .

vii:5–10

When it was dawn and Re-Harakhti rose over the horizon, Bata argued his case with his older brother in broad daylight. "Why are you hunting me? Why do you want to kill me without giving me a chance to speak in my defense? I am still your younger brother. You and your wife are like father and mother to me . . . ." Then Bata told him everything that had happened. He swore to the truth of his story with an oath and an or-deal. (Num 30:2; 2 Chr 6:22–23)

"So help me Re-Harakhti, only an unfaithful wife could get you to take up your spear and try to kill me for no reason at all." Then he took his knife, cut off his penis and threw it into the lake where a catfish swal-lowed it . . . .

viii:7–10

Bata went into exile in the Valley of the Cedars in Syria-Palestine, and Anubis set off for home in the morning. He struck his forehead with his hand and smeared his face with dirt (2 Sam 1:2; 13:19). When he got home, he killed his wife and fed her body to the dogs (2 Kgs 9:30–36). Then he mourned his younger brother. . . .

≋ *The story concludes when the divine assembly provides Anubis with another wife. Eventually Anubis becomes pharaoh. Later Bata is reconciled with Anubis and succeeds him as pharaoh.*

STORIES OF AQHAT

Ugarit was an important commercial center on what is today the northern coast of Syria. It connected the trade lanes between Egypt to the south, islands like Crete to the west, and Mesopotamia to the east. Culture followed Ugarit's prosperity, especially between 1400 and 1250 BCE. Among this period's magnificent works of art and tradition recovered by a French excavation directed by C. A. Schaeffer during twenty-two seasons (1929–1960) are the Stories of Aqhat. They are written on three baked clay tablets (CTA 17-19) in Ugaritic, a Semitic language like Hebrew. Ugaritic uses wedge-shaped, cuneiform characters, but the characters represent individual sounds from an alphabet, rather than syllables, which was the earlier method used in Mesopotamian cuneiform writing and the hieroglyphics of Egypt as well. The tablets are preserved today in the Louvre Museum in Paris.

Aqhat is a wise son and a wise hunter. Danil is Aqhat's father. Danatiya is his mother. Paghat is his sister. Danil and Danatiya were unable to have a son until Baal, their divine patron, helped them. When Aqhat reached puberty, Kothar-wa-hasis, the divine metalworker, made the boy a unique and powerful bow and arrows. Angry that Aqhat would not sell her his weapons, Anat, divine patron of love and war, hired Yatpan to assassinate him. Paghat subsequently avenges his death.

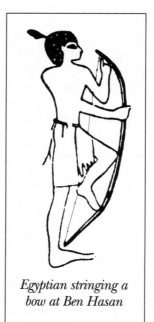

Egyptian stringing a bow at Ben Hasan

70

There are parallels to the barren-wife motif in the Stories of
Aqhat in the books of Genesis (Gen 15:1-4, 16:1-15, 18:9-15, 25:21,
30:1-24), of Judges (Judg 13:2-3), and of Samuel-Kings (1 Sam 1:2-17;
2 Kgs 4:8-17). The motif describes a couple that wants, but cannot have, a child. Yahweh intervenes to announce the impending
birth of a child. Miraculous events highlight the birth of their
child, who is destined to deliver the people. Some of the episodes
from the Stories of Aqhat also appear in a story of Hagar (Gen
21:9-21) where Ishmael plays Aqhat's role of the great hunter whose
life is threatened by Sarah, playing the role of Anat, and whose life
is saved by Hagar, who plays the role of Paghat. In the stories of
Jacob and Esau (Gen 27:1-45), it is Esau who plays Aqhat the
hunter, whose mother Rebekah, playing the role of Anat, tries to
take away his inheritance.

A i:1–42

The Stories of Aqhat open with Danil engaged in a ritual of incubation. He sleeps in the sanctuary and prays that he and Danatiya will be able to have a son. For seven days, Danil feeds the
members of the divine assembly. Then, on the seventh day, Baal,
the divine patron of Ugarit, stands and addresses El, the ruler of
the divine assembly.

On the first day, Danil prepared food for his divine patrons to eat,
        The Powerful One mixed wine for the divine assembly to drink.
Then the Son of Harnam spread his garment in the sanctuary,
        Danil lay down and went to sleep.... (1 Sam 3:3; Amos 2:8)
On the seventh day, Baal answered Danil's lament. (Neh 8:18)
        The divine patron of Ugarit showed mercy to the Son of Harnam.
"Surely, Danil should have a son like his brothers;
        He needs an heir like his covenant partners.
He has blessed the divine assembly with food;
        He has filled their sanctuaries with drink.
Bless him and show that you are El the Bull.
        Bless him, O my father, creator of all things. (Isa 40:28)
Raise up a son for his household.
        Establish an heir in his palace.
Give Danil a son to erect a stela for the divine patrons of his ancestors,
        To build a shrine for the household of Danil in their sanctuary.
Give Danil a son to burn incense for him,
        To chant beside his grave.

Lift up a son to silence the voices of his father's enemies,   (Ps 63:11)
    To drive away those who trouble him.
To give Danil a hand when he is in ecstasy,
    To support him when he is full of spirits,   (Isa 51:17–18; Hos 7:5)
To eat a sacrificial meal for him in the sanctuary of Baal,
    To consume his portion in the House of El,   (Deut 32:38; 1 Sam 1:4)
To repair Danil's roof after it rains,
    To purify his clothes from spells."

El took his servant by the hand
    He blessed Danil the powerful,
    He showed favor to the brave Son of Harnam.
"Let Danil enjoy the bliss of his bed.
    When he kisses his wife, she will become pregnant.
    When he holds her in his arms, she will conceive.
Let her conceive and give birth.
    Let there be a son in the household of Danil.
    Let there be an heir in his palace . . . ."

A ii:8–15, 25–42

Danil lifted up his face.
    His skin was glowing.   (Exod 34:29–30)
Danil put his head back and laughed,   (Gen 17:17)
    Put his feet up on his footstool and roared.
Danil began to sing: "Now I can sit and rest.
    Now my spirit can be at ease.
For a son like those my brothers have will be born to me.   (Isa 9:6)
    I will have an heir like those of my covenant partners."

≍ *For seven days, Danil entertains the divine midwives [Ugaritic: Kotaratu], who will assist him and Danatiya with the birth of Aqhat.*

Danil went home,
    He entered his palace.
On the first day, the divine midwives arrived;
    The radiant daughters entered his house.
Danil the Powerful roasted an ox for the midwives;
    The brave Son of Harnam threw a feast for them.

He gave wine to the skillful midwives,
    He provided food and drink for the radiant daughters....
On the seventh day, the midwives left his house,
    The radiant daughters departed.
Then Danil and Danatiya experienced the joy of sex,
    They enjoyed the bliss of bed.
Danil began to count her months....

 *Parts of the tablet are missing. When the story picks up again, Aqhat has reached puberty and is about to become a man. Kothar-wa-hasis, the divine craftsman, is talking about making a bow and arrows for him.*

A.v:2–28

...Kothar-wa-hasis announced: "I will deliver a bow to Aqhat."
    The divine craftsman will present him with many arrows.
On the seventh day, Danil was in the gate,   (2 Sam 15:2; Amos 5:10)
    The powerful one sat at the threshing floor with the elders.
Here, Danil judged the widow's complaint,
    Here, he heard the orphan's case.   (Deut 10:18; Isa 1:17)
In the distance, Kothar-wa-hasis appeared running with giant strides.
    Danil saw him carrying a bow and a quiver of arrows.
The powerful one called to Danatiya, his wife:
    "Prepare a lamb from the flock.   (Gen 18:2, 6–7; 19:1)
    Cook Kothar-wa-hasis his favorite meal.

Godmother of Lachish

Kothar-wa-hasis is hungry;
    The clever one wants something to eat...."
Kothar-wa-hasis put the bow in Danil's hands;
    He laid the arrows in his lap....

⏑ *Aqhat uses his divine bow and arrows to become a mighty*
    hunter (Gen 10:9; 21:20-21). Anat, the divine patron of love and
    war, wants his bow and arrows.

A.vi:18–45

Anat promised Aqhat: "Ask for silver and I'll give it to you.
    Ask for gold and it will be yours.
Just give Anat your bow.
    Let the Young Warrior have your arrows."

"No, Anat," Aqhat replied.
    "I will bring you yew trees from the mountains of Lebanon,
I will harvest sinews from wild oxen,
    And horns from mountain goats.
I will collect tendons from the legs of bulls,
    The strongest reeds from the marshes.
You can give them to Kothar-wa-hasis.
    Let the divine craftsman build a bow and arrows for Anat."

Anat continued: "Ask for life without end, and I will give it to you,
    Ask for immortality and I will grant it to you.   (Ps 21:4)
Your years will be as countless as the years of Baal,
    Your months like the son of El.
You will be like Baal, who was raised from the dead.
    You will be like Baal, who is honored with a feast.
As Baal is honored in endless song,
    So I will grant life to you, Aqhat."   (2 Kgs 5:7)

"Do not lie to me, Anat," Aqhat replied.
    "Do not waste your breath lying to a hero."
Mortals cannot become immortals.
    What becomes of mortals?   (Eccl 6:12)
We are faces to be masked with plaster;
    We are skulls to be daubed with lime.

*Semitic war bow
at Beni Hasan*

All mortals die,
    And death is my mortal end. (Ps 82:7)
My bow is the weapon of a man at war,
    Shall women now go hunting?"

Anat laughs. She exclaims, "Listen to me, Aqhat,
    Listen for your own good.
Your arrogance will cross my path again;
    Your presumption will lead you back to me. (Ps 10:6)
I will overthrow you; (Isa 14:25; 41:25)
    I will trample you under my feet, my valiant hero."

🔖 *Anat storms off to the divine assembly where she tries to get El to punish Aqhat. El refuses, but also agrees not to stand in Anat's way of getting revenge. So, Anat designs a plan to gain Aqhat's confidence so that she can murder him and take his bow. Anat sets her plan in motion by showing Aqhat a good place to hunt. Leaving him there to enjoy himself, she goes off and changes Yatpan, her accomplice, into a vulture. While Aqhat is preparing to cook one of his kills, Yatpan, now disguised as a vulture, approaches him without arousing his suspicion (Gen 15:11). Swooping in behind him, Yatpan changes back into a human and stuns Aqhat with two blows to the head. He then murders him with three surgically placed blows to the temple.*

B.iv:28–40

Anat orders Yatpan, her bodyguard, to kill Aqhat.
    She disguises him as a bird of prey in her belt,   (Isa 46:11)
    As a vulture placed in her pouch....
When Aqhat sat down to eat,
    When the son of Danil was preparing his meal,
Vultures circled over his head,
    Birds of prey soared in the sky above.   (Deut 32:11)
Anat hid Yatpan among the birds of prey,
    Camouflaged him among the vultures swooping down on Aqhat.
Yatpan struck Aqhat twice on the head;
    He hit him three times behind the ear.
Aqhat's blood ran down the arms of his assassin,
    Aqhat's blood drenched the legs of his murderer.
Aqhat's breath departed like the wind,
    He exhaled his last breath like a gentle breeze;
    His last breath left his nose like a wisp of smoke.
Anat watched Aqhat die,
    Anat began to weep....

≋❙ *With Aqhat dead, there are no harvest rains. The crops of Ugarit
wither. As he sits among the elders at the city gate, Danil becomes aware that drought is destroying his land.*

C.i:32–38

Crops dry on the threshing floor;
    Fresh ears of grain droop....
Birds begin to soar above the palace,   (Job 39:26; Hos 8:1)
    Vultures coast in the wind.
Deep within her heart Paghat began to weep,   (Lam 2:11)
    Unnoticed, the sister of Aqhat began to cry.
She tore the garments of Danil the powerful,   (2 Sam 3:31; Job 1:20)
    She rent the robe of brave Danil the son of Harnam.

≋❙ *Neither Danil nor Paghat was yet aware that Aqhat had been
killed. By tearing Danil's garments, Paghat is not mourning the
death of her brother, but officially filing a gloomy economic fore-
cast with the head of state. Danil accepts her analysis, and pre-
dicts the drought will last for seven years.*

C.i:38–C.ii:55

Then Danil declared that the land was cursed,
>The powerful announced that a prolonged drought had begun.
"For seven years Baal will disappear,   (Ps 68:4; 104:3)
>For eight years the Rider of the Clouds will dispatch no dew or rain.
Rivers and springs will dry up;
>The voice of Baal will not signal a single thundershower...."

Danil called to Paghat, who carries water,
>Who collects dew for the barley,
>Who knows the course of the stars,
"Saddle an ass, and harness my mount.
>Use my reins of silver, my bridle of gold."

    After Paghat saddles an ass, she and Danil set off to survey the drought damage.

C.ii:89–C.iii:127

Suddenly, Paghat saw two messengers appear.
>They began to weep and lament....
"Hear our words, Danil the powerful,
>Aqhat the hero is dead.
Anat made Aqhat's life depart like the wind,
>The Young Warrior made him exhale his last breath...."

Danil saw vultures appear in the clouds.
>He began to lament: "May Baal break their wings.

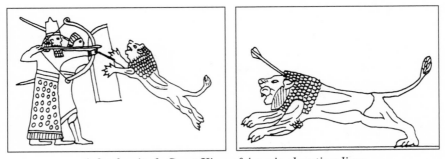

Ashurbanipal, Great King of Assyria, hunting lions

May Baal pluck the feathers from their wings,
    Let them fall at my feet.   (2 Sam 22:39)
I will split them open,
    To find Aqhat's flesh and bone.
I will mourn for him and will bury him.
    I will lay him in his grave at the sanctuary."   (2 Sam 1:27)

≋ *Baal responds to Danil's plea and each time a bird is killed it is examined. When he finally finds the remains of Aqhat, Danil mourns him, buries him in an unmarked grave, and curses the land and its inhabitants where Aqhat was murdered (Gen 4:10-12; Deut 21:1-9). After seven years of mourning, Paghat asks Danil to appoint her to avenge her brother's death.*

C.iv:190–98

"My father," Paghat said, "you have completed your sacrifices,
    You have left food and drink for the divine assembly,
    You have sent the smell of incense to the stars.
Now, bless me, father, and I will be blessed.   (Gen 24:60; 27:29)
    Choose me, and I will be chosen.
I will kill my brother's killer;
    I will murder the one who murdered my brother."

≋ *Danil commissions Paghat by breathing into her nostrils and thereby infusing her with his own strength (Gen 2:7; Ezek 37:9).*

C.iv:203–9

In the sea, Paghat bathes,
    She dyes her skin a rich purple.
Paghat puts on the clothes of a warrior;
    She thrusts a knife into her belt.
Paghat hangs a sword on her side.
    Then she covers her weapons with a woman's clothes.

≋ *At dusk, Paghat enters Yatpan's camp and asks to be taken to his tent, where she finds him drunk.*

Sickle sword from Gezer

C.iv:210–24

A messenger said to Yatpan: "The one we hired has come;
    She is outside your tent."

Yatpan replied: "Let her come into my tent."
    Anat's accomplice boasted: "She can serve me wine.   (Judg 4:19)
She can take the cup from my hand;
    She can fill the drinking horn in my right hand."

Paghat entered the tent of Yatpan;
    She began to serve him wine.   (Judg 5:24–27)
Paghat took the cup from his hand;
    She filled the drinking horn in his right hand.

Then Yatpan began to brag: (Gen 4:23–24)
    "This hand which killed Aqhat has killed a thousand."
Paghat served Yatpan more and more wine....   (Gen 9:20–21)

The end of the tablet is missing. However, there are two similar stories in the Bible, which may suggest conclusions for the Stories of Aqhat. The book of Judges (Judg 4:17-22) recounts that as Sisera was lying fast asleep, Jael took a tent peg and hammer and drove the peg into his temple. The book of Judith (Jdt 13:2-9) tells how, when Holofernes collapsed drunk on his bed, Judith took his sword and cut off his head.

STORIES OF KIRTA

The Stories of Kirta, like the Stories of Aqhat, were recovered at Ugarit in Syria by C. A. Schaeffer and his French team (1929-1960). They are written on three clay tablets (CTA 14-16; KTU 1.14-16) in the Ugaritic language using an alphabetic cuneiform script. They are preserved today in the Louvre Museum in Paris. Although the Stories of Kirta probably developed as early as 2000 BCE, this version is signed by Ilimilku, a scribe of Niqmaddu II (1375-1345 BCE).

Kirta is a monarch who has no son. He is ill and his land is in revolt. The stories open with Kirta engaged in a ritual of incubation during which he sleeps in a sanctuary of El to ask his divine patron to restore his household. In his dream, El tells him to go to war, capture a bride, and begin a new household. Kirta obeys, but fails to thank Asherah, his godmother, for her help. To punish Kirta, Asherah destroys his health. Nonetheless, El once again inter-

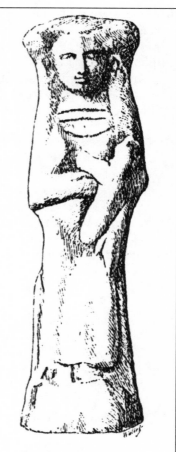

Small terra-cotta statue of a godmother

venes and Kirta recovers only to have his own son, Yassib, revolt against him.

The death of Kirta's first household and its replacement with a second is parallel to the reversal in the book of Job (Job 42:10-17). Kirta's dreams are parallel to those of Jacob (Gen 28:10-17), and those of Solomon (1 Kgs 3:4-15). The revolt of his son, Yassib, parallels the revolt of David's son, Absalom (2 Sam 15:1-6).

I.i:8–42

The household of the king was destroyed;
    The home of his seven brothers vanished.
The household of eight sons of the same mother was ruined;
    Their home was no more.   (2 Kgs 9:8; Job 1:13–19; Mic 5:5)

Kirta's first wife was infertile;
    His father's niece did not bear him a child.
He married again, but his second wife vanished childless;
    His mother's niece disappeared.
His third wife died childless in apparent good health,   (Job 21:23)
    His fourth wife died childless of disease.
His fifth wife perished childless from fever;
    His sixth wife drowned childless at sea.
His seventh wife died childless during wartime . . .

Kirta locked himself in the sanctuary and mourned,
    Going over each tragedy again and again . . . .

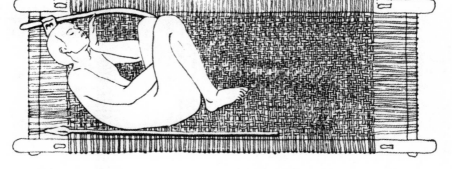

Warrior from Syria-Palestine buried on his bed with a spear and ax

Exhausted from weeping, he fell asleep,   (Gen 28:10–17)
   His couch soaked with tears, he began to dream....

El appeared to Kirta in his dream,   (Job 33:15)
   His Godfather came to him in a vision....
"Kirta, why are you crying?
   Why is the son of El in tears?
Do you want to be a king like your father, El the Bull,   (2 Sam 7:14)
   Do you want to be powerful like the Father of All?..."

I.ii:5–24

"Do I need silver or gold?   (2 Sam 21:3–4; Prov 22:1)
   Do I need land or slaves or horses?"
"Give me sons," Kirta pleaded.   (1 Sam 1:11)
   "I need a household," he begged.

El replied: "Stop your mourning, Kirta,
   Dry your tears, son of El.
Wash your face with water,   (Exod 29:4)
   Anoint your face with oil.
Bathe your arms to the elbows,
   Scrub the dirt from your fingertips to your shoulders.
Go to the shade of your tents.
   Prepare a sacrifice.
Pick out the sheep with your right hand;
   Select a lamb with each hand.

Sumerians bring offerings to a sanctuary

City with a lower wall and an upper wall

Assemble all the food needed for a sacrifice.
  Find a bird suitable for sacrifice,
Pour wine from a silver cup,
  Drip honey from a golden bowl.
Climb to the top of the tower,
  Climb to the heights of the wall.
Raise your hands to heaven,
  Sacrifice to your father, El the Bull."

🖹 *After El teaches Kirta how to offer sacrifice, he tells him to*
gather a six-month supply of food for an army of 300,000 soldiers
and lay siege to Udum. The vast army is not to attack the walls
of the city, but cut the inhabitants off for seven days until Pabil,
the ruler of Udum, sues for peace (Josh 6:1-16).

I.iii:1–49

Your army will cover the fields like locusts,   (Joel 1:4; Nah 3:15–17)
  Like crickets carpet the fringe of the steppe.
March for seven days until you reach the great city of Udum.
  Pillage its cities and villages.

Women gathering wood will run from the fields,
    Women picking up straw will abandon the threshing floor.
Women drawing water will flee the well,   (Gen 24:11)
    Women filling jars will escape from the spring.
Then wait for six days;
    Shoot no arrows into the city;
    Let no slinger throw a stone.

On the seventh day, King Pabil will not be able to rest,
        For the cries of his animals...
The King of Udum will send Kirta the message: "Accept peace offerings.
    Spare my palace. Leave my land!"...

Send the two messengers back to King Pabil with this demand:
    "Give me what the household of Kirta lacks,
        Give me Hurriya, your first-born child....
    Who will bear a child for Kirta?
        Let her give birth to a son for the Son of El."

≋❚ *El tells Kirta to seal the covenant between Ugarit and Udum by marrying Hurriya, a daughter of Pabil. On the third day of the march, Kirta stops at a sanctuary of Asherah and makes a vow (Judg 11:30-31; 1 Sam 14:24).*

I.iv:38–43

"By the power of Asherah, divine patron of Tyre,   (Judg 8:19; Ruth 3:13)
    By the power of the divine patron of Sidon,   (1 Sam 19:6)
If I can marry Hurriya,
    If I can bring this woman into my palace,
Then I will give Asherah double her bride price in silver,
    I will give you three times the value of Hurriya in gold."

≋❚ *Kirta and Hurriya celebrate their marriage before the divine assembly.*

II.ii:12–iii:16

When the divine assembly convenes   (Ps 82:1)
    The mighty Baal proposes a toast.

"May El the kind, the compassionate, bless Kirta the powerful,
    Show favor to the son of El."

El takes his cup in his hand;
    He takes his goblet in his right hand.
El blesses his servant, Kirta the powerful,
    He shows favor to the son of El.
"Kirta, you have obtained a wife,
    You have taken a woman into your household,
    and you have brought a young woman into your palace.
She will bear you seven sons,   (Ruth 4:11–12; Isa 32:15)
    Eight sons she will bear for you.   (Job 42:10–15)
She will bear for you Yassib,
    Who will be nursed by Astarte,
    Will suck from the breast of Anat."

✈ *Hurriya has many sons and daughters. Kirta, however, does not fulfill his vow to endow the sanctuary of Asherah. To remind him of his vow, Asherah inflicts Kirta with a fever no one can cure. Royal officials and the household of Kirta go into mourning to prepare for his death. Finally, El hears their prayers and responds by polling the other members of the divine assembly to see if any of them will cure Kirta. None in the divine assembly wishes to undertake so dangerous a mission, so El commissions Shataqat to cure him (2 Kgs 4:34-37; 5:10-14).*

III.vi:1–18

El orders: "Death, be vanquished!"
    He commands: "Shataqat, be strong!"
Shataqat sets out from the divine assembly;
    She arrives at the household of Kirta.
She enters to the sounds of mourning,
    Weeping fills the palace....
Shataqat wipes the sweat from Kirta's brow,
    She lets his appetite return,
    and she returns his taste for food.
Death is vanquished.
    Shataqat is victorious.   (2 Kgs 20:1–11)

Then Kirta the powerful commands,
    He shouts in a mighty voice:

"Hear me, Hurriya,
>Butcher a lamb for me to eat,
>Prepare a sheep for my supper."

⬛ *Kirta once again sits upon his throne and all appears to be well. Kirta's illness, however, has given his son, Yassib, a chance to seize the throne, so he demands that Kirta abdicate (2 Sam 15:1-14).*

III.vi:41–54

Yassib indicts Kirta:
>"If enemies had invaded the land while you were ill,
>They would have driven you out,
>>They would have forced you into the hills.
>Your illness made you derelict.

You did not hear the case of the widow.	(Deut 10:18; Isa 1:17)
You did not hear the case of the poor.	(Amos 2:6–7; 5:12)
You did not drive out the oppressor.	(Ps 82:2)
You did not feed the orphan in the city.	(Isa 10:2; Ezek 22:7)
You did not feed the widow in the country.	(Ps 68:5; Prov 29:14–16)
The sickbed has become your brother,	(Ps 41:3)

>>The pallet is your best friend.
>Step down from the kingship,
>>Allow me to reign.
>Relinquish your power;
>>Let me sit on the throne...."

⬛ *The story breaks off with Kirta pronouncing a curse on his rebel son. The failure to keep his vow to Asherah cost him his household and his health, and left him with only his youngest daughter as heir of his household (Josh 6:26).*

EXODUS

Bronze sculpture of Sargon, Great King of Agade

STORY OF SARGON
OF AGADE

Sometime after 3000 BCE, Agade was founded near the current city of Baghdad, Iraq. Agriculture, trade, and war soon made Agade an empire, and Sargon (2334-2279 BCE) one of the greatest rulers of the Sumerian or "black-headed" people [Akkadian: sag gig ga*].*

By 1900, British archaeologists had recovered three copies of the Story of Sargon celebrating the humble beginnings of this great king. All three were written in cuneiform. Two were written in the Assyrian dialect of the Akkadian language and one in the Babylonian dialect. They are preserved today in the British Museum in London.

A parallel to the Story of Sargon of Agade can be found in the story of the birth of Moses (Exod 1:22–2:10), where the motifs of unwanted pregnancy, secret birth, abandoning a newborn, being drawn out of the water, and adoption by a stranger also appear. The Story of Sargon is an apology defending the Great King against claims that he is not a legitimate ruler, which parallels the stories of Moses (Exod 1:22–4:26) defending him against claims that he has no legitimate authority.

Call me Sargon.
    I am the one and only Great King of Agade.

My mother was a priest,
    My father was an unknown from the mountains.

My mother gave birth to me in secret at Asupiranu, the city of saffron,
    She hid me in a basket woven from rushes and sealed with tar.

My mother abandoned me on the bank of the Euphrates
    The Euphrates carried my basket away,   (Exod 2:2–3)

Akki, the royal gardener, lifted me out of the water
    Akki reared me as his own,   (Exod 2:5–10)

Akki trained me to care for the gardens of the Great King.
    Ishtar, my divine patron, cared for me.

Then, I became a Great King
    I ruled the Sumerian peoples for fifty-five years.

I blazed trails through mountains with copper axes.
    I scaled high peaks....

Three times I conquered Dilmun on the Persian Gulf
    I laid siege to Dor and Kazallu on the Mediterranean Sea....

I challenge the kings who come after me:

Rule for fifty-five years!
    Become Great King of the Sumerian peoples!

Blaze trails through mountains with copper axes!
    Scale high peaks....

Conquer Dilmun three times!
    Conquer Dor and Kazallu....

TREATY BETWEEN RAMESSES II AND HATTUSILIS III

For more than one hundred years, Egypt and Hatti struggled for control of the eastern Mediterranean. The conflict drained the resources of both superpowers. Following a famous, but inconclusive, battle at Qadesh, Syria in 1285 BCE, the Treaty of Ramesses II and Hattusilis III was negotiated. This remarkable treaty was motivated both by Egypt's and Hatti's need for economic recovery, as well as by the increasing military threat of the Sea Peoples migrating into the eastern Mediterranean. The treaty kept the peace for the next fifty years and brought the Late Bronze period (1550–1200 BCE) to an end.

In the early 1900s archaeologists recovered both Egyptian and Hittite editions of the treaty. In the Egyptian edition,

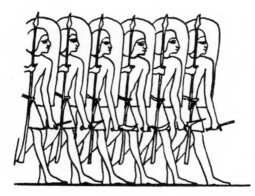

Infantry of Ramesses II

Ramesses II flamboyantly elaborates the role that he played in negotiating the treaty. He had one copy carved in hieroglyphics on the walls of the House of Amun in Karnak and another on the walls of his own funeral chapel, the Ramesseum, in the valley of the pharaohs, both located near today's Luxor in central Egypt. The Hittite edition is a more sober legal document written on clay tablets in cuneiform, using Akkadian, which was the diplomatic language of the ancient Near East. German archaeologists recovered the tablets from the archives of Hattusas, the Hittite capital, located in today's Turkey. They are preserved in the Ankara Museum in Turkey. This is a translation of Ramesses II's version of the treaty.

The Hittites developed the treaty form, which other cultures used. Standard Hittite treaties contained at least six components. They opened by giving (1) the credentials of the signatories to the treaty and issued (2) a new and official history of the relationship between the covenant partners. Then they laid out (3) the terms in careful legal language. These were followed by (4) a list of witnesses to the treaty, (5) a litany of curses for treaty violations and blessings for treaty compliance, and finally (6) provisions to record and promulgate the treaty. Covenants in the Bible parallel Hittite treaties. Simple covenants appear in negotiations between Jacob and Laban (Gen 31:44-54). The Covenant Code (Exod 21–23), the Holiness Code (Lev 17–26) and the Deuteronomic Code (Deut 12–26) and the covenant between Yahweh and Israel at Shechem (Josh 24:1-28) are more complex examples of the genre.

CREDENTIALS

Inscribed on this silver tablet is the treaty creating peace and eternal alliance between Hattusilis, Great King of Hatti, son of Mursilis, Great King of Hatti, grandson of Suppiluliumas, Great King of Hatti, and Ramesses, Pharaoh of Egypt, son of Seti, Pharaoh of Egypt, son of Ramesses, Pharaoh of Egypt.

HISTORY

In the beginning, the divine assembly decreed that there be peace between the Pharaoh of Egypt and the Great King of Hatti. Then Muwatallis, my brother and Great King of Hatti, declared war on

Ramesses II at the Battle of Qadesh

Ramesses. From this day forward, Hattusilis will observe the decree of Re and Seth, which prohibits war between Egypt and Hatti forever.

TERMS
(Deut 23:15–16; 2 Kgs 9:16–26)

Current Relations

Hattusilis agrees to this treaty with Ramesses, creating peace and an eternal alliance between us. We are brothers and are at peace with each other forever. I, Hattusilis, came to the throne of Hatti when Muwatallis died. Therefore, I agree to this treaty with Ramesses, creating peace and an alliance between us. The state of peace and alliance between our lands is now better than in former times.

I, Ramesses, agree to peace and an alliance. The successors of the Great King of Hatti will be allies with the successors of Ramesses. The relationship between Egypt and Hatti shall be like our relationship, one of peace and eternal alliance. There will never again be war between us.

Non-Aggression

In the future, the Great King of Hatti shall neither invade nor raid Egypt.

Ramesses shall neither invade nor raid Hatti.

Existing Treaties

I, Hattusilis, reaffirm the treaties of Suppiluliumas and of Muwatallis, Great Kings of Hatti.

I, Ramesses, affirm the treaty I make with Hattusilis this day, and will observe it and act accordingly from now on.

Defense

If a foreign army invades the lands of Ramesses, and he sends a message to the Great King of Hatti, saying: "Come and help me against this enemy," the Great King of Hatti shall come and fight against the enemy of Egypt, his ally. If the Great King of Hatti does not wish to come personally, he may send infantry and chariots to fight against the enemy of Egypt, his ally.

Likewise, if Ramesses is trying to put down an armed revolt, the Great King of Hatti shall help him until all the rebels have been executed. If a foreign army attacks the Great King of Hatti, Ramesses shall come and fight against the enemy of Hatti, to aid his ally. If Ramesses does not wish to come personally, he may send infantry and chariots, as well as word to this effect, to Hatti.

Succession

When Hattusilis dies, the son of Hattusilis shall be crowned Great King of Hatti in his father's place. If the people of Hatti revolt against his son, Ramesses shall send soldiers and chariots to protect the son of Hattusilis. Once order has been restored in Hatti, they shall return to Egypt.

Extradition

...If one, or even two, powerful Egyptians, or anyone from Egypt, seeks asylum in Hatti, the Great King shall extradite them to Ramesses, Pharaoh of Egypt.

...If one, or even two, powerful Hittites, or anyone from Hatti seeks asylum in Egypt, Pharaoh shall extradite them to the Great King of Hatti.

List of Witnesses
(Gen 31:51–53)

Thousands of divine patrons of Hatti and Egypt are witnesses to the treaty between the Great King of Hatti and Ramesses inscribed on this silver tablet.

Teshub,
Divine Patron of Storms in Hatti

Re, Divine Patron of the Sky
Re, Divine Patron of Arinna
Seth, Divine Patron of Storms
Seth, Divine Patron of Hatti
Seth, Divine Patron of Arinna
Seth, Divine Patron of Zippalanda
Seth, Divine Patron of Pettiyarik
Seth, Divine Patron of Hissashapa
Seth, Divine Patron of Sarissa
Seth, Divine Patron of Aleppo
Seth, Divine Patron of Lihzina
The Divine Patron of Zitharias
The Divine Patron of Karzis
The Divine Patron of Hapantaliyas
The Divine Patron of Karana
The Queen of the Sky
The Divine Patrons of Oaths
The Divine Patron of the Earth
Ishara, Divine Mother of Oaths
Ishara, Divine Mother of Mountains and Rivers of Hatti
The Divine Assembly of Kizuwanda
Amun-Re
Seth
The Divine Patrons of the Mountains and Rivers of Egypt
The Divine Patron of the Sky
The Divine Patron of the Earth
The Divine Patron of the Sea
The Divine Patron of the Winds
The Divine Patron of the Clouds

LITANY OF CURSES AND BLESSINGS
(Gen 31:50–54)

The households, lands and slaves of those who do not observe the treaty between Hatti and Egypt inscribed on this silver tablet will be cursed by the divine assemblies of Hatti and Egypt.

The households, lands and slaves of those Egyptians and Hittites who observe and carry out faithfully the treaty between Hatti and Egypt inscribed on this silver tablet will be blessed by the divine assemblies of Hatti and Egypt with prosperity and long life....

ANNALS OF
MERNEPTAH

In 1896, Flinders Petrie from England recovered a stela of granite almost seven and one-half feet high and three and one-quarter feet wide from the funeral chapel of Merneptah (1224–1214 BCE) in the Valley of the Pharaohs (KV8) at Luxor, Egypt. The stela was originally inscribed by Amenophis III (1391–1353 BCE), but was recycled by Merneptah to celebrate his victory over Libya and Syria-Palestine. These annals are written in hieroglyphics on twenty-eight lines. The stela is now in the Egyptian Museum in Cairo (34025 verso).

The Annals of Merneptah contain the only mention of Israel during the New Kingdom (1550–1070 BCE) recovered in Egypt. The annals refer to "Israel" as a "people," rather than as a "state." The stela is used to date the exodus of the Hebrews from Egypt to the reign of Ramesses II (1290–1224 BCE) and the appearance of Israel in Syria-Palestine to 1250 BCE.

Parallels to the Annals of Merneptah appear in the books of Joshua and Judges, and in the annals of rulers of Israel and Judah in the books of Samuel-Kings.

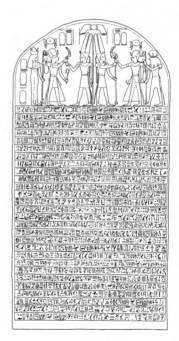

Stela of Merneptah

Hieroglyphics for "Israel" in the Annals of Merneptah

The rulers of my enemies now lie prostrate before me and beg for peace. Not one of my enemies [Egyptian: "nine bows"] raises his head in revolt. I have devastated Tehenu and put down a revolt against the Great King of Hatti. I have plundered Syria-Palestine from one end to the other, taken slaves from the city of Ashkelon (Josh 13:3), and conquered the city of Gezer (Josh 10:33). I have razed Yanoam to the ground. I have decimated the people of Israel and put their children to death [Egyptian: "its seed is not"]. Hurru is a widow. All lands have been pacified. Every rebel is now prostrate before Merneptah, pharaoh of Upper and Lower Egypt, the divine presence of Amun-Re [Egyptian: Ba-en-Re], beloved of the divine assembly [Egyptian: *Meri-Amun*], who dawns each day like Amun-Re the sun.

LEVITICUS,
NUMBERS,
DEUTERONOMY

CODE OF SHULGI

Shulgi (2094-2047 BCE) ruled during the Third Dynasty of Ur, in southern Iraq today. He authorized the publication of the Code of Shulgi, formerly attributed to Ur-Nammu (2112-2095 BCE). Two fragments were recovered at Ur [Arabic: Tell al-Muqay-yar] during the 1922-1934 excavations of the British Museum and the University of Pennsylvania directed by C. Leonard Wooley (1880-1960). Both tablets, including the prologue and articles #7-37, are written in Sumerian using the cuneiform script. There were originally eight columns of writing, four on each side of the tablets. They are preserved today in the British Museum in London. The first ten articles contained in the code have been reconstructed from tablets discovered at Nippur, also in the British Museum.

The Code of Shulgi is the oldest system of laws recovered by archaeologists from the world of the Bible. It established an enduring legal tradition that applies uniform principles of justice to a wide range of social institutions, from the standardization of weights and measures to the protection of widows and orphans. The code also limited capital punishment to murder, robbery, and other serious crimes. Most sentences have to do with fines paid to victims, rather than revenge

Seal of Nammu,
Servant of King Shulgi

101

taken on criminals. These fines, however, are not determined by the principle of proportionality or talion.

In the Bible, the Covenant Code (Exod 21—23), the Holiness Code (Lev 17—26) and the Deuteronomic Code (Deut 12—26) are parallel to the Code of Shulgi.

art 1 (Exod 20:13)

If the father of a household commits murder, then the sentence is death.

art 6 (Deut 22:23–24)

If the father of a household rapes a marriageable and engaged woman, then the sentence is death.

art 8 (Lev 19:20–21)

If the father of a household rapes a marriageable slave of another, then the fine is one and two-thirds ounces [Akkadian: "five shekels"] of silver.

art 17 (Deut 23:15–16)

If a slave runs away from his household and his city, and the father of another household returns the slave, then the owner shall pay a reward of two-thirds ounces of silver.

art 25 (Gen 16:4–6)

If a slave shames the mother of her household by speaking insolently to her, then the mouth of the slave shall be scrubbed with . . . salt.

art 28 (Deut 19:16–19)

If the father of a household is guilty of perjury, then the fine is five ounces of silver.

SUMERIAN CODE

⧄ *The Sumerian Code, preserved today at Yale University (YOS 1.28), is an exercise done by a student preparing for a government job in Sumer or Babylon around 1800 BCE. Candidates wrote out, again and again, the technical terms and phrases that would appear in the examinations at the end of their training. The site where the tablets were recovered is unknown.*

Parallels to the Sumerian Code appear in the Covenant Code (Exod 21—23), in the Holiness Code (Lev 17—26) and in the Deuteronomic Code (Deut 12—26).

art 1 (Exod 21:22)

If one father of one household accidentally strikes the daughter of another, and she miscarries, then the fine is three and one-third ounces of silver [Akkadian: "ten shekels"].

art 4 (Deut 21:18–21)

If an adopted son disowns the father and mother of his household with the oath: "You are not my father. You are not my mother," then he forfeits his right to inherit their land and property, and can be sold as an ordinary slave at full market value.

art 5

If the father and mother of a household disown their adopted son with the oath: "You are not our son," then they shall forfeit the land and property that he will inherit from them.

art 7 (Gen 34:1–12)

If the father of one household rapes the daughter of another, while she is in the street without the knowledge of the father and mother of her household, and if he swears: "I will marry her," then her father and her mother shall give her as a wife to the man who raped her.

art 8 (Gen 34; Exod 22:16; Deut 22:23–24)

If the father of one household rapes the daughter of another, who, with the knowledge of the father and the mother of her household, is walking about the city, and if he swears at the sanctuary gate that he did not know she was the daughter of a household, then he is not guilty.

Ur-Ninu, King of Lagash, with his cupbearer and four sons

CODE OF HAMMURABI

The Code of Hammurabi is a treatise on legal theory, political science, and social organization. It reflects the legal thinking and moral values of Babylon. In 1901, French excavators recovered a copy of the code at Susa on the border between Iraq and Iran today where it had been taken by the Elamites, who were Babylon's enemies. The code was inscribed in cuneiform on an eight-foot pillar of black diorite and is preserved today in the Louvre Museum in Paris.

A catalog of the military victories and political endorsements of Hammurabi, Great King of Babylon (1792-1750 BCE), introduces 282 case laws. Each case law has two parts. First, a dependent clause introduced by "if" describes a situation: "If the father of one household charges another with murder, without the evidence to prove it...." Second, a main clause introduced by "then" imposes a sentence: "...then the sentence is death" (CH 1). Distinct social groups, like laborers, slaves, fathers of households, and priests, appear in the laws. Punishments are based on the social status of the persons involved. The code concludes with an essay on the role of law in a state.

In ancient Israel, the Covenant Code (Exod 21–23), the Holiness Code (Lev 17–26) and the Deuteronomic Code (Deut 12–26) are parallel to the Code of Hammurabi.

Prologue

In both the Code of Hammurabi and the Middle Assyrian Code, prologues place the promulgation of a code of law within the context of a ruler's rise to power. The prologue in the Code of Hammurabi begins at the point in the dim past when Anu and Enlil delegated Marduk, divine patron of Babylon, to govern all nations and Hammurabi to "...to establish justice" in Babylon. (2 Sam 8:15; 1 Kgs 10:9; Ps 15; Ps 111:10)

What follows is a litany of Hammurabi's titles and the services that he performs for the cities under his rule and the temples of his divine patrons.

Good Shepherd—wearing Enlil's crown . . . ,	(1 Chr 11:2)
Great King—campaigning to the ends of the earth . . . ,	
Net—trapping his enemies . . . ,	(Hos 7:12)
Raging Bull—tossing challengers over his head . . . ,	(Isa 10:13)
Wise Mediator—equitably allotting pasture and water rights . . . ,	
Competent Administrator—getting things done . . . ,	
Deliverer—rescuing his people from affliction . . . ,	
Judge—establishing justice,	
Guide—leading his people in right paths,	(2 Chr 9:8)
Faithful—restoring the statues of Ashur to his temples,	
Mediator—quieting all who raise objections . . . ,	

At the time when Marduk chose me to lead the people,
    And show them the path of right behavior,
I caused the land to resound with justice and truth,   (Prov 8:20–21)
    And improved the lot of the people.
Therefore I set forth these laws:

art 1 (Exod 23:1–3; Deut 19:16–19)

If the father of one household charges another with murder, but has no evidence, then the sentence is death.

art 2

If the father of one household charges another with witchcraft, but has no evidence, then the defendant is tried by ordeal in a river.

If the defendant drowns, then the plaintiff inherits the defendant's household.

If the defendant survives, then the sentence is death for the plaintiff, and the defendant confiscates the plaintiff's household.

Seal from Alalakh belonging to a citizen of Karana, with the arrow of Marduk, patron of Hammurabi, whose empire ruled Alalakh and Karana

art 3 (Deut 19:16–19)

If the father of a household commits perjury before the city assembly in a case involving the death penalty, then the sentence is death.

art 5 (Exod 23:6–8; Lev 19:15; Deut 16:19)

If a judge accepts a bribe to render and seal a decision, then the judge is fined twelve times the settlement ordered in the decision, is expelled from the bench, and cannot serve as a judge again.

art 8 (Exod 20:15; Lev 19:11 + 13; Deut 5:19; 22:1–4)

If the father of a household steals an ox, a sheep, a donkey, a pig, or a boat from a state or temple official, then he is fined thirty times the value of the stolen property.

Likewise, if the father of a household steals one of these items from a laborer, then the fine is ten times the value of the stolen property.

If the father of a household fails to pay the fine, then the sentence is death.

art 14 (Exod 21:16; Deut 24:7)

If the father of one household kidnaps the child of another, then the sentence is death.

art 15 (Deut 23:15–16)

If the father of a household helps state slaves or household slaves to escape through the city gates, then the sentence is death.

art 16 (Deut 23:15–16)

If the father of a household harbors slaves who have run away from the temple or from a household, and if he disobeys a court order to produce them, then the sentence is death.

art 17

If the father of a household captures a runaway slave in the open and returns the slave to the owner, then a reward of two-third ounces [Akkadian: "two shekels"] of silver is paid by the slave's owner to the father of the household that caught him.

art 21 (Exod 22:2–3)

If the father of a household tunnels through the wall of another's house and robs it, then he is sentenced to death. The execution shall take place outside the tunnel, and the body shall be hung in front of the tunnel.

art 24 (Deut 21:1–9)

If a murderer is not caught, then a fine of eighteen ounces [Akkadian: "one mina"] of silver is paid by the state to the household of the victim.

art 25

If the father of one household steals property from another while fighting a fire, then the looter shall be cast into that fire.

art 57 (Exod 22:5)

If a herder does not have a covenant with the owner of a field to graze his sheep on it, but has grazed his sheep on the field without the consent of its owner, then, when the owner of the field harvests the field, a fine of one-hundred forty bushels [Akkadian: *kur*] of grain for every sixteen acres [Akkadian: *iku*] of land is imposed on the herder.

art 94 (Deut 25:13–15; Amos 8:5)

If bankers use a light scale to measure the grain or the silver that they lend and a heavy scale to measure the grain or the silver that they collect, then they shall forfeit their investment.

art 117 (Exod 21:2–11; Deut 15:12–18)

If a destitute father of a household sells his wife, his son, or his daughter into slavery to pay a debt, then the creditor cannot keep them as slaves for more than three years and must free them at the beginning of the fourth year.

art 125 (Exod 22:7–8)

If father of one household stores property in the warehouse of another, and if the property is stolen by a thief who tunnels through the wall or climbs over it, then the owner of the warehouse whose carelessness allowed the robbery to take place must make every effort to find the thief and recover the stolen property. In any case, the warehouse owner must make full restitution of the value of the stolen property to its owner.

art 129 (Deut 22:22)

If a wife of a father of the household is arrested in the act of committing adultery, then she and her partner are to be tied up and tried by ordeal in the river.

If, however, the woman's husband pardons her, then the monarch can pardon his subject.

art 130 (Deut 22:23–27)

If the father of a household rapes a woman who is marriageable and engaged, then the man is sentenced to death, but the woman is exonerated.

art 131 (Num 5:12–22)

If the father of a household accuses his wife of adultery without evidence, then she shall swear an oath of innocence before the divine patron of her household, and she may return home.

art 132 (Num 5:11–31; Shulgi 10–11)

If a wife of the father of a household is charged with adultery, but there is no evidence, then she is to be tried by ordeal in the river to restore the honor of her husband.

art 141 (Deut 24:1–4)

If a wife of the father of a household leaves her husband's house on her own business, and if she neglects the house, and shames her husband, then her husband may either divorce her without paying a divorce settlement, or may marry another woman while his former wife is to live in the house as a slave.

art 142–43

If a woman so hates her husband that she says: "You may not have intercourse with me!"—and if the elders conclude that she is a faithful wife, despite the false accusations of her husband, then the woman may take her dowry and return to the household of her father.

If the elders conclude that the woman is unfaithful, that she leaves the house of her husband on her own business, that she neglects the house and shames her husband, then she is to be drowned in the river.

art 146 (Gen 16:1–15; Gen 21:9–21)

If the slave with whom a Naditu priest negotiates a covenant to bear children for her husband considers herself to have the same status as the Naditu priest once she has borne children, then the Naditu priest may pierce her ear and downgrade her status in the household, but the Naditu priest may not sell her.

art 154 (Lev 18:6–18; 20:10–21; Deut 27:20 + 22–23)

If the father of a household has sexual intercourse with his daughter, then he is to be exiled from the city.

art 155 (Lev 18:15; 20:12)

If the father of a household chooses a bride for his son and if his son has intercourse with her, but later it is proven that the father of the household also has had intercourse with her, then the father of the household is to be drowned in the river.

art 156 (Lev 19:20–22)

If the father of a household chooses a bride for his son and if his son does not have intercourse with her, but the father of the household does have intercourse with her, then a fine of nine ounces of silver is paid to the household of her father, her dowry is returned, and she may marry the man of her choice.

art 157 (Lev 18:8; 20:11; Deut 27:20)

If the father of a household has intercourse with his mother after the death of his father, then both are to be burned at the stake.

art 170 (Gen 21:9–21)

If the father of a household who has children by his wife and by his slave adopts the slave's children, then his household shall be divided evenly between the children of both, after his wife's first-born son has received the preferential share.

art 195 (Exod 21:15)

If the father of a household strikes his father, then his hand is to be cut off.

art 196 (Exod 21:24; Lev 24:20; Deut 19:21)

If the father of a household blinds an eye of another of equal status, then his eye is to be blinded.

art 197

If the father of one household breaks a bone of another, then his bone is to be broken.

art 198

If the father of a household blinds the eye or breaks a bone of one of his laborers, then the fine is eighteen ounces of silver.

art 199 (Exod 21:26; Lev 24:19–20; Deut 19:21)

If the father of one household blinds the eye or breaks the bone of a slave of another household, then the fine is one-half the price of the slave.

Stela with Hammurabi
before Shamash,
Divine Patron of Justice

art 206–7 (Exod 21:18–19)

If the father of a household accidentally hits another and causes injury, then he must swear: "I did not strike him deliberately" and must pay his medical expenses.

If the victim dies from the blow, then the father of the household must swear the same oath and pay a fine to the household of the victim of nine ounces of silver.

art 209 (Sumerian Code 1; Exod 21:22–23)

If the father of a household beats the daughter of another and causes her to miscarry, then the fine is six ounces of silver.

art 233 (Deut 22:8)

If a builder constructs a house and does faulty work resulting in an unsafe wall, then the builder must strengthen that wall at his own expense.

art 244 (Exod 22:14–15)

If the father of a household rents an ox or an ass, and if a lion kills it while it is out in the open, then there is no fine.

art 249 (Exod 22:14–15)

If the father of a household rents an ox and a member of the divine assembly strikes it with lightning and it dies,then, to avoid a fine, he must swear that a member of the divine assembly killed the ox.

art 251 (Exod 21:28–36)

If the father of a household has neither tethered nor blunted the horns of his ox, even after the city assembly has put him on notice that the animal was dangerous, and the ox gores a state official, then the fine is eighteen ounces of silver.

art 266 (Gen 31:39; Exod 22:10–13)

If a member of the divine assembly or a lion kills a sheep, then the shepherd must take an oath of innocence before his divine patron and turn the remains of the animal over to its owner.

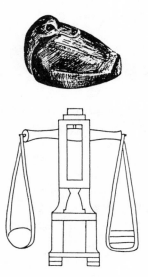

*Assyrian duck-shaped weight
and balance scales*

HITTITE CODE

After 1893 archaeologists excavated some ten thousand baked clay tablets from Hattusas, the 419-acre site of the Hittite capital in Turkey. They included samples of the Hittite Code. These two-hundred case laws were written on two baked clay tablets in Neshili Hittite using cuneiform script. By 1915, Bedrich Hrozny, a Czech scholar, was able to translate the language.

The Hittite Code represents legal thinking in Hatti between 1650 and 1200 BCE. It prefers sentences that compensate victims for loss, rather than sentences that punish convicts for crime. It also regularly commutes death sentences to corporal punishment and reduces corporal punishment sentences to fines. To make these changes, the Hittite Code simply inserts "Formerly" at the beginning of the old law and then introduces the new law with "but now." Certain cases are reserved to a royal court (Deut 17:8-11).

Parallels to the Hittite Code appear in the Deuteronomic Code (Deut 12–26) and in the Holiness Code (Lev 17–26). These parallels are especially clear in each code's use of similar technical terms. The terms "brother" and "brother-in-law" identify fathers of households who are covenant partners, rather than simply individuals who are kin to one another by birth. For example, in the book of Deuteronomy (Deut 25:5-10), a "brother-in-law" is a legal guardian. The same legal connotations appear in the English use of "sons" in the titles of businesses like "J. R. Everitt & Sons." Although the terms "sister" and "daughter" in English are used only to identify members of one's family of origin, in Semitic languages the same words often carry important legal connotations as well. Another strong parallel appears in the practice of sealing a covenant, which exchanges food and weapons, with a marriage.

art 4 (Deut 21:1–9)

If the body of the father of one household is found on the property of another, then the property owner shall forfeit his property, his house, and pay twenty-four ounces of silver [Hittite: "sixty shekels"].

If the deceased is a woman, then the property owner shall simply pay forty-eight ounces of silver [Hittite: "one hundred twenty shekels"].

If the body is not found on private property, but in open country, then the authorities shall measure eleven miles [Hittite: three *dannas*] in every direction, and any village or city within this distance shall pay the fine.

If no village or city lies within this distance, then the household of the deceased may make no claim.

art 10 (Exod 21:18–19)

If the father of one household beats another and makes him an invalid, then the assailant shall take care of his victim. He shall also pay someone to look after the victim's household until he recovers. When the victim recovers, the assailant shall give him two and one-half ounces of silver [Hittite: "six shekels"] and pay his medical expenses.

Bulls in a frieze of shell inlay at Temple of Ubaid, Sumer

art 17 (Exod 21:22–23)

If the father of a household causes a free woman in her tenth month of pregnancy to miscarry, then he shall pay a fine of four ounces of silver [Hittite: "ten shekels"].

If the woman is in her fifth month of pregnancy, then he shall pay a fine of two ounces of silver [Hittite: "five shekels"] or put his own land and children up as collateral.

art 67 (Exod 21:37 [Heb], 22:1–4)

If the father of a household steals a cow, formerly, the thief was fined twelve head of cattle, but now, the fine is six head of cattle—two two-year-old calves, two one-year-old calves, and two calves who have just been weaned—or put his own land and children up as collateral.

art 94 (Exod 22:1 [Heb], 22:2–3, 7)

If the father of a household breaks into a house . . . , formerly, the fine was sixteen ounces of silver [Hittite: "forty shekels"], but now, the fine is five ounces of silver [Hittite: "twelve shekels"].

art 98 (Exod 22:6)

If the father of a household sets fire to the house of another, then he must rebuild the house and compensate the household for every person or animal killed by the fire.

art 111 (Exod 22:18; Deut 17:8–11; 18:10–14; 1 Sam 28:3)

If the father of a household makes a clay figurine and uses it to make magic, then he is guilty of sorcery, and the case must be tried in a royal court.

art 189 (Lev 18:6–18)

The father of a household may not have sexual intercourse with his mother, his daughter, or his son.

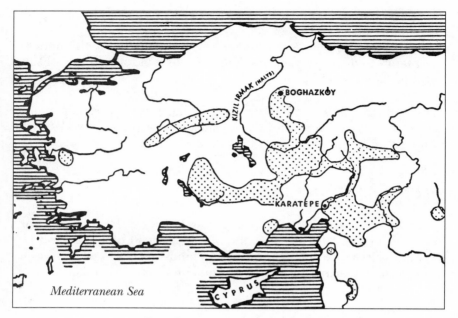

Dotted area shows Hittite ruins

art 193 (Gen 38; Deut 25:5–10; Ruth 4)

If the father of a household dies, then his legal guardian [Hittite: "brother"] marries the widow.

If the father of a household and his legal guardian die, then the guardian's father marries the widow.

If the father of a household, his legal guardian, and his father die, then one of his brother's sons marries the widow....

art 195 (Lev 18:6–18)

The father of a household may not have sexual intercourse with his brother's wife while his brother is still alive.

The father of a household may not have sexual intercourse with the daughter of his wife or with his mother-in-law or his sister-in-law.

art 197 (Deut 22:22–27)

If the father of a household rapes a woman while they are in the mountains together, then his sentence is death; the woman is not guilty.

If the father of a household rapes a woman while they are in her house together, then the sentence for the woman is death.

If the woman's husband discovers them in the act, then he may kill them without committing an offense.

MIDDLE ASSYRIAN CODE

The Middle Assyrian Code was developed during the reign of Tiglath-pileser I, Great King of Assyria (1114-1076 BCE). In 1903, German archaeologists found part of the code at Ashur, Iraq. It was written in the Assyrian dialect of the Akkadian language in cuneiform script on fifteen baked clay tablets. The tablets are preserved today in the Staatliches Museum in Berlin.

The Middle Assyrian Code may have been four thousand lines long and probably followed the same literary pattern as the Code of Hammurabi. An inspiring recitation of the military and political accomplishments of Tiglath-pileser I introduces a major section of case laws aimed at clarifying guilt and responsibility.

Parallels to the Middle Assyrian Code appear in the Covenant Code (Exod 21—23), in the Holiness Code (Lev 17—26) and in the Deuteronomic Code (Deut 12—26).

A, art 1

If the wife or daughter of the father of a household enters a temple, steals something, and either it is found in her possession or the charge is proven against her, then she shall be brought before the divine patron of the temple, who will determine her sentence.

A, art 2 (Lev 24:16; Deut 24:16)

If a wife or daughter of the father of a household blasphemes or gossips, then she alone is guilty. Her husband, sons, and daughters are not guilty.

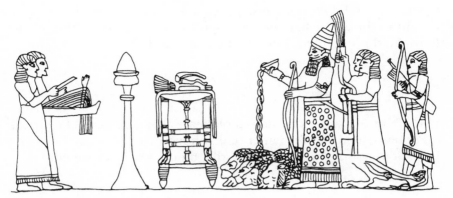

Accompanied by sacred music (left), Ashurbanipal, Great King of Assyria, stands with hunters (right) to offer wine for the lions killed

A, art 8 (Deut 25:11–12)

If a woman ruptures one of the testicles of a man of a household during a fight, then one of her fingers is amputated.

If a woman ruptures one of the testicles of the father of a household during a fight and, even after medical treatment, his other testicle also ruptures, then both of the eyes of the woman are gouged out.

A, art 9

If the father of a household forces the mother of another household to let him fondle her, then, following due process, one of his fingers is amputated.

If the father of a household forces the mother of another household to let him kiss her, then his lower lip is drawn along the edge of an ax blade and cut off.

A, art 12 (Deut 22:23–27)

If the father of a household forces himself on the mother of another household when she is walking along a street and says, "Have intercourse with me," and he has intercourse with her, even though she resists him and does not consent, regardless of whether he has been caught in the act or has been accused by witnesses, the father of the household is executed. The woman is not guilty.

A, art 13 (Deut 22:22)

If a wife of the father of a household leaves her own house to visit another household and the father of that household has intercourse with her, knowing that she is another's wife, then both are executed.

A, art 14

If the father of a household has intercourse with the mother of another household at an inn or in the street, knowing that she is another's wife, then her husband shall sentence both of them to similar punishments.

If the father of a household did not know that the woman with whom he had intercourse was another's wife, then the father of the household is not guilty. The woman's husband shall charge his wife and punish her as he sees fit.

A, art 15 (Deut 22:22)

If the father of a household catches the father of another household having intercourse with his wife, then, after due process, both the father of the household and the woman are executed. The woman's husband is not guilty.

If the father of a household catches the father of another household having intercourse with his wife, then the plaintiff is to charge the defendant before the ruler or the elders.

If, following due process, the plaintiff asks to have his wife executed, then the ruler or the elders are to also execute the defendant.

If the plaintiff asks to have his wife's nose cut off, then the ruler or the elders are to castrate the defendant and mutilate his face.

If the plaintiff asks to have his wife go free, then the ruler or the elders shall let the defendant go free.

A, art 16

If a wife of the father of a household asks the father of another household to have intercourse with her, then that man is not guilty. The husband of the woman is to punish his wife as he sees fit.

If the father of a household forces the mother of another household to have intercourse with him, then, following due process, both are to receive similar punishments.

A, art 17 (Num 5:11–31)

If the father of one household says to another: "Men are repeatedly having intercourse with your wife," but there are no witnesses, then the matter will be settled by ordeal in the river.

A, art 18 (2 Sam 10:4)

If the father of one household says to another, either in private or during a brawl: "Men are repeatedly having intercourse with your wife and I will charge her myself," but there is no proof, then the plaintiff is flogged forty times with staves, is to serve as a slave for the state [French: *corvée*] for a month, have his beard shaved, and be fined 75 pounds [Akkadian: "one talent"] of lead.

A, art 19 (2 Sam 10:4)

If the father of one household starts a rumor against another by saying: "Men are repeatedly having homosexual intercourse with him," or says to him during a brawl in the presence of other people, "Men are repeatedly having homosexual intercourse with you and I will charge you myself," but there is no proof, then the plaintiff is flogged fifty times with staves, is to serve as a slave for the state for a month, have his beard shaved, and be fined 75 pounds of lead.

A, art 20 (Lev 18:22; 20:13)

If the father of one household has homosexual intercourse with the father of another household, then, following due process, the defendant is raped and castrated.

A, art 21 (Exod 21:22)

If the father of a household physically abuses the daughter of a free man until she has a miscarriage, then, following due process, he is fined 225 pounds [Akkadian: "three talents"] of lead, flogged fifty times with staves, and is to serve as a slave for the state for a month.

A, art 24 (Lev 20:10–21)

If a wife of a father of a household runs away, enters the household of another, whether in the same city or in a neighboring city, stays with the mother of the household, spending the night three or four times, without the knowledge of the father of the household, and later that woman is caught, then the husband of the fugitive woman is to cut off her ears and not take her back. The husband of her accomplice is to cut off the ears of his wife, but may pay a fine of 320 pounds [Akkadian: "four talents, 12 minas"] of lead to redeem her and take her back.

If the father of the household knew that the fugitive wife was staying in his house, then he is fined three times her bride price.

If the father of the household pleads not guilty and swears: "I did not know there was a fugitive in my house," then he is tried by ordeal in the river.

If the father of the household refuses to go to the river, then he is fined three times the bride price of the fugitive wife.

If the father of a household whose wife deserted him refuses to go to the river, then the father of the household where she took refuge does not have to undergo the ordeal.

If a father of a household whose wife deserted him does not cut off her ears and takes her back, then no penalties are imposed.

A, art 30

If the father of a household pays the bride price for one son, but the wedding has not yet been celebrated, and another son who is already married dies, then he is to appoint the still unmarried son as the widow's legal guardian.

Like cherubim guarding the Jerusalem Temple, lamassu—
winged bulls with human heads—guard Assyrian sanctuaries

If, after he accepts the bride price, the father of a woman's household becomes unwilling for his daughter to be married to the legal guardian for another woman, then the father of the household of the dead man may arrange for his surviving son to marry the widow, and may abrogate the marriage covenant with the other household, taking back the lead, silver, gold, and inedible portion of the bride price. He must not take back any part of the bride price that was edible.

A, art 33 (Gen 38:1–30; Deut 25:5–10)

If, after her husband dies, a woman with sons is living in the household of her father, then, if he chooses, her father may send her to live in the household of her father-in-law.

If both the father of her household and the father of her husband's household are also dead, and she has no sons, then she becomes a widow and she may go wherever she wishes.

A, art 37 (Deut 24:1)

If the father of a household wishes to divorce his wife, he may do so with alimony or without alimony.

A, art 40 (Gen 38:14–15)

Mothers of households, widows, and other free women are to wear veils when they go out into the street.

Marriageable women are to wear veils...when they go out into the street during the day.

Concubines are to wear veils when they go out with the mothers of their households.

Women vowed to temple service [Akkadian: *qadishtu*] who are married are to wear veils when they go about in the streets. Unmarried women vowed to temple service are not to wear veils when they go about in the streets. Prostitutes are not to wear veils.

If the father of a household sees a prostitute wearing a veil, then she is arrested, witnesses are subpoenaed, and she is charged before the assembly at the palace gate. Her jewelry is not confiscated, but the plaintiff is to confiscate her clothing. She is flogged fifty times with staves, and tar is poured into her hair.

If the father of a household sees a prostitute who is wearing a veil, and does not charge her at the palace gate, then he is flogged fifty times with staves, his clothes are confiscated by the informant, his ears are pierced and tied with a cord behind his head, and he is to serve as a slave for the state for one full month. Slaves are not to wear veils.

If the father of a household sees a slave wearing a veil, then she is arrested, charged before the assembly at the palace gate, her ears are cut off, and her clothes are confiscated by the plaintiff.

If the father of a household sees a slave wearing a veil and does not arrest her and charge her at the palace gate, then, following due process, he is flogged fifty times with staves, his ears are pierced and tied with a cord behind his head, his clothes are confiscated by the informant, and he is to serve as a slave for the state for one full month.

A, art 41

If the father of a household wishes to marry a captured woman, then he is to ask five or six of his neighbors to be present and he shall veil her in their presence while swearing: "She is my wife," and she becomes his wife.

If the father of a household wants to make a secondary wife the mother of the household, he must veil her in the presence of five or six witnesses and declare: "This woman is the mother of my household."

If the father of a household dies and the mother of his household has no sons, then his sons by his secondary wives become eligible for a share of the household.

A, art 45

If the husband of a married woman becomes a prisoner of war, and the father of her husband's household is dead, and she has no son, then she is to remain faithful to her husband for two years....

If, during those two years, the woman swears before witnesses that she does not have enough to live on, then the state is to appoint a legal guardian to support her, and for whose household she is to work....

If, during those two years, the woman swears before witnesses that she does not have enough to live on, but that her husband's household cannot support her, then the ruler and the elders of the city are to accept his field and house as collateral and pay for her support....

...after two years, the ruler and the elders are to declare her a widow; then she may go to live with the husband of her choice.

If a husband who becomes a prisoner of war returns after his wife has been declared a widow and has remarried, then he is to take her back.

He may not claim the sons whom she has had with her second husband. Their sons belong to his household. He is to repay the ruler and the elders of the city for everything they spent to support his wife, and thus recover his right to his field and house.

If a husband who becomes a prisoner of war dies in a strange land, the ruler is to reassign his field and house to whomever he wishes.

A, art 47 (Exod 22:18; Lev 20:27; Deut 18:10–14; 1 Sam 28:3)

If the father of a household or the mother of a household is discovered working magic, then, following due process, the defendants are sentenced to death.

If the father of a household witnesses a man or a woman working magic, or if he hears of it from an eyewitness who swears: "I have seen it myself," then he is to come forward and testify before the ruler....

A, art 50 (Exod 21:22–25)

If the father of a household physically abuses the wife of another until she has a miscarriage, then her husband is to physically abuse the wife of the

The Great King of Assyria (right) prays to his divine patron—appearing as a fish (left)—for rain to water the crops (center)

defendant until she has a miscarriage. The defendant is to also compensate the victim by giving her household a child from his household.

If the father of a household physically abuses the wife of another until she has a miscarriage and dies, then the defendant is executed, and his household is to compensate the victim by giving her household a child.

If the father of a household physically abuses the wife of another until she has a miscarriage and her husband has no sons, then the defendant is executed. If the fetus is female, he need only compensate the victim by giving her household a child.

A, art 53

If a woman has an abortion, then, after due process, she is impaled on a stake and left unburied.

If a woman has an abortion and dies, then her body is impaled on a stake and left unburied.

If the father of a household hides a woman so that she can have an abortion, and does not charge her before the ruler....

A, art 55 (Deut 22:23–27)

If a marriageable woman, who is the daughter of a man of a household, who is living in her father's house, who is not engaged or married, and who is not collateral for any of her father's debts, is kidnapped and raped by another, either in the city, in the country, in the street at night, in a granary or at a city festival, then the father of her household is to kidnap and rape the wife of his daughter's assailant and keep her in his custody.

If the assailant has no wife, the father of the daughter who was kidnapped and raped may give his daughter to her assailant in marriage, and the assailant is to pay three times more than the standard bride price in silver to her father as the bride price for a marriageable woman, and marry her without the opportunity for divorce.

If the father does not wish to marry his daughter to her assailant, he is to accept three times more than the standard bride price in silver as a fine and then may marry his daughter to whomever he wishes.

A, art 56 (Exod 22:16–17; Deut 22:28–29)

If a marriageable woman freely consents to have intercourse with a married man, then the man is to swear that he did not force himself on her, and the father of the woman is not to touch the man's wife. The man is to pay three times more than the standard bride price in silver for a marriageable woman, and the father of her household may punish his daughter as he wishes.

A, art 59

Except in those instances prescribed by law, a husband may punish his wife, without liability, whipping her, pulling out her hair, or mutilating her ears.

STORIES OF BALAAM

In 1967 Hendricus Jacobus Franken excavated a twenty-room sanctuary at Deir 'Alla in the Jordan Valley. First, a bit of plaster with writing in red and black ink on it, and then two large, fragmentary inscriptions were recovered. The plaster may have been applied to the walls inside the sanctuary. The sanctuary was dedicated to the members of the divine assembly named in the Stories of Balaam, and intended to protect the people of Deir 'Alla from the natural disasters they describe. The stories are written in a local dialect of the Aramaic language common to southern areas of Syria-Palestine. The artifacts found with the plaster and the style of writing date it to the eighth century BCE.

The fragments have been reassembled in more than one sequence. In one combination, Balaam has a dream that the divine assembly is planning to destroy his city. The assembly orders Sha-

Late Bronze period vase from Syria-Palestine with antelopes grazing

131

*Satire with wolves and cats herding goats and ducks
on papyrus from reign of Ramesses III*

gar, divine patron of light, to turn off the sun and turn nature
upside down. Tame animals would become wild. Wild animals
would become tame. The next morning Balaam goes into mourning. When the people ask him why he is mourning, he tells them
about the dream so that they will repent and call on the divine
assembly to spare the city. The plans of the divine assembly are
thwarted and the disaster is averted.

  The world-turned-upside-down motif in the book of Lamentations parallels the Stories of Balaam from Deir 'Alla. The motif in
which a divine patron warns a human protégé of an impending
disaster also appears in the Stories of Atrahasis, the Stories of Gilgamesh, and the flood stories (Gen 6:1–11:26). Another series of stories of Balaam appears in the book of Numbers (Num 22:1–24:25).

lines 5–10

This is a story of Balaam, a seer.   (1 Sam 9:9; Isa 30:10)
      At night the son of Beor saw the divine assembly.   (Num 24:2–4)
He dreamed that El pronounced a death sentence on his city.   (Lam 2:8)
      The divine assembly decreed a disaster without equal.

When Balaam got up the next morning,
      He began to fast and to lament bitterly.   (2 Sam 12:16; Jon 3:5)
The people of the city asked: "Balaam, son of Beor, why do you fast?
      Why do you mourn?"   (Lam 2:10)
So Balaam agreed to tell them about his dream.

Let me tell you what the Shadday have done,   (Exod 6:3)
    Let me describe what the divine assembly has decided.
The Shadday convened a divine assembly,
    They decreed that Shagar
Sew up the heavens,   (1 Kgs 17:1)
    Fasten the doors of the clouds.
Bring darkness,   (Lam 3:2; Joel 2:10)
    Instead of light.
Let the enveloping darkness
    Keep you silent forever!

Let the sparrow hunt carrion like a vulture,
    Let the vulture chirp for its food like a sparrow....
Let the stork steal the young of the cormorant,
    ...claw the marsh bird and the sparrow.
Let herds run wild, sheep be scattered, not led by the staff. (Jer 25:34)
    Let rabbits graze in peace.
Let the hyena become tame,
    Let the pups of a fox run wild.

The people respond to Balaam's warning by praying to avert the disaster. The divine assembly hears their prayers and allows Shagar to open the gates for the sun, and nature returns to its proper balance.

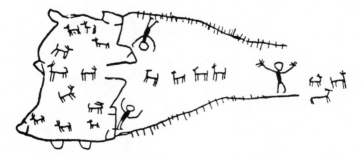

Petroglyph of a sheepfold fenced with mud and thorns

JOSHUA,
JUDGES

STORIES OF SINUHE

The Stories of Sinuhe are preserved today on five papyri in the Berlin Museum, the two most important being P. Berlin 3022 (B) and P. Berlin 10499 (R), and at least seventeen ostraca elsewhere.

Sinuhe is an official of Pharaoh Amenemhet I (1991-1962 BCE). Sinuhe serves the pharaoh's daughter, Neferu, and her husband, Senwosret. When Amenemhet dies, Sinuhe inadvertently witnesses a plot to take over Egypt. Afraid that the traitors will assassinate him to protect themselves, he goes into exile in Syria-Palestine, away from the Egypt he loves. The story ends when Senwosret becomes pharaoh and invites Sinuhe to return to Egypt.

Cartouches of Senwosret I with two of his names: Kheperkara and Senwosret

The Stories of Sinuhe have parallels in the stories of Abraham and Sarah (Gen 11:27–25:18), the stories of Jacob, Leah and Rachel (Gen 25:20–37:2), and the teachings of Joseph (Gen 37:3–Exod 1:6), which describe many of the same places and customs. The adoption of Sinuhe by herders from Syria-Palestine and his marriage to their leader's daughter parallel Moses' experience with Jethro the Kenite (Exod 2:11-22). Sinuhe describes his duel in Syria-Palestine in much the same language as that in the story of how David delivers Israel from Goliath (1 Sam 17:17-58).

B: 20–35

... I traveled away from Egypt throughout the night, and by dawn I had reached Peten. I collapsed on an island in the Bitter Lakes. My throat was so dry and parched that I thought I was going to die from thirst. ...

I told myself: "I am about to taste death!" Suddenly, I heard the sounds of livestock, so I got control of myself and pulled myself to my feet. Some herders from Syria-Palestine were approaching. The head of their household, who had been to Egypt on other occasions, recognized me. He gave me water and yogurt and I traveled with his tribe. They were good hosts to me. I was the guest of one household after the other until I reached Byblos on the coast of Syria. I lived there in the Eastern Desert for one and one-half years.

Then Ammunenshi, who was ruler of northern Syria-Palestine, invited me to live in his land. "You shall be happy with me," he said, "...because you shall hear the language of Egypt again!" Ammunenshi extended this invitation to me because the other Egyptians in his land had told him that I was both honest and wise.

> Sinuhe marries the oldest daughter of Ammunenshi, and settles in his land. He lives like the herders and becomes famous for his wealth and the strength of his household. He also serves as host to travelers as repayment for the hospitality he received during his flight from Egypt.

B: 78–100

Ammunenshi took me into his household and gave me his oldest daughter as my wife (Exod 2:21). He let me choose my own land from

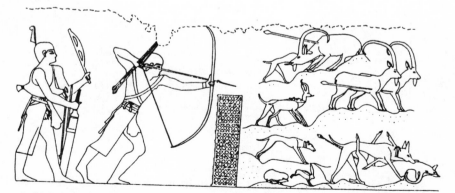

A depiction on the walls of Senbi's tomb at Meir shows him hunting with his armor-bearer and his dogs

among his holdings within the Land of Yaa. It was a land overflowing with figs and grapes. It had more wine than water, honey and oil in abundance (Exod 3:8; 13:5).

Every messenger, and all those from Egypt who traveled through my lands, were invited to my house. I gave water to the thirsty, directions to the traveler, help to those who had been robbed (Gen 18:1–8). I counseled the herders during times of unrest.

B: 110–150

One day a strong man from Syria-Palestine pushed his way into my tent and challenged me to a duel (1 Sam 17:4–10). He was a warrior without equal. He had never lost a duel. His household had encouraged him to pick a fight with me, and, once he had shamed me, to plunder my livestock. Ammunenshi asked me how I had caused this strong man to lose face. I swore to him: "I do not even know this man. I am not his covenant partner, and I have never raided his camp. I have never been a guest of his household, and I have never stolen livestock from his pens. He is angry with me for being your obedient servant...."

That night I strung my bow and checked my quiver of arrows. I took my knife out of its scabbard and sharpened it. By dawn, half of all Syria-Palestine had arrived and pitched camp to watch the duel.

As the strong man advanced, I waited for him. Everyone wanted me to win. Men and women groaned. Every heart embraced me as the underdog. Everyone wondered: "How can anyone defeat such a strong man?" He was armed with a shield, an ax, and a whole armful of javelins (1 Sam 17:5–7). One after the other, I dodged his javelins and side-stepped his arrows. I waited until finally the strong man rushed me, then I shot him in the neck with an arrow. With a loud cry he fell on his face, mortally wounded. I finished him off with his own ax (1 Sam 17:49–51), and then stood on his back and let out my battle cry while all the people of Syria-Palestine thundered their applause. I sang hymns to Montu, the Divine Warrior, while the household of the strong man sang their laments.

≋ *In spite of the wealth, the respect, and the adventure that Sinuhe enjoys in Syria-Palestine, he is homesick. In response to discreet inquiries, Senwosret I invites him to come home to Egypt. In preparation for his departure, Sinuhe leaves his eldest son in charge of his household (Deut 21:15-17).*

B: 248–84

At dawn, I was escorted by ten elders and ten soldiers to the palace of Pharaoh. I prostrated myself between the long rows of sphinxes, while Pharaoh's children watched from a balcony in the pylon gate overhead. The elders and soldiers escorted me as far as the grand hall, and then told me to present myself to Pharaoh in his private audience hall. I found Pharaoh seated on a great throne in a room paneled with gold and silver. At once I prostrated myself before him (Gen 42:6). I had forgotten how to behave in his presence. Nevertheless, Pharaoh the Divine addressed me kindly. Immediately, I began having seizures. My *ba*-soul left my body. My arms and legs trembled. I fell unconscious.

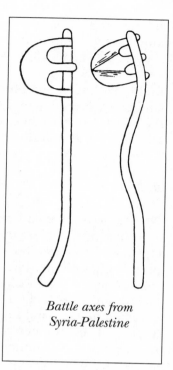

Battle axes from Syria-Palestine

At that moment, Pharaoh ordered one of the soldiers: "Wake him up. I want to speak with him." Then Pharaoh said to me: "Look, you have just made a frightening journey through strange lands (Ps 107:4–5). Old age is your enemy. Feebleness has caught up with you. Your burial is no small affair. You should not be buried by strangers. No, no indeed.... Why do you not answer, when I speak to you?"

I was almost too terrified to answer. "I do not understand what my lord is saying to me. I want to answer, but I cannot. I am possessed with terror.... I can only stand here in front of you (Gen 45:3). My life is in your hands. Pharaoh may do with me as he wishes."

Then, Pharaoh sent for Queen Neferu and her daughters. "Look, this is Sinuhe, disguised as one of the people of Syria-Palestine, a herder." Neferu shouted with joy, and all her daughters began to laugh.

Neferu and her daughters kept asking Pharaoh: "Is this really Sinuhe?"

Pharaoh kept reassuring them: "It really is he." (Gen 45:1–4)

A hymn is sung to the accompaniment of rattles and sistra, acknowledging Sinuhe's return to Egypt and his restoration to royal favor (Exod 15:20).

B: 285–310

I left the audience chamber with the daughters of Pharaoh holding my hands. I was given a luxurious house with a bath, fit for a prince. I was also given robes of purest linen, myrrh, and the scents used by Pharaoh and his court. I had slaves to perform my every wish. My years melted away as I was shaved and my hair combed. I washed the filth of a strange land from my body; I discarded my desert clothes. I was clothed in the finest linen and anointed with the choicest oil, and I slept on a bed. I returned the sand to those who dwell in it and the wood oil to those who grease themselves with it.

Typical clothing worn by Egyptian men

ANNALS OF
TUTHMOSIS III

≋ *The Annals of Tuthmosis III (1479-1425 BCE) were discovered by German archaeologists and first published by C. R. Lepsius. Tuthmosis III had ordered that the annals be carved in hieroglyphics on the walls the great temple at Karnak, on the north wall of the eastern hall in the temple of Amon (Pylon VI). The temple and its inscriptions remain in their original location on the east bank of the Nile in Luxor, Egypt. Subsequently, German archaeologists recovered another copy of the annals on a granite stela from Jebel Barkal near the fourth cataract of the Nile. That copy is preserved today in the Cairo Museum. British archaeologists recovered yet another copy of the annals on a red granite stela from the temples at Armant in southern Egypt. The Armant stela is preserved today in the Cairo Museum.*

Annals are the reports that rulers in the world of the Bible make to their divine patrons as evidence that they have protected the land and provided for the people with whom they have been entrusted. Tuthmosis III reported to his divine patron, Amun-Re, that he had rebuilt Egypt's empire in Syria-Palestine, where he waged sixteen campaigns. Tuthmosis III shared the rule of Egypt with Hatshepsut from 1479 to 1458 BCE, so 1458 BCE [Egyptian: "Year 22"] was the first year he ruled Egypt by himself.

The battle for Megiddo (1468 BCE) was Tuthmosis III's greatest victory. The annals on the Jebel Barkal stela say the battle lasted seven months. During the battle the Egyptian army harvested Megiddo's wheat, and after the battle, they took Megiddo's chariots as war trophies.

Parallels to the Annals of Tuthmosis appear in the books of Samuel-Kings where similar reports are filed by the rulers of Israel and Judah with Yahweh.

Armant Stela:8–17

TENTH DAY OF MONTH TWO, SECOND SEASON, YEAR 22 OF THE REIGN OF TUTHMOSIS III

His majesty, Tuthmosis III, marched into Syria-Palestine [Egyptian: "crossed the River"] to crush the traitors [Egyptian: *retenu*], utterly destroying their cities with fire, and then erecting a victory stela on the eastern bank of the river.... After slaying the traitors that had rebelled against him, his majesty rewarded those who were loyal to him. Their names are here listed here (1 Kgs 15:16–22). After each victorious campaign, he returned to Egypt, which prospered as it did during the epoch primeval when Re, its divine patron, ruled the land alone.

Tuthmosis III

*Section of a wall in Sebekhotep's tomb at Thebes
depicting rulers of Syria-Palestine paying tribute to Egypt*

SECOND DAY OF MONTH FOUR, SECOND SEASON, YEAR 22 OF THE REIGN OF TUTHMOSIS III

His majesty, Tuthmosis III, won a great victory when he marched from Memphis into Syria-Palestine to punish traitors. After his army regained control of all the roads, these traitors took refuge in Megiddo. His majesty led his army through the narrow pass along the Wadi Ara against traitors from all over Syria-Palestine who were waiting for him on the plain of Megiddo (2 Kgs 23:29–30)...but they fled headlong into the city with their leader.... They bargained for their lives with everything they owned. His majesty jubilantly returned to Egypt with every ruler of Syria-Palestine bringing him tribute (2 Kgs 18:14–16).

Karnak (Urk. IV 649 ff.)

TWENTY-FIRST DAY OF MONTH ONE, THIRD SEASON, YEAR 23

...when Tuthmosis III led his army to victory over the traitors, they fled in terror into the city of Megiddo. Because the gates of the city had already been bolted shut, they abandoned their gold and silver inlaid horse-drawn chariots. They were pulled up over the walls of Megiddo, holding onto garments thrown over the walls.

If the soldiers of Tuthmosis III had not been so interested in plundering everything the traitors had abandoned on the plain of Megiddo, they could have captured the city itself on that first day of battle while the traitors from Qadesh and Megiddo were being hauled up over the walls, paralyzed by fear of the Great Serpent, Uraeus, riding on the forehead of his majesty....

...addressing his troops, his majesty told them, "My valiant soldiers, today, Re has trapped all of the peoples of Syria-Palestine in this city. Because all the rulers of Syria-Palestine are trapped here in one place, the capture of Megiddo, is equal to the capture of a thousand cities!"

📜 *The annals do not describe the capture of Megiddo, but the list detailing tribute paid by the rulers of Syria-Palestine to Tuthmosis III—silver, gold, lapis lazuli, turquoise, grain, wine, cattle, horses, chariots, the rulers' armor, as well as their tents and household goods—indicates that the victory was significant. Tuthmosis III appointed as governor of Megiddo a ruler from Syria-Palestine who was loyal to him. He assigned Egyptian inspectors to ensure that a large portion of the harvest would be set aside as yearly tribute to Egypt.*

EL-AMARNA LETTERS

The first tablets containing the el-Amarna letters were found in 1887 by a woman from the neighboring Egyptian village of el Till. She sold some three hundred tables for about one dollar. Eventually, 540 tablets and fragments would be recovered by archaeologists through excavation or purchase. So far, 382 tablets have been published, of which 350 are diplomatic communiqués. Today they are preserved in the Pergamon Museum in Berlin, the British Museum in London, the Cairo Museum, and the Louvre Museum in Paris. They were written in a dialect of Akkadian using cunei-

People from Syria-Palestine as depicted on the wall of an Egyptian tomb

form script, but they include many words and expressions unique
to Syria-Palestine.

Amenophis IV (1353-1335 BCE), also known as Akhenaten,
built the royal city of Akhetaten—the Horizon of Aten—at el-
Amarna to replace Thebes as the capital of Egypt. The site he
chose was about 150 miles south of Cairo today at the exact geo-
graphical center of the Egypt of his day. The letters were written
to Amenophis III (1391-1353 BCE) and Akhenaten by their governors in Syria-Palestine. Neither of these pharaohs managed Egypt's
domestic or foreign policy well. Consequently, governors throughout Egypt itself and its trade empire in Syria-Palestine seized the
herds and crops of villages for raw materials and caravans for
trade goods. In the letters, governors protest their loyalty to
Pharaoh, and repeatedly ask for soldiers to protect themselves
from their fellow governors, whom they label traitors [Akkadian:
'apiru].

There is little evidence today for identifying the 'apiru in
the el-Amarna letters with the Hebrews in the Bible. Nonetheless, the social unrest of 1550-1150 BCE in these letters is parallel
to the social unrest of 1150-1000 BCE in the books of Joshua-
Judges.

Letter 244:1–30

To: Pharaoh, Ruler of the Heavens and Earth
From: Biridiya, Governor of Megiddo

I am your slave, and I renew my covenant with you as my pharaoh by
bowing before you seven times seven times. (Esth 3:2)

Pharaoh should know that, since he recalled his archers to Egypt,
Labayu, the governor of Shechem, has not stopped raiding the land of
Megiddo. The people of Megiddo cannot leave the city to shear your
sheep for fear of Labayu's soldiers. (1 Sam 25:7)

Because you have not replaced the archers, Labayu is now strong
enough to attack the city of Megiddo itself. If Pharaoh does not reinforce the city, Labayu will capture it.

The people of Megiddo are already suffering from hunger and disease.
I beg Pharaoh to send 150 soldiers to protect Megiddo from Labayu or
he will certainly capture the city. (1 Sam 11:3)

Letter 254:1–40

> To: Pharaoh, Ruler of the Heavens and Earth
> From: Labayu, Governor of Shechem

I am your slave, who is less than the dust under your feet, and I renew my covenant with Pharaoh by bowing before you seven times seven times. (Isa 45:23)

I have received Pharaoh's letter. Your fears are unfounded. I am far too insignificant to be a threat to the lands of Pharaoh in Syria-Palestine.

I am, and always have been, loyal to Pharaoh. I am neither a traitor nor a rebel. I pay tribute on time, and I obey every order that the ambassador of Pharaoh here in Syria-Palestine gives me. If Pharaoh will personally look into the case, he will see that I am the victim of malicious lies (Ps 35:11; 1 Macc 7:25). My only crime is that I invaded the land of Gezer in compensation for the land of Shechem, which Pharaoh confiscated from me. Milkilu, the governor of Gezer, has committed even worse offenses than I, and Pharaoh has not confiscated his land.

Pharaoh has also indicted my heir as a traitor [Akkadian: *'apiru*]. I had no idea that my son was consorting with traitors. I have since handed him over to Addaya. Even if Pharaoh were to indict my wife, I would hand her over for trial. (Judg 15:11–13)

I would not even refuse your order to thrust a bronze dagger into my own heart.

Letter 286:1–64

> To: Pharaoh, Ruler of the heavens
> From: 'Abdi-Heba, Governor of Jerusalem

I am your slave, and I renew my covenant with you as my pharaoh by bowing before you seven times seven times (Gen 43:28; Isa 60:14). What have I done to displease Pharaoh? The charge circulating in your court, that "'Abdi-Heba is a traitor," is destroying my good name. I am well aware that I owe my authority to the mighty hand of Pharaoh (Deut 4:34; Jer 21:5), and not to an inheritance from my parents. Why should I rebel against Pharaoh, my lord? (1 Sam 24:9; Micah 6:3)

Egyptian soldier
saluting Pharaoh

Over and over I have asked the ambassador of Pharaoh: "Why do you support traitors who raid the lands of your governors in Syria-Palestine?" (1 Kgs 11:26) Now he charges me with treason. Enhamu blames me for failing to protect the lands of Pharaoh, but it was he who recalled the soldiers whom Pharaoh sent to protect these lands. Today there are no soldiers left to protect the lands of Pharaoh. It is now entirely up to Pharaoh to deal with the traitors whom Ili-Milkilu, the Governor of Gezer, has incited to seize Pharaoh's lands.

On many occasions I have asked for an audience with Pharaoh, but the present hostilities against me have prevented me from coming. Only if Pharaoh sends soldiers to protect his lands will I be able to come to court to speak with him. I swear by the life of Pharaoh that soon all the lands of Pharaoh in Syria-Palestine will be lost, and not a single governor will remain loyal to Pharaoh (Gen 42:15–16; 2 Sam 15:21).

May it please Pharaoh to send the archers needed to reinforce the garrison. Without opposition, traitors will continue to plunder the lands of Pharaoh at will. The only hope Pharaoh has to keep his lands under control and end the plundering of the *'apiru* is if archers are sent this year.

Note to the scribe of Pharaoh: Be sure that at least this much of my message is brought to the immediate attention of Pharaoh, Ruler of all the Earth:
"The lands of Pharaoh, my lord, in Syria-Palestine are lost."

Letter 289:1–51

To: Pharaoh, Ruler of the Heavens
From: 'Abdi-Heba, Governor of Jerusalem

I am your slave, and I renew my covenant with you as Pharaoh by bowing before you seven times seven times (Gen 43:28; Isa 60:14). Milkilu continues his conspiracy with Labayu of Shechem and Arsawa to take Pharaoh's lands for themselves. Why does the pharaoh not call him to account for these deeds?

Milkilu and Tagi...have taken Rubbutu. Now, with Jerusalem threatened, why does the pharaoh not show the same concern expressed for Gaza [Akkadian: Hazzatu]?...

Now Milkilu has written to Tagi and Labayu instructing them, "Let both of you obey me and re-enforce our soldiers at Keilah [Akkadian: Qiltu]. In this way we will isolate Jerusalem."

Addayu, your ambassador, has withdrawn the garrison you had assigned to Haya, son of Miyare, and stationed it in his own palace in Gaza. In addition, he sent twenty men on to Egypt. This means, my lord Pharaoh, that I now have no soldiers at all!

I swear, as Pharaoh lives (Gen 42:15–16; 2 Sam 15:21), that Pu'uru, your ambassador, has also left me and departed for Gaza. May it please the pharaoh, my lord, therefore to send fifty men to protect the land. The entire land of Pharaoh is left undefended!

Please send Yenhamu, your ambassador, to inspect the land of Pharaoh, my lord.

Note to the scribe of Pharaoh: Assure Pharaoh, my lord that:
    "Your Servant, 'Abdi-Heba, is loyal." (Prov 20:28)

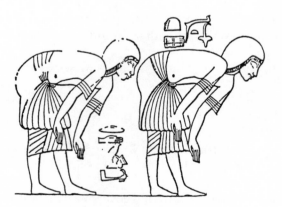

Officials bow before Akhenaten

ANNALS OF
RAMESSES III

When Napoleon invaded Egypt (1798-1803), the members of his expedition included 167 scholars to study and catalog its antiquities. Dominique Vivant Denon sketched the reliefs and inscriptions at Medinet Habu in the Valley of the Pharaohs at Luxor, Egypt. A high pylon gate opens into a broad courtyard with another pylon gate ninety feet high leading to the holy of holies. Emphatically carved on both sides of the entrance pylon, more than eight inches deep into the walls, are the annals of a pharaoh conquering his enemies. Jean François Champollion was only eight years old when Denon sketched these reliefs, but in 1822, at the age of thirty-two, he deciphered hieroglyphics for the first time. By 1829, he had conclusively identified the pharaoh of Medinet Habu as Ramesses III (1194-1163 BCE) and translated his annals describing the defense of Egypt under attack by the Sea Peoples. Although Ramesses III proclaims a total victory over the Sea Peoples, he probably only won a single sea battle against them. The language of annals regularly exaggerates the accomplishments of rulers.

Parallels to the Annals of Ramesses III appear in the saga of Samson (Judg 13:1—16:31), in the stories of Samuel (1 Sam 1:1—4:1+7:3—8:13), and in the stories of David's rise to power in the books of Samuel-Kings (1 Sam 8:4—2 Sam 8:13). The Philistines and the Hebrews were peoples brought together in the same land at the same time by Egypt, their common enemy. The Philistines settled the southern coast of Syria-Palestine, which others would call "Philistia" or "Palestine." The Hebrews settled in the land later called "Israel." Philistines and Hebrews appear in Syria-Palestine for the first time at the end of the Late Bronze period

Ramesses III presiding over a sacrifice with his Kherep *scepter,*
which identified pharaohs as high priests

(1550-1200 BCE), when the empires of Mycenae, Hatti, and Egypt collapsed. As the Iron Age I period (1200-1000 BCE) opened, these two peoples would share a common border in a common land, which would lead to competition and conflict. The struggle between Dagon, the divine patron of the Philistines, and Yahweh, the divine patron of the Hebrews, would last 250 years. The most famous Philistine in the Bible is Goliath (1 Sam 17:17-58).

a:1–26

YEAR 8 OF THE REIGN OF RAMESSES III...

...strangers from the Islands formed a federation with one another. Suddenly, their warriors were invading and destroying every land. No land could defend itself against them. In one campaign, they cut down Hatti, Kode, and Arzawa in Turkey, Carchemish in Syria, and Alashiya in Cyprus. They pitched their battle camp at Amor, and began slaying the peoples of Syria-Palestine and devastating their lands as no one had ever done before. Then they turned toward Egypt, whose fire was preparing to devour them. In this federation were the Peleset, the Tjekker, the Shekelesh, the Dannuna, and the Weshesh. They attacked every land on the face of the earth, confidently boasting: "We will be victorious!"

Now my divine heart was plotting how I was going to snare them like birds.... (Ps 91:3)

I, ruler of the divine assembly, ordered my governors and commanders in Syria-Palestine to deploy their soldiers and charioteers [Akkadian: *maryanu*] at Djahi on the coast. I ordered them to outfit every warship, freighter, and transport from stem to stern with heavily armed, hand-picked troops, and to blockade the mouth of every river along the coast. These ships were the pride of Egypt, and they roared like lions in the mountains (Isa 5:29). Runners led the chariots manned by the best hand-picked soldiers. The bodies of the horses quivered as they waited to crush these strangers under their hoofs (Ezek 26:11). Like Montu, the divine warrior, I led them into battle, so that they could see my outstretched hand.... (Jer 21:1–10)

Those who reached the border of Egypt by land were annihilated. Their hearts and souls will never rise again. Those who attacked by sea were devoured at the mouths of the rivers, while the spears of the soldiers on shore tightened like the wall of a stockade around them (2 Macc 5:3). They were netted, beached, surrounded, put to death and stacked, head to foot, in piles. Their ships and cargo drifted aimlessly on the water.

I decreed that no one in the lands of these strangers was to even say the word "Egypt." Whoever pronounced the word was to be burned alive. Since the day I ascended to the throne of Re-Harakhti, the divine patron of pharaohs, since the first day the divine power of the uraeus serpent rode like Re upon my brow, I have not let a single stranger see the border of Egypt, or any of the Nine Bows even boast of having fought against it. I have seized their lands and crossed their borders. Their rulers and their people all sing my praises, for I have walked in the ways of Re, ruler of all the earth, my incomparable godfather, who rules the divine assembly.

Ramesses III defending Egypt against the Sea Peoples

GEZER ALMANAC

The Coastal Highway was an important north-south trade lane that ran along the Mediterranean Sea from Egypt to the Carmel Mountains. Midway up the coast, an east-west cut-off connected that highway to Jerusalem. The ancient city of Gezer guarded the intersection. Here, around 925 BCE, a student practiced writing Hebrew on a piece of soft rectangular limestone about four inches long and four inches wide. R. A. S. Macalister recovered the artifact during his excavation in 1908. The student copied an almanac identifying each portion of the farmer's year with specific chores. In Syria-Palestine, the agricultural year begins in the fall, when olives are harvested and the October rains soften the sundried soil enough so that planting can start.

The Gezer Almanac
in archaic Hebrew script

Farmers harvesting and plowing at Beni Hasan

Parallels to the Gezer Almanac appear in the Bible in agricultural contexts. The importance attached to learning these skills and being attuned to the seasons is summed up in the adage: "The lazy person does not plow in season; harvest comes, and there is nothing to be found" (Prov 20:4).

The Gezer Almanac does not contain month names, but they have been added below to indicate the normal cultivation and harvesting cycles during the agricultural year. In some cases, particular crops are also suggested.

August and September to pick olives,	(Deut 24:20; Isa 24:13)
October to sow barley,	(Eccl 11:6; Isa 28:25)
December and January to weed,	
February to cut flax,	(Exod 9:31; Josh 2:6)
March to harvest barley,	(Ruth 2:23)
April to harvest wheat and to pay tithes,	(Deut 26:12; 1 Sam 6:13)
May and June to prune vines,	(Isa 5:6; 18:5)
July to pick the fruit of summer.	(Jer 40:10; Amos 8:1)

RUTH

Cast of a woman's face from Petra

ARCHIVES OF BABATHA

Near the end of the second war between Judah and Rome (132–135 CE), Jews from Ein Gedi took refuge in a cave on the cliffs above the Dead Sea, which archaeologists call the "Cave of Letters." These refugees were eventually discovered and killed by the Romans. Among them was a widow named Babatha. She and other civilians left Ein Gedi with the Jewish troops commanded by her brother-in-law, Jonathan. Babatha expected to survive the Roman attack and had brought with her a packet of legal documents that she had filed in courts of law between 94 and 132 CE.

The thirty-five documents that comprise the Archives of Babatha were recovered in 1962 by an Israeli archaeological expedition led by Yigael Yadin. They were written in Greek, Nabataean, and Aramaic. There were twenty-six documents in Greek, which was the official language of the eastern provinces of the Roman Empire. Some had been annotated in Aramaic and Nabataean. There were six documents in Nabataean, which was the language of the people of Petra. Three documents were written in Aramaic, which was the everyday language spoken by Jews throughout the Roman provinces of Judaea and Syria at the beginning of the Common Era.

The archives are a unique source from which to reconstruct everyday life in Judea and Nabatea. They shed light on such subjects as the legal system, economics, religious observances, agriculture, linguistics, and geography. For example, the village of Babatha—Mahoza or Zoar—grants Lot and his daughters asylum (Gen 19:22-23). The archives also demonstrate the tenacity of this widow before courts of law. Like Tamar (Gen 38:1-30) and Ruth and Naomi (Ruth 1:1—4:22), Babatha was a persistent widow dedicated to protecting the legal rights of her household.

Deed to a Plantation in Zoar (July 13, 120 CE)

◣ *Babatha was born into a wealthy household in Zoar, south of the Dead Sea. A deed to a plantation in Zoar, dated July 13, 120 CE, is part of a trust created by Simeon for his wife, Miriam, and his daughter, Babatha. Simeon provides that if Babatha becomes a widow she may live in one of the houses on the plantation until she remarries.*

P. Yadin 7: Upper Version, Verso Lines 1–10

... in the second consulship of Lucius Catilius Severus and Marcus Aurelius Antoninus, in the third year of Imperator Caesar Traianus Hadrianus Augustus, and on the twenty-fourth of Tammuz in the year fifteen in this province of Arabia....

... issued in Mahoz of 'Eglatain

... of my own free will, I, Simeon, son of Menahem, who live in Mahoz, give in perpetuity to you, Miriam, my wife, daughter of Joseph, son of Menasheh, all that I possess in Mahoz: the courtyards and the lower and upper floors in all my houses, all utensils, the produce of all my date palms, both on the ground and in the trees, as described within this document, and whatever else I possess, not specifically described here, together with all I may acquire in the future. The boundaries (Gen 23:17–18) of this estate extend east into the desert as far as the land of Joseph, son of Dormenes; to the west, as far as the cliffs owned by the heirs of Menahem and others; to the north; and to the south as far as the land of Joseph, son of Baba'.

... water rights (Gen 26:18–25; Judg 1:15): one hour and one-half of three hours allotted ...

... water rights: Sunday, one-half hour of stream water

... Monday, one-half hour

... water rights: Wednesday, one hour....

Recto Lines 24–26

After my death ... it shall be the confirmed right of our daughter Babatha, if she is widowed and has no husband, to reside in the storage area attached to my house. She may have free access to the courtyard of the storage area, but she may not bring a new husband into my house.

*Painted pottery
bowl from Petra*

A TRIAL OF JONATHAN EGLA (OCTOBER 12, 125 CE)

Babatha was married twice. Her first husband was Joshua. They had one son and named him Joshua. After the death of her husband, the senate of Petra appointed two guardians for her son: Jonathan Egla, who was Jewish, and Abdobdas Illoutha, a Nabataean. The senate's decision followed the tradition that a widow's care lay in the hands of her legal guardians. Several of Babatha's archives document her legal battle against Egla and Illoutha for control of her deceased husband's land. On October 12, 125 CE, Babatha filed suit against Egla and charged him with failing to pay her child support. She wanted the land held in trust by her son's guardians to be turned over to her and, in return, she would pay her legal guardians a higher rate of interest on it than the guardians could get on the open market.

P. Yadin 15: Lines 7–22

...since you, Jonathan Egla, did not pay adequate child support for my orphaned son, Joshua... only one-half a per cent interest on his money, and since the remainder of his inheritance is insufficient....

...Abdobdas Illoutha has given me...power of attorney over Joshua's inheritance and allowed me to use my own property as a bond. I shall pay him an interest of one and one-half days' wages in silver [one denarius] a month for every one hundred days' wages in silver in the inheritance. This arrangement to provide for my son was negotiated during the happy days when Julius Julianos was governor.

...therefore, in the presence of Julius Julianos, I, Babatha, charge you, Jonathan, my son's legal guardian, for failing to pay child support....

Pre-Nuptial Agreement of Judah and Babatha

≋ *After the death of her first husband, Babatha remarried. A pre-nuptial agreement [Aramaic: ketubba] between Babatha and Judah negotiates this second marriage, which was officially celebrated on February 2, 127 CE. Judah died almost immediately after the wedding, leaving Babatha a large estate. His relatives, however, contested the agreement.*

P. Yadin 10: lines 5–6

...a pre-nuptial agreement with Babatha, the daughter of Simeon...who will be my wife, according to the law of Moses and the people of Judah. Based on this pre-nuptial agreement, I will feed you and clothe you and I will bring you into my house. I will pay your father fifty ounces of silver [four hundred denarii] as a bride price....

lines 10–16

...If you are taken as a prisoner of war, my estate will redeem you, and restore you as my wife....

...If you predecease me, our sons shall inherit your portion of our pre-nuptial agreement as well as the share of my estate that will be allocated to all my sons. Our daughters will continue to live in my house and be supported by my estate until they marry.

...if I die before you, you may continue to live in my house and be supported by the income from it and from my other possessions, until my heirs pay you the settlement stipulated in our pre-nuptial agreement.... My possessions stand as collateral, pledged to pay our pre-nuptial agreement. I, Judah son of Eleazar, bind myself to what is written within this document.

SAMUEL, KINGS

ANNALS OF TIGLATH-PILESER I

The Annals of Tiglath-pileser I are written in cuneiform using the Assyrian dialect of Akkadian. The inscription was recovered by German archaeologists and is preserved today in the Pergamon Museum in Berlin (VAT 13833).

The annals ask: "Is it possible for a wild ass to escape a hunter sent by the divine assembly?" The protagonist in the parable is Tiglath-pileser I who is cast as a hunter [Akkadian: ba'iru]. The antagonist is the ruler of Murattash and Saradaush, who is a wild ass [Akkadian: imeri sadi]. The hunter stalks the ass into the mountains (Gen 16:12), where a fierce battle takes place. There

A wall relief depicting Assyrian soldiers battling their enemies

is a graphic description of the ripping open of the wombs of preg-
nant women, a military tactic that kills soldiers to be born. An-
other version of these annals appears on a cylinder carved in year
5 of his reign (ARI 2.25).

Obv. 21–22; Rev 1—4, 6—7

...after the hunter consulted the prophets,   (Gen 10:9)
    He hitched his horses faster than a storm and a sunrise.
He set out before the sun rose.
    He marched three days' distance before dawn....
The hunter cut open wombs   (2 Kgs 8:11–12; 15:16; Amos 1:13)
    He blinded infants.   (Isa 13:16)
He slit the throats of warriors....
    Whoever offended Ashur was executed.

Sing of the power of Assyria,
    Ashur the strong, who goes forth to battle.... (Exod 15:3; Ps 24:8)

ANNALS OF MESHA

▰ *Mesha of Moab inscribed his annals on a curved topped, rectangular block of basalt three feet high and two feet wide. The thirty lines are written in Moabite using the Hebrew alphabet. The grammar, syntax, and vocabulary of Moabite and Hebrew are similar. The stela was located in Dibon, Jordan in 1868 by F. A. Klein, a German missionary. Subsequently, Charles Clermont-Ganneau (1846-1923), a French scholar, had a paper squeeze made of the inscription. Reacting to the attention these Europeans were giving their artifact, local people heated the stela in a fire and then smashed it into pieces with cold water, hoping to find treasure inside. A third of the stela was permanently destroyed. In 1870, the remains were restored by the Louvre Museum in Paris.*

Ivory inlay of a sphinx from furniture at Samaria, Omri's royal city

> *The Annals of Mesha mention Omri of Israel (886–875 BCE), the fighting of a holy war [Hebrew:* herem*], and the use of prisoners of war to rebuild captured cities. They are parallel to the annals of the rulers of Israel and Judah in the books of Kings (1 Kgs 11:44–2 Kgs 25:30), especially the annals of Omri (1 Kgs 16:21-28).*

I am Mesha from Dibon, ruler of Moab (2 Kgs 3:4). My father, Chemoshyat, ruled Moab for thirty years, and then I became king....

Omri, ruler of Israel, invaded Moab year after year because Chemosh, the divine patron of Moab, was angry with his people (Judg 2:14). When the son of Omri succeeded him during my reign, he bragged: "I too will invade Moab." However, I defeated the son of Omri and drove Israel out of our land forever. Omri and his son ruled the Madaba plains for forty years, but Chemosh dwells there in my time. I built the city of Baal-Ma'on with its reservoir, and the city of Qiryaten.

Long ago the tribe of Gad invaded Ataroth, but I defeated them and captured the city of Ataroth, which the ruler of Israel had fortified. I sacrificed all of the people of Ataroth to Chemosh (Josh 6:24). I brought the altar of Israel [Moabite: *dwd*] from the sanctuary of Ataroth and mounted it before Chemosh in the sanctuary of Qiryat (1 Sam 5:1–2). Finally, I settled the tribes of Sharon and Maharith in the land which I had taken from Israel to claim it for Moab.

At that time, Chemosh said to me, "Go! Take Mt. Nebo from Israel" (Josh 8:1–2, 18, 24–27; 10:42; 1 Sam 23:4). So I deployed my soldiers at

Wall relief at Beni Hasan depicts Egyptians defending their city

night and attacked Nebo from dawn until noon (Josh 7:19–22). I won a great victory and I sacrificed seven thousand men, women, and children from Nebo to Chemosh. I brought sacred vessels from the sanctuary of Yahweh and laid them before Chemosh (Jer 28:3, 6; Dan 1:2).

The king of Israel was invading Moab from Jahaz, which he had fortified. Chemosh, my divine patron, drove him out before me. I settled the households of two hundred of my best soldiers in Jahaz to claim it for Dibon.

I built Qarhoh with gates and towers, a palace and reservoirs. I also decreed: "Every household in Qarhoh is to have its own cistern." I had my prisoners of war from Israel dig the cisterns of Qarhoh (2 Sam 8:2). I built Aroer and a highway through the Arnon valley [Arabic: Wadi el-Mujib]. I also rebuilt the cities of Beth-bamoth and Bezer for fifty households from Dibon.

I reigned in peace over hundreds of villages which I had conquered . . . and Chemosh dwelt there in my time. . . . (1 Kgs 16:23–24)

TELL DAN ANNALS

In 1966, Avraham Biran took his Israeli team into the field at Tell Dan in northern Israel for the first time. Thirty seasons of work at the site have produced remarkable finds for understanding the world of the Bible between 1000 BCE, when David established a state in Israel, and 720 BCE, when Shalmaneser V of Assyria conquered more than half of the land ruled by David (2 Kgs 17:1-41; 18:1-12). In 1993, Biran's team recovered a basalt stela inscribed in Aramaic that had been recycled as a paving stone. The stela is only eight and one-half inches wide, but originally it may have been twenty inches wide. Only thirteen lines are preserved. There are three letters in the first three lines and five letters in the last line. The longest line has only fourteen letters. Words are separated from each other with dots. Two smaller fragments from the same stela were recovered in 1994. The stela is preserved today in the Israel Museum in Jerusalem.

The stela may have been erected by either Hazael (842-800 BCE), a ruler of Aram in today's Syria, or by Jehu (844-815 BCE), a ruler of Israel. Hazael may have erected the stela to celebrate a victory over Israel and Judah. Jehu may have erected the stela to celebrate his revolt against the kings of Israel and Judah, whom he killed in a single battle in the Jezreel Valley (2 Kgs 9:1—10:28). Here the Tell Dan Annals are read as the Annals of Jehu. Curiously, Jehu acknowledges Hazael, the ruler of Aram, and Hadad, the divine patron of Aram, as covenant partners in his struggle with Jehoram, father of the household of Ahab, and Ahaziahu, father of the household of David, for control of Israel.

The Tell Dan Annals are only the fourth tradition outside the Bible to mention Israel. The others are the Annals of Merneptah of Egypt (1224-1214 BCE), the Annals of Mesha of Moab (830 BCE), and the Annals of Shalmaneser III (858-824 BCE) of Assyria. They are also the only tradition outside the Bible that mentions the "...house of David."

Tell Dan Inscription

I, Jehu, commanded the soldiers of Jehoram, ruler of Israel.... Hazael, my patron, invaded Israel when Jehoram declared his independence from Aram, but he was seriously wounded and retreated to his palace.... When Jehoram invaded Aram, Hadad, my divine patron, made me king of Israel. With Hadad riding before me (Deut 31:8; Isa 45:2), I liberated Israel from two ruthless monarchs by destroying their chariots and cavalry and killing Jehoram, son of Ahab and ruler of Israel, and Ahaziahu, son of Jehoram and ruler of the household of David. I destroyed their cities and left their lands barren....

KARATEPE ANNALS OF AZITIWADA

The University of Istanbul (1945-1947) recovered five copies of the Annals of Azitiwada (730-710 BCE) at Azatiwaqadiya in Karatepe, Turkey. Two were written in Luwian hieroglyphics and three in Phoenician, a West Semitic language. The only complete copy was carved across four adjoining columns and one of the two stone lions flanking the gate. This copy contains sixty-two lines, the longest known inscription in Phoenician.

Azitiwada was appointed by Awariku [Assyrian: Urriki], the king of Que, to be governor of Adana. Que and Adana are located in Cilicia, a southeastern region of Turkey. The annals describe the steps that Azitiwada took to meet the needs of his people and to maintain good relations with other states. Its first-person style is similar to that of the Annals of Mesha (840-820 BCE).

Titles, formulas like "...from sunrise to sunset," descriptions of worship and trade, and the use of curses and blessings in the Annals of Azitiwada have biblical parallels like Solomon's prayer for wisdom (1 Kgs 3:5-15).

Queen of Karatepe nursing her son

*Divine patron
of Amrith
[Phoenicia]
riding on a
lion*

col i:1–3

I am Azitiwada, the blessed steward of Baal. I have been raised to my position of authority by my father, Awariku, king of the Danunians. With Baal's blessing I have become both father and mother of the Danunians in the plain of Adana (Isa 22:21), giving them all they needed to live (Gen 50:21), and extending their land from sunrise to sunset (Isa 45:6; Mal 1:11).

col i:3–col iii:2

In my time, Adana enjoyed all the good things in life, full storehouses, and general prosperity. I filled the storehouses of Pahar (Gen 41:47–49) and greatly increased the number of horses and supplies of arms as well as the size of the army at the command of Baal and the divine assembly (1 Kgs 10:26).

I dealt harshly with traitors, expelling all troublemakers from the kingdom (Ps 101:8). I restored the household of Mopsos to power in Adana, ensured an orderly succession (1 Kgs 2:24), and maintained good diplomatic relations between Adana and its covenant partners. My deeds caused me to be held as a father by other rulers (Gen 45:8). My righteous and blameless actions were the outgrowth of my wisdom and my listening heart (1 Kgs 3:6–12).

On all the borders of Adana, I built strong fortresses to guard against traitors who had never served the household of Mopsos (1 Kgs 9:15–19). I, Azitiwada, placed all these traitors under my feet (Josh 10:24; 1 Kgs 5:3) and Adana was at peace within the shelter of my fortresses.

I, Azitiwada, conquered the lands to the west, which no one before me had conquered. I subdued them and deported their populations to the eastern frontiers. I settled the Danunians in their place.

Throughout Adana (2 Kgs 17:24), even in those places that had been without peace, where men were afraid to leave their houses (Judg

Hittite gate inscription at Karatepe

19:22), now, with the help of Baal and the divine assembly, women can walk alone carrying their spindles.

In my days there was abundance, life was good, and the Danunians lived without care or fear. Baal and Resheph, divine patron of stags, commanded me to build this city and name it "Azitiwada" (Gen 4:17; 1 Kgs 16:24). Its abundance, prosperity, law and order provide protection for Adana and for the household of Mopsos. In my day, the sun never set on the Danunians.

I established the worship of Baal Krntrys [Luwian: Tarkhunza; Latin: Tarsus] in Azitiwada. On their feast day every year (1 Sam 1:21), the river-land shall offer an ox before the statues of all the members of the divine assembly (1 Kgs 3:4). At the time of plowing and at the time of harvesting, a sheep shall be sacrificed.

col iii:4–11

May Baal Krntrys and the divine assembly of Azitiwada bless Azitiwada with many years of life, authority to rule, and strength beyond that of any king (Ps 29:11; 61:6–7). May this city and the people who dwell here possess storehouses full of grain and wine (Prov 3:10), oxen and livestock in abundance. May they have many children and in their strength of numbers become powerful. May they all serve Azitiwada and the House of Mopsos as Baal and the divine assembly have ordered....

col iii:12–iv:1

If any monarch, prince, or strong man removes the name of Azitiwada from this gate or its statues and puts his own name on it, or if in renovating the city he tears down this gate made by Azitiwada and replaces it with a new gate containing his own name, whether with good or evil intent, may Baal, the Cloud Rider, and El, the creator of the heavens and the earth (Gen 14:19), and every member of the divine assembly erase the name of that state and its ruler... (Josh 6:26). May only the name of Azitiwada endure forever, like the names of the sun and the moon (Ps 72:17; 89:35–37).

ANNALS OF
SHALMANESER III

After 1250 BCE, when the Mycenaean, Hittite, and Egyptian empires collapsed, there were no world powers for the next 350 years in Syria-Palestine. Small states like Syria, Ammon, Moab, Edom, Israel, Judah, and Philistia began to appear. After 900 BCE, Ashurnasirpal II (883–859 BCE) and Shalmaneser III (858–824 BCE), great kings of Assyria, laid the foundations for a new age of empires. Two important copies of Shalmaneser's annals were preserved on a stela at Kurkh on the Tigris River in Turkey and an obelisk at Nimrud in Iraq.

On a single round-topped stone stela, Shalmaneser III describes his first six campaigns into Syria-Palestine. There are 102 lines of cuneiform. British archaeologists recovered the stela, which they called the "Monolith Inscriptions," in 1861. It is preserved today in the British Museum (No. 11884). With his victory at the Battle of Qarqar (853 BCE) on the Orontes River over a coalition of twelve states, including Hadad-ezer of Syria and Ahab of Israel, Shalmaneser established a permanent Assyrian presence west of the Euphrates River.

In 1846 Austen Henry Layard (1817–1894) recovered a four-sided obelisk of black limestone, six and one-half feet high. It is preserved in the British Museum. There are five titled columns of cuneiform. The stepped ziggurat on the top of the obelisk and about one-third of its base are also inscribed. On the obelisk, Shalmaneser reports on the achievements of his fifth western campaign in 845 BCE, including Assyria's covenant with Israel. In 841, Assyria collected tribute from its new vassals and recognized Jehu as king of Israel (842–815 BCE). Jehu, in return, declared an armistice with Syria and abrogated Israel's covenant with Judah.

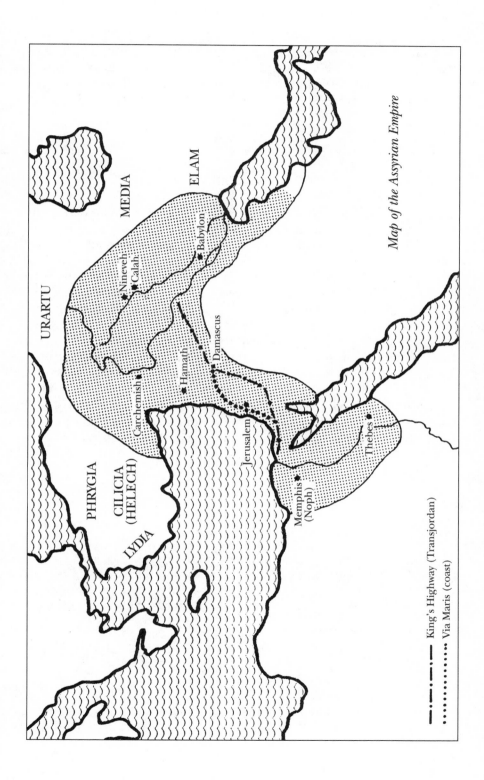

URARTU

PHRYGIA

CILICIA
(HELECH)

LYDIA

MEDIA

ELAM

Nineveh●
Calah●

Babylon●

Carchemish●

Hamath●
Damascus■

Jerusalem●

Memphis●
(Noph)

Thebes●

Map of the Assyrian Empire

—·—·— King's Highway (Transjordan)

·············· Via Maris (coast)

> The covenant is described, not only in writing, but also in a re-
> lief that shows Jehu kneeling before Shalmaneser as his client.
>   Parallels to the Annals of Shalmaneser III appear in the
> books of Samuel-Kings (1 Kgs 16:29—22:40; 2 Kgs 9:1—10:33).

Kurkh Stela (ii:78–102)

YEAR SIX

After departing Nineveh, I crossed the Tigris River and marched to the
towns of Giammu on the Balikh River. My terror-inspiring presence and
the array of my weapons frightened the inhabitants so much that they
killed Giammu, their leader.

   I passed on to the towns of Sahlala and Til-sha-Turahi and installed
the images of my divine patrons in their palaces. I celebrated my victory,
and then looted the palace treasury, sending the booty back to my capital at Ashur.

   ...I crossed the flooding Euphrates River twice using goat-skin
boats. I marched west of the Euphrates and camped at Ana-Ashur-uter-
asbat on the Sagura River... to collect tribute of gold, silver, tin, bronze
ingots, and bronze vessels from Sangara, the ruler of Carchemish;
from Kundashpu, the ruler of Commagene; from Arame, the son of
Guzi; from Lalla, the ruler of Melidea; from Hayani, the son of Gab-
bari; from Qalparuda, the ruler of Pattina; and from Qalparuda, the
ruler of Gurgum.

*A relief in Sennacherib's palace depicting soldiers swimming a river
on inflated goat skins*

I marched west to Aleppo [Akkadian: Halman]. Afraid to fight, the people surrendered [Akkadian: "seized my feet"] and paid tribute in gold and silver. I recognized Aleppo as a new member of the empire by sacrificing to Adad, its divine patron.

I marched into the land of Irhuleni, the ruler of Hamath (2 Sam 8:9; 2 Kgs 14:28). I captured the cities of Adennu, Parga, and Argana, and plundered his palaces before setting them on fire.

I marched to Qarqar and laid siege to the city. Once it was captured, I set it on fire. Irhuleni, the ruler of Qarqar, mustered only 700 chariots, 700 cavalry and 10,000 soldiers, but his twelve covenant partners also fielded armies against me (Josh 10:1–28; 11:1–12):

Hadad-ezer, the ruler of Aram
    1,200 chariots
    1,200 cavalry
    20,000 soldiers   (Num 31:3–6; 2 Sam 10:6)
Ahab, the ruler of Israel   (2 Kgs 16:29)
    2,000 chariots
    10,000 soldiers
Byblos
    500 soldiers
Egypt
    1,000 soldiers
Irqanatu
    10 chariots
    10,000 soldiers

Israelites deliver gold and silver vessels to Shalmaneser,
as depicted on the Black Obelisk

Matinu-Baal, the ruler of Arvad   (Ezek 27:8)
    200 soldiers
Usanata
    200 soldiers
Adon-Baal, the ruler of Shianu
    30 chariots
    ... soldiers
Gindibu, the ruler of Arabia
    1,000 camels
Ba'asa, son of Ruhubi, the ruler of Ammon
    ... soldiers

With the help of Ashur, my divine patron whose divine standard goes
before me, I routed all these rulers, killing and wounding 14,000 soldiers. Like Adad, divine patron of the thunderstorm, I rained destruction upon them. Their corpses covered the battlefield, and their blood
filled the valleys (Ezek 37:1–2). The dead were too many to bury (Jer
7:33), and bodies formed a bridge across the Orontes River. I plundered their chariots and war horses.

YEAR EIGHTEEN

Black Obelisk (base lines 97–99)

My sixteenth campaign west of the Euphrates took place eighteen years
after I became the Great King of Assyria (845 BCE). Hazael, king of
Damascus, revolted against me. I attacked and defeated him, taking
1,121 chariots, 470 horses, and his supply train.

Epigraph 2: (RIMA #88)

Jehu, king of Israel, ransomed his life with silver, with gold bowls, vases,
cups and pitchers, with tin, a royal scepter, and spears.

YEAR EIGHTEEN

Schramm EAK 2.77–78: iii.45b–iv.15a

My sixteenth campaign west of the Euphrates took place eighteen years
after I became the Great King of Assyria. Hazael, king of Damascus,

Depiction on the Black Obelisk of Jehu surrendering to Shalmaneser III

mustered a large army, and fortified Mt. Senir (2 Kgs 10:34). I fought and defeated him, killing 16,020 of his soldiers. I took 1,121 chariots, 470 horses, and his supply train. He ran from the battle to save himself, and I besieged his capital city of Damascus. After cutting down his orchards and burning his fields, I marched as far as the mountains of Hauran. Along my line of march I destroyed every town, taking vast amounts of booty.

Eventually, I marched as far as the mountains of Ba'li-ra'si and erected at the seashore a stela containing my royal image. Having demonstrated my power, I accepted the surrender of the people of Tyre and Sidon, and from Jehu, the son of Omri (1 Kgs 16:17–28; 2 Kgs 9:1—10:36).

ANNALS OF
TIGLATH-PILESER III

Between 1845 and 1851, Austen Henry Layard excavated Tell Nimrud at Calah for the British Museum. Founded by Ashurnasirpal
II (883–859 BCE), and expanded by Shalmaneser III (858–824 BCE),
Tiglath-pileser III (744–727 BCE), and Esarhaddon (680–669 BCE),
the city was eventually destroyed in 612 BCE. The Annals of
Tiglath-pileser III were engraved on slabs in the Assyrian dialect
of Akkadian using the cuneiform script. Only a portion of the
original monumental inscription survives.

Tiglath-pileser III formally inaugurated a new age of empires
in the world of the Bible. He completely reorganized Assyria's bu-
reaucracy to gain political and economic control of the trade
routes running from the Mediterranean coast inland in order to
prevent any cut-off of Assyria's imports of metals, lumber, and
horses.

Tiglath-pileser III

*On a palace relief, a depiction of Tiglath-pileser III attacking a city and
beheading and impaling prisoners*

Tadmor 69–71

I, Tiglath-pileser III, received tribute from:
    Kushtashpi of Commagene,
    Resin of Damascus,
    Menahem of Samaria,   (2 Kgs 15:14–19)
    Hiram of Tyre,
    Sibittibi'li of Byblos,
    Urikki of Qu'e,
    Pisiris of Carchemish,
    Eni'il of Hamath,
    Panammuwa of Sam'al,
    Tarhulara of Gurgum,
    Sulumal of Melidene,
    Dadilu of Kaska,
    Uasurme of Tabal,
    Ushitti of Tuna,
    Urballa of Tuhana,
    Tuhamme of Ishtunda,
    Urimme of Hubishna,
    and Zabibe, the queen of Arabia,

... which included gold, silver, tin, iron, elephant-hides, ivory, linen garments embroidered with different colors, blue wool, purple wool,
ebony, boxwood, luxury items like ... wild birds mounted with their

wings extended and tinted blue, as well as horses, mules, large cattle, small cattle and camels, some already bred.

Tadmor 78–81

I dyed the river red with the blood of Rezin of Damascus's soldiers (2 Kgs 3:22) .... I captured his archers, his spearmen, and their supply train. In order to save his life, Rezin fled the battlefield and fled into his city like a mongoose. I impaled his generals alive on stakes (Num 25:4) and I laid siege to his city for forty-five days, confining him like a bird in a cage. I cut down his orchards.... I captured the village of the household of Rezin and took 800 prisoners, their cattle and sheep as spoil. I took 750 captives from Kurussa and Sama, and another 550 from Metuna. In all, I destroyed 591 villages in the sixteen districts around Damascus, leaving them like mounds created by the Great Flood.

ANNALS OF SARGON II

In 713 BCE, Sargon II (721-705 BCE), Great King of Assyria, founded a new city called the "Mountain of Sargon" [Akkadian: Dur-Sharrukin; Arabic: Khorsabad]. When he died, his successor, Sennacherib, moved the capital back to Nineveh. Sargon's capital was excavated between 1842 and 1844 by Paul Emile Botta (1802-1870) and Eugene Napoleon Flandin (1809-1876) for the Louvre Museum in Paris. The Annals of Sargon were among the inscriptions in the Assyrian dialect of Akkadian using cuneiform. The Annals were carved into the reliefs on Sargon's palace walls, on the thresholds of public buildings, and in the Khorsabad Display Inscription.

Covenant partners of Assyria that were unable to meet their quotas lost their self-determination and became Assyrian vassals or colonies. In a colony, native officials retained their titles and offices, but Assyrian personnel reviewed all domestic policies to guarantee the colony would meet the empire's military budget. Only states with healthy economies, efficient governments, and popular rulers managed to maintain their self-determination. Assyria's budget requirements increased continually and few states could meet its expectations and avoid a revolt. Depositions and revolutions were frequent. Any reticence or refusal on the part of local officials left an Assyrian colony subject to outright foreclosure. Assyria would deport all government personnel, redistribute the colony's population in developing regions of the empire, and assign the colony a military governor, incorporating it completely into the empire as a province.

The Annals of Sargon II chronicle the days when Israel went from the status of an Assyrian ally in 738 BCE to that of an Assyrian colony in 732 BCE and finally to that of an Assyrian province in 720 BCE. Shalmaneser V (729-722 BCE) reduced the Israel of Hoshea from the status of a covenant partner of Assyria to its colony. Sargon, who called himself "Conqueror of Samaria,"

converted Israel into an Assyrian province after Hoshea defaulted
on his tax payments. It took Assyria more than three years to win
its war against the Land of Omri [Akkadian: bit hu-um-ri-ia], and
to deport its people from the capital city of Samaria to faraway
places like "...Halah...the Habor, the river of Gozan, and the cities
of the Medes (2 Kgs 17:6)." Others were deported to nearby rural
sections of Israel itself, and descendants of these people as well as
others who remained in the land during the Babylonian exile became known in the New Testament as "Samaritans."

FIRST YEAR OF THE REIGN OF SARGON II

Assyrian Annals 10–18

The ruler of Samaria, in conspiracy with another king, defaulted on his
taxes and declared Samaria's independence from Assyria (2 Kgs 17:4–6).
With the strength given me by the divine assembly, I conquered Samaria
and its covenant partner, and took...prisoners of war...as spoil (2 Kgs
17:23; 18:11). I conscripted enough prisoners to outfit fifty teams of chariots. I rebuilt [Samaria], bigger and better than before. I repopulated it
with people from other states that I had conquered, and I appointed one
of my officials over them, and made them Assyrian citizens....

SECOND YEAR OF THE REIGN OF SARGON II

Khorsabad, Display Inscriptions 33–36

In the second year of my reign, Yau-bi'di, a Hittite conspirator and an
imposter to the throne of Hamath in Syria, formed an alliance [Akka-

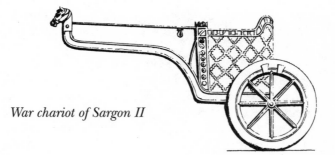

War chariot of Sargon II

Sargon II attacks Philistines at Gaza with a battering ram

dian: "made them one mouth"] with Arvad, Simirra, Damascus, and Samaria, and declared their independence from Assyria. Together they raised an army and attacked me. At the command of Ashur, my divine patron, I, Sargon II, mustered an army and laid siege to Qarqar, the city of Yau-bi'di. After I burned Qarqar to the ground and skinned Yau-bi'di alive, I executed the rebels in these cities to restore peace and harmony once again. I assigned two hundred of their chariots and six hundred of their cavalry to my army.

SEVENTH YEAR OF THE REIGN OF SARGON II

Assyrian Annals 120–23

With the assistance of Ashur, my divine patron, I campaigned against the Tamudi, Ibadidi, Marsimani, and Hayappa, the Arab tribes who inhabit the desert and who have never submitted to the word of any official or paid tribute to any king. Those that survived were deported and settled in Samaria (2 Kgs 17:24).

ELEVENTH YEAR OF THE REIGN OF SARGON II

Assyrian Annals 249–62

Aziru, the ruler of Ashdod, defaulted on his taxes and conspired with his covenant partners to rebel against Assyria (Isa 20:1). In response to the crimes he committed against his people, I deposed him and placed his brother Ahimiti on the throne. The people of Ashdod [Akkadian: Hittites] conspired against his rule and raised up the usurper Yadna as their king. My anger was kindled and I marched my army to Ashdod, besieging it along with Gath [Akkadian: Gimtu] and Ashdod-Yam. Among the spoils I took from them were the images of their gods, Aziru and his people, gold, silver, and the treasury of the palace. I settled prisoners of war on their lands, appointed ... governors over them, and imposed tribute on them as a province of the Assyrian empire.

AZEKAH TABLET

📜 *The Azekah Tablet describes the campaign of Sargon II in 712 BCE against Philistia and Judah. The tablet (K 6205) was first published in cuneiform in 1875 by George Smith, and then translated in 1870 by Henry Rawlinson. An additional fragment (BM 82-3-23, 131), published in 1898 by Henri Winckler, made it possible to associate the text with the reign of Sargon II.*

Two sieges are described on the Azekah Tablet. The first is against Azekah, an important border town in Judah (2 Chr 11:5-10; Jer 34:7). The other siege is most likely against the Philistine city of Ekron, which is explicitly mentioned in the Annals of Sargon II. The tablet describes Hezekiah's revolt against Assyria and his invasion of Philistia (2 Kgs 18:7-8).

In the course of my campaign,
    I approached Judah and received tribute from kings...
With the powerful assistance of my divine patron, Ashur,   (Ps 83:15)
    I ravaged the land of Hezekiah of Judah like a hurricane....
Azekah sat on a ridge of mountains, like knives pointing to heaven,
    The walls of the fortress are as tall as mountains touching the sky.
I laid siege to Azekah between my land and the land of Judah,
    I attacked the city with ramps, battering rams, and infantry....
At the sight of my... and my cavalry,
    At the roar of my troops, their hearts failed them....

I took this fortress and carried off its spoil,
    I utterly destroyed it with fire.

I approached Ekron, city of the Philistines,
    Which Hezekiah had taken and fortified....
Mighty towers surrounded it,
The city stood on a slope....
    The palace stood like a great mountain....
Hezekiah defended the city with seasoned troops,
    These seasoned soldiers were equipped with the best weapons....
On the seventh attempt...I smashed through the walls like a clay pot
    I took their herds of sheep and counted as spoil.   (Isa 30:14)

Winged Disc—Symbol of the Divine Patron Ashur

ANNALS OF
SENNACHERIB

Sennacherib, Great King of Assyria (704-681 BCE), inscribed annals for eight military campaigns on a six-sided clay prism about
fifteen inches high. They are written in the Assyrian dialect of
the Akkadian language using the cuneiform script. R. Taylor recovered this prism in 1830 from Nineveh [Arabic: Nebi Yunus] in
Iraq. The Taylor Prism is now at the British Museum in London.
Another prism containing these annals is at the Oriental Institute at the University of Chicago (OIM A2793).

   When Hezekiah declared Judah's independence from Assyria
after 715 BCE, Sennacherib sent an army into Judah in 701 BCE
to put down the revolt. He laid siege to Jerusalem and devastated
the surrounding countryside and nearby cities like Lachish. Par-

Refugees from Lachish flee Assyrians

190

allels to the Annals of Sennacherib appear in the annals of Hezekiah (2 Kgs 18:1—20:21) and the trial of Hezekiah (Isa 36:1—39:8).

THIRD YEAR OF THE REIGN OF SENNACHARIB

22–34

The official and ranking citizens of Ekron deposed Padi, their king, and put this loyal covenant partner of Assyria in chains. They placed him in

Sennacherib at his headquarters during siege of Lachish

the custody of Hezekiah, the king of Judah. Once they realized what they had done, they called on the pharaohs of Egypt for assistance.

Although the Egyptians marshaled a large army against me, I inflicted a great defeat upon them in the Plains of Eltekeh with the help of Ashur, my divine patron (2 Kgs 19:9). I personally captured the Egyptian and Ethiopian chariots and their commanders, and then laid siege, conquered, and looted the cities of Eltekeh and Timnah.

Advancing to Ekron, I slew its rebellious officials and ranking citizens and impaled their bodies on the towers of the city (1 Sam 31:10). All the rest of the people who had raised a hand against me were taken captive. The innocent were spared. King Padi was released from prison in Jerusalem and once again placed on his throne and his tribute payments were reinstated.

Because Hezekiah of Judah did not submit to my yoke, I

laid siege to forty-six of his fortified cities and walled forts and to the countless villages in their vicinity. I conquered them using earthen ramps and battering rams. These siege engines were supported by infantry who tunneled under the walls. I took 200,150 prisoners of war, young and old, male and female, from these places. I also plundered more horses, mules, donkeys, camels, large and small cattle than we could count. I imprisoned Hezekiah in Jerusalem like a bird in a cage. I erected siege works to prevent anyone escaping through the city gates. The cities in Judah which I captured I gave to Mitinti, king of Ashdod, and to Padi, king of Ekron, and to Sillibel, king of Gaza. Thus I reduced the land of Hezekiah in this campaign, and I also increased Hezekiah's annual tribute payments.

Hezekiah, who was overwhelmed by my terror-inspiring splendor, was deserted by his elite troops, which he had brought into Jerusalem. He was forced to send me 420 pounds [Akkadian: "thirty talents"] of gold, 11,200 pounds [Akkadian: "eight hundred talents"] of silver, precious stones, couches and chairs inlaid with ivory, elephant hides, ebony wood, boxwood, and all kinds of valuable treasures, his daughters, wives, and male and female musicians. He sent his personal messenger to deliver this tribute and bow down to me (2 Kgs 18:14–16).

SILOAM STORY

The annals of Hezekiah (715–687 BCE), king of Judah (2 Kgs 18:1–20:21; 2 Chr 29:1–32:33: Isa 39:1-8; Sir 48:17-22) describe the construction of a channel to bring water from the Gihon Spring outside Jerusalem to the Siloam Reservoir inside the city in the event of an Assyrian attack. The builders of the Siloam Channel left a detailed story of how their work progressed in a dedication discovered in 1880 by children playing in the Siloam Reservoir. The inscription is nineteen and one-half inches wide and twenty-six inches long and was cut into the face of the rock wall of the tunnel. It is written in Hebrew, using cursive or longhand script. Half has been removed and is still missing; the rest is now in the Istanbul Museum, Turkey.

Siloam Inscription

It is unclear just how the builders laid out the route of the tunnel. They may have simply enlarged a fault in the bedrock through which water was already seeping. The course of the tunnel indicates that the two teams were about to dig past one another, but they made ninety degree turns and connected the two channels. The story describes these exciting moments. Water tunnels from the same period (1000–587 BCE) have also been found at Gezer, Hazor, and Megiddo, demonstrating that they were a common feature of a royal city's defenses. Curiously, the story mentions neither Hezekiah nor Yahweh and, despite the fine execution of the letters, the inscription does not fill the space prepared for it on the rock. These experts at digging tunnels seemingly were amateurs at carving inscriptions.

... this is the story of how these two tunnels were joined together. The two teams working in opposite directions were digging toward one another with picks. The workers began shouting to each other when they realized they were four and one-half feet apart. Then, the teams turned toward one another following the sounds of their picks until they cut through the remaining rock and joined the tunnels. Thus, the water was able to flow through this tunnel one-hundred fifty feet underground for some eighteen hundred feet from the Gihon Spring outside the city wall to the Siloam Reservoir (2 Kgs 20:20; 2 Chr 32:30; Sir 48:17).

ANNALS OF
NEBUCHADNEZZAR II

⌁ *The Annals of Nebuchadnezzar II, Great King of Babylon (605-562 BCE) contain summaries of military campaigns during his fourth through seventh years (601-598 BCE). At this time, Egypt and Babylon both claimed Syria-Palestine as their territory. Therefore, Nebuchadnezzar and his predecessors mounted yearly raids into the area as a way of enforcing their claim.*

Mushashu dragon of glazed tiles on the walls of Nebuchadnezzar's Babylon

The annals are inscribed in the Akkadian language in cuneiform script on baked clay tablets a little more than three inches high. The British Museum recovered the tablets from Babylon, about fifty-five miles south of Baghdad, Iraq, and began publishing them in 1887 as The Babylonian Chronicle.

As was the case with many rulers of Mesopotamia, Nebuchadnezzar used the title "King of Agade" as a way of creating a line of succession from Sargon of Agade. Nebuchadnezzar refers to the area where he and his army campaigned as "Hatti," a name originally given to Syria-Palestine by the Egyptians. By Nebuchadnezzar's time, this name was used by scribes throughout the ancient Near East as a generic term for the region to the west of Mesopotamia. His campaigns generally took place during December [Akkadian: Kislimu] as in the books of Zechariah and Chronicles (Zech 7:1; Neh 1:1), or March [Akkadian: Adar] as in the books of Ezra and Esther (Ezra 6:15; Esth 3:7).

Annal 5, BM 21946: 5–7

YEAR 4

Nebuchadnezzar, the king of Agade, marched his army uncontested into Hatti. In November [Akkadian: Kislimu] he led his army toward Egypt. When Pharaoh heard of this, he sent out his own army. In the resulting battle heavy losses were inflicted on both sides. The king of Agade then returned with his army to Babylon. (2 Kgs 24:1–7; Jer 37:7–10)

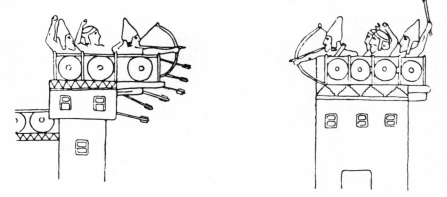

Soldiers of Judah defend Lachish against Assyrians

Annal 5, BM 21946: 8

YEAR 5

Nebuchadnezzar, the king of Agade, remained in his own land outfitting chariots and their horses.

Annal 5, BM 21946: 9–10

YEAR 6, NOVEMBER

Nebuchadnezzar, the king of Agade, marched his army into Hatti. He raided the desert taking a great deal of plunder from the herds of the Arabs and the statues of their divine patrons. The king returned to his own land in February [Akkadian: Adar].

Annal 5, BM 21946: 11–3

YEAR 7, NOVEMBER

≋ *In his seventh year, 598 BCE, Nebuchadnezzar II put down a revolt by Jehoiakim, king of Judah (2 Kgs 24:10). According to the books of Samuel-Kings, the invasion took place in the eighth year of his reign. Jehoiakim died during the siege of Jerusalem and was succeeded by Jehoiachin. Nebuchadnezzar took Jehoiachin and his household back to Babylon as hostages and appointed Mattaniah as king of Judah. Mattaniah took the throne name "Zedekiah."*

In November [Akkadian: Kislimu], Nebuchadnezzar, the king of Agade, marched his army into Hatti. He laid siege to the city of Judah. He captured the city and its king on the second day of February [Akkadian: Adar]. He appointed a new king to his liking and carried away a great amount of plunder from Judah to Babylon. (2 Kgs 24:13–17; 2 Chr 36:10; Jer 29:1–2)

ARAD LETTERS

⟫ From 1962 to 1967, Yohanan Aharoni directed an Israeli excavation of Tel Arad and recovered some 200 ostraca. These broken pieces of pottery have writing on them in Hebrew and Aramaic. Some are only 2.5 inches high. They are preserved today in the Israel Museum in Jerusalem.

The majority of the letters date to 650–600 BCE when Judah was continuously threatened by Babylon. Most of the letters order commanders to issue rations of grain, wine, and oil to the troops under their command. One curious letter writes the name "Arad" backward seven times.

Fortresses like Arad, Ramoth-Negev [Hebrew: horvat 'uza] and Kinah [Arabic: khirbet taiyib] guarded the Edom Highway like stagecoach stops and cavalry forts in the American West (2 Kgs 3:8). This east-west trade route connected the Coast Highway in the west (Josh 19:8; 1 Sam 30:27) with the Royal Highway in the east. From Arad, the Edom Highway descends to the northern end of the Jebel Usdum Mountains and from there into the Arabah Valley.

Parallels to the Arad letters appear in the books of Samuel-Kings, Ezra-Nehemiah, and Jeremiah. Some letters refer to the households of priests like Pashhur and Meremoth mentioned in the Bible (Jer 20:1; Ezra 8:33).

ostracon 2

⟫ Ostracon 2 orders the commanding officer at Arad to issue rations to the Kittim, who were mercenaries from Crete and Cyprus. A four-day ration for seventy-five soldiers was three hundred loaves of bread and eighty-five quarts of wine. Therefore, each soldier received one loaf of bread per day (Jer 37:21) and eight ounces of wine.

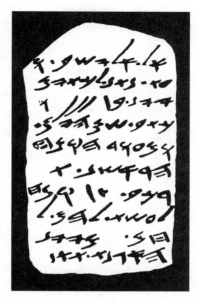

Arad letter ordering Eliashib to ship oil and wine

New wine was recently fermented (Deut 32:14). Old wine was stale or, at least, past the date when it was best to drink it (Ps 69:21).

To: Eliashib, commanding officer at Arad
From:...commanding officer at...

Issue the Kittim 2 bat rations of wine and three hundred loaves of bread for the next four days, and another *homer*-ration of wine for the rest of the garrison. Deliver the rations tomorrow. Do not be late. Fill some of the jars with old wine (Ruth 2:14), if there is any left.

ostracon 18

Ostracon 18 is written by a professional scribe in good biblical Hebrew using the ancient Hebrew script. The letter, sent by an unidentified officer to Eliashib at Arad, contains the earliest reference to the Temple [Hebrew: beth YHWH] outside the Bible. The "sons of Keros" also appear in the Bible at the Temple (Ezra 2:44; Neh 7:47).

On an ivory inlay, a depiction of prisoners and plunder being presented to the ruler of Megiddo, who sits on his cherubim throne

To: Eliashib, my Lord at Arad.
From . . .

May Yahweh take good care of you.
     Issue Shemaryahu one *lethech*-ration of flour. Issue the Kerosite one homer-ration of flour. I have carried out your orders. The person about whom you asked is housed in the Temple of Yahweh . . . . (Neh 13:4)

ostracon 24

📜 *Arad was the headquarters for its sector of the Negev. Ostracon 24 is an order to reinforce Ramoth-Negev, six miles southeast of Arad. Apparently, when Babylon invaded Judah from the north in 594 BCE, Edom invaded from the south (Ps 137:7-9; Lam 4:22). Whether or not the troops from Arad and Kinah, four miles northeast of Arad, were successfully deployed to Ramoth-Negev is unclear. The destruction level at Arad where this letter was recovered indicates that Edom overran both Ramoth-Negev and Arad.*

To . . . commanding officer at Arad
From . . . commanding officer at Jerusalem

. . . dispatch five soldiers from Arad and from Kinah . . . send them to Ramoth-Negev, under the command of Malkiyahu, the son of Qerabur, and he shall turn them over to Elisha, the son of Jeremiah, in Ramoth-Negev (2 Sam 18:2; 30:27), before anything happens to the city. You are to carry out these orders of the king of Judah under penalty of death. This is my last warning (Deut 8:19): Get those soldiers to Elisha before Edom attacks.

LACHISH LETTERS

British archaeologists J. L. Starkey, Henry Wellcome, and Charles Marston recovered nineteen inscribed pieces of broken pottery at Lachish [Arabic: Tell ed-Duweir] in Israel (1932-1938). Some of the pieces were about four inches high. The inscriptions were written in Hebrew in a longhand script using a reed pen and a black ink made from soot and gallnut juice. The letters were found in the ruins of a guard room at the western gate of the city, where they had been buried when Azekah and Lachish were destroyed by the Babylonian army of Nebuchadnezzar in 587 BCE. Azekah is eighteen miles southwest of Jerusalem; Lachish is thirty miles away. Lachish covered about thirty acres on the Wadi Ghafr. The letters are preserved today in the British Museum in London.

Four letters are illegible; four are lists of names; one is written on a jar; and five are written on pieces of pottery from the same jar. The letters reflect the breakdown in discipline in the face of Babylon's invasion. Yaush is a military commander. Hoshayahu

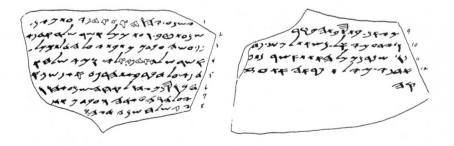

Front side (left) and back side (right) of Letter 4 from Lachish

201

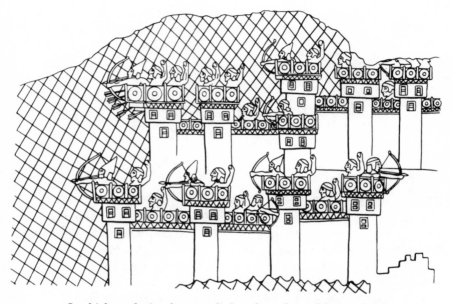

Lachish as depicted on a relief at the palace of Sennacherib

is his subordinate. Yaush has reprimanded Hoshayahu for insubordination, and Hoshayahu is defending himself.

The style of writing is similar to that in the books of Deuteronomy, Jeremiah, and Samuel-Kings, but there are several stock phrases as well as numerous misspellings.

Letter 3

To: Yaush, my commanding officer
From: Hoshayahu, your servant

May Yahweh send my lord good news!

I have received your letter, but I do not understand my commander's instruction: "If you did not understand my orders, have a scribe read them to you!" I have been sick at heart over such an accusation (Isa 1:5; Jer 8:18).

As Yahweh lives, I do not need a scribe to read your orders for me. When an order comes, I read it carefully and can repeat it down to the smallest detail.

I have received the following intelligence report: "Konyahu son of Elnatan, an army commander, has arrived on his way to Egypt (Jer 26:22; Ezek 17:15) and has sent messengers to bring Hodavyahu son of Ahiyahu and his men to him."

I have intercepted a letter sent by Tobyahu, a royal official, to Shallum, son of Yada. The prophet who delivered it said: "Beware!" (2 Kgs 6:9) I am forwarding the letter to my lord.

Letter 4

May Yahweh bless you with good news.

I have posted your orders in writing. Following your orders to make a reconnaissance of Beth-haraphid, I discovered that it had been abandoned.

Semayahu has taken Semakyahu into custody so that he can be transferred to Jerusalem for court-martial. I could not get him through the lines to Jerusalem today, but I will try again tomorrow morning.

This letter certifies to my commanding officer that I remain on duty to carry out your orders to keep the signal fire burning at Lachish (Judg 20:38; Jer 6:1) because the fire at Azekah has been put out (Jer 34:6–7).

CHRONICLES, EZRA, NEHEMIAH

DECREE OF CYRUS II

🏳 Hormuzd Rassam (1826-1910) recovered a cylinder inscribed with a decree of Cyrus II, ruler of Persia (559-530 BCE), for the British Museum (BM 90920) from the library of Ashurbanipal (668-627 BCE). Cyrus had promulgated the decree shortly after his conquest of Babylon in 539 BCE. The decree was written in the Akkadian language using cuneiform script on a cylinder about nine inches long. Few Persians understood Akkadian, but it was the official language in which all formal documents were published.

The decree indicts Nabonidus, Great King of Babylon (555-539 BCE), whom Cyrus defeated, for failing to protect and provide for the land and people of Babylon. It then orders the repatriation of the hostages in Babylon, whom Nebuchadnezzar and Nabonidus had deported from the lands that they had conquered. Households from Judah had been deported in 597 BCE and again in 587 BCE following their failed revolts against Babylon (2 Kgs 24-5;

Decree of Cyrus on a barrel-shaped clay cylinder

Jer 34:1-7). The decree also provides royal subsidies to these peoples who were to rebuild their cities and the sanctuaries of their divine patrons (Ezra 1:1-4; 6:3-5).

Parallels to the Decree of Cyrus appear in the books of Isaiah and Ezra. The book of Isaiah (Isa 45:1) acknowledges the decree by giving Cyrus the title of "Anointed" or "Messiah." He is the only non-Israelite to be given such an honor. The Second Temple in Jerusalem was not actually completed until 516 BCE during the reign of Darius I (522-486 BCE). The book of Ezra (Ezra 6:1-15) describes how Darius searched the royal archives for a decree of Cyrus, which may well have been a copy of this decree.

Nabonidus turned the worship of Marduk, ruler of the divine assembly in Babylon, into an abomination ... celebrating rituals incorrectly and failing to offer sacrifices at the proper time with the intent of completely eliminating the worship of Marduk. He also enslaved the people of Babylon to work for the state year-round (1 Kgs 12:4) ....

Marduk, the ruler of the divine assembly, heard the people of Babylon when they cried out, and became angry. Therefore, he and the other members of the divine assembly left the sanctuaries which had been built for them in Babylon (Ezek 10:18–19). Marduk ... searched all the lands for a righteous ruler to lead the *akitu* New Year procession in Babylon. He chose Cyrus, ruler of Anshan. Marduk called his name and made him ruler of all the earth (Isa 44:28; 45:4) .... Because Marduk ... was pleased with Cyrus's good deeds and upright heart, he ordered him to march against Babylon. They walked together like friends, while the vast army of soldiers accompanying Cyrus marched into Babylon without fear of attack. Marduk allowed Cyrus to enter Babylon without a battle (Isa 45:1–2) ... and delivered Nabonidus, the king who would not revere Marduk, into the hands of Cyrus.

≋ *The elders and soldiers of Babylon surrendered [Akkadian: "bowed and kissed his feet"] to Cyrus and his son, Cambyses, who resumed the worship of all the members of the divine assembly with sanctuaries in the city.*

I entered Babylon as a friend of Marduk and took my seat in the palace. Every day I offered sacrifice to Marduk, who made the people love and obey me. Therefore, I ordered my soldiers not to loot the streets of Babylon, nor to molest the people of Sumer and Akkad. I no longer en-

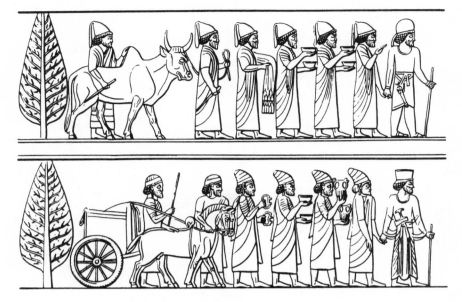

Tribute from Babylon and Persia,
as depicted in the palace of Xerxes (485–465 BCE) at Persepolis

slaved the people of Babylon to work for the state, and I helped them to rebuild their sanctuaries, which had fallen into ruin.... Every ruler from the Mediterranean Sea to the Persian Gulf, rulers who dwell in palaces in the east and rulers who live in tents in the west came to Babylon to bring me tribute and to kiss my feet (Ps 2:12).

I returned the statues of the divine patrons of Ashur, Susa, Agade, Eshnunna, Zamban, Meturnu, Der, and Gutium to their own sanctuaries. When I found the sanctuaries across the Tigris in ruins, I rebuilt them. I also repatriated the people of these lands and rebuilt their houses (Isa 45:13). Finally, at Marduk's command, I allowed statues of the divine patrons of Sumer and Akkad, which Nabonidus had moved to Babylon, to be returned to their own sanctuaries...which I rebuilt.

May all the members of the divine assembly whose statues I have returned to their sanctuaries ask Bel and Nebo for a long life for me every day. May they remember me to Marduk, my divine patron, with the prayer: "Remember Cyrus, the ruler who reveres you, and his son, Cambyses."

ELEPHANTINE LETTERS

≋ Six papyrus letters belonging to Yedoniah, son of Gemariah, the leader of a community from Judah on Elephantine Island on the southern border of Egypt, were discovered in 1907 by German archaeologists. They are currently housed in the Berlin Museum. The letters are written in Aramaic, the international language of the Persian Empire, and date to the period between 420 and 407 BCE.

The Elephantine letters explain how to determine the date for Passover. They also describe the destruction of the Jewish temple on Elephantine by Egyptian soldiers. Curiously, at no point do these letters refer directly to traditions in the book of Deuteronomy that call for the celebration of Passover only in Jerusalem, and for the closing of all sanctuaries to Yahweh except the Temple in Jerusalem.

The concerns of the community from Judah on Elephantine parallel some of the problems faced in Jerusalem and Judah under the Persians in the books of Ezra, Nehemiah, and Chronicles. It is possible that the Hananiah mentioned in these letters as a senior Persian administrator in Egypt is the same as Hanani, the brother of Nehemiah (Neh 1:2; 7:2).

Text 30, AP 21, St. Mus. P. 13464, restored version

≋ The letter is not teaching the Jews in Egypt how to celebrate Passover for the first time, but rather how to date their celebration more accurately (Ezra 6:20).

To: The household of Yedoniah and the soldiers of Judah on Elephantine Island

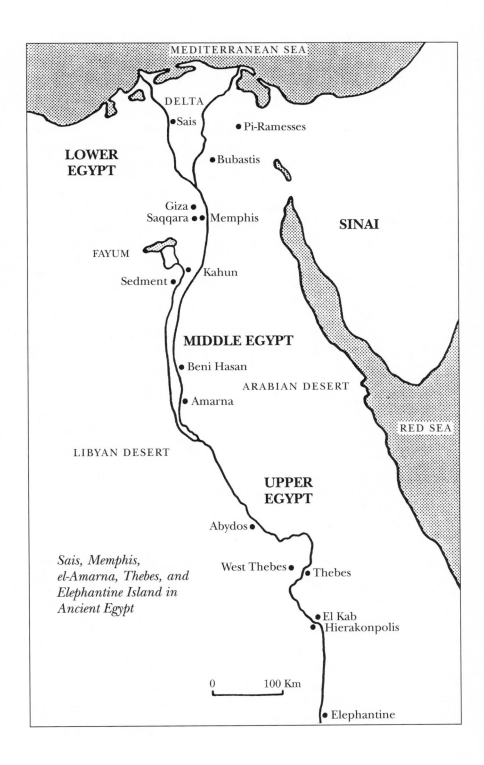

MEDITERRANEAN SEA

DELTA

• Sais

• Pi-Ramesses

LOWER EGYPT

• Bubastis

Giza •
Saqqara • • Memphis

SINAI

FAYUM

Sedment • • Kahun

MIDDLE EGYPT

• Beni Hasan

ARABIAN DESERT

• Amarna

RED SEA

LIBYAN DESERT

UPPER EGYPT

Abydos •

*Sais, Memphis,
el-Amarna, Thebes, and
Elephantine Island in
Ancient Egypt*

West Thebes • • Thebes

• El Kab
• Hierakonpolis

0   100 Km

• Elephantine

From: Hananiah, your brother

May Yaho and the Creator of the Heavens always bless you.
...Darius the king sent this message to Arshama, the governor:...begin the celebration of Passover on the fourteenth of March
[Aramaic: Nisan] at sunset. You shall celebrate the Feast of Unleavened
Bread from the fifteenth to the twenty-first day of March. You shall eat
unleavened bread for seven days (Exod 12:15; Lev 23:5–8).
     Maintain strict ritual purity. Do not work on the fifteenth or the
twenty-first of March. Do not drink any wine or beer. Do not eat or keep
any leavened bread in your house from sunset on the fourteenth of
March until sunset on the twenty-first of March (Deut 16:3–4, 8)....

Text 34, AP 30/31; Berlin, St. Mus. P. 13495/ Cairo P. 3428

▰ *Text 34 describes the destruction of the temple on Elephantine
   by the priests of Khnum and Vidranga the governor. Syene, the
   city of Aswan today, is the larger settlement on the banks of the
   Nile River around Elephantine Island.*

To: Our Lord Bagavahiah, governor of Judah

From: Yedoniah and the priests of the military outpost on Elephantine
Island

May Yaho and the Creator of the Heavens bless our lord forever, and
grant you favor with King Darius a thousand times greater than now.
May you have a long, healthy, and happy life!
     ...during the month of June [Aramaic: Tammuz] in year fourteen
of Darius [410 BCE], when Arshama, the Persian governor [Aramaic:
satrap] of Egypt, was out of the country, the priests of Khnum... issued
an ultimatum: "The Temple of Yahweh [Aramaic: YHW] on Elephantine
Island must be destroyed!" So, Vidranga, the governor of Elephantine Island, sent a letter to his son, Nafaina, the commander of Syene, ordering him to destroy the temple. Nafaina responded by leading his soldiers
to Elephantine Island with weapons and axes.
     The soldiers forced their way into the temple and completely de-
stroyed it. They smashed its stone pillars, wrecked its five stone gate-
ways, and burned the doors in their bronze pivots, the cedar roof, and
all of the fixtures. They looted the temple, taking the gold and silver
basins and everything else of value.

Temple on Elephantine Island modeled on the Temple in Jerusalem (above)

Our ancestors built the temple on Elephantine Island when the pharaohs ruled Egypt. When Cambyses entered Egypt he found it already there. Although he destroyed all the Egyptian temples, our temple was left undisturbed.

After our temple was destroyed, we and our households put on sackcloth, fasted, and prayed to Yahweh, Creator of the Heavens (Ezra 8:23; Neh 9:1; Lam 2:10): "...may Vidranga be eaten by dogs (1 Kgs 14:11; 21:23–24, 27; 2 Kgs 9:36–37), may all his property be destroyed, may all those who plotted evil against the temple be killed (Ps 59:5), and may we live to see it happen!"

It has now been some time since we sent this news to you, to Yehohanan the high priest, to the other priests in Jerusalem, to Avastana, brother of Anani, and to the other officials of Judah [Aramaic: Yehuda]. We have received no reply.

So we have worn sackcloth and fasted since June, Year 14 of Darius. For three years, we have abstained from intercourse with our wives, from anointing ourselves with oil, and from drinking wine. We have not offered grain or animals in the temple.

If it pleases our lord, since we have not been allowed to rebuild the temple all this time, may you now give us permission to rebuild it (Neh 2:5). Consider the faithfulness of your servants and friends in Egypt. May a letter be sent from your hand which gives us permission to rebuild the Temple of Yahweh on Elephantine Island. If you agree to do this, then offerings of incense and animals will be brought in your name to the altar of Yahweh. We and our entire households will pray constantly for you. If you do this, it will be a truly righteous action before Yahweh, worth more than one thousand silver and gold talents of offerings and sacrifices.

The details of these events have also been sent in a letter to Delaiah and Shelemiah, sons of Sanballat [Aramaic: Sin-uballit], governor of Samaria (Neh 4:1). Note that Arshama was unaware of these actions taken against us.

Text 35, AP 32, Berlin, St. Mus. P. 13497

Text 35 contains an agreement between Bagavahia of Jerusalem and Delaiah of Samaria to rebuild the Temple of Yahweh on Elephantine Island. Presumably, Arshama, the Persian governor of Egypt, also agreed. What is interesting is that animal sacrifices are not mentioned, possibly as a way of minimizing the importance of the temple on Elephantine Island in relation to the Temple in Jerusalem.

To: Arshama, governor of Egypt...

From:

The Temple of the Creator of the Heavens was built prior to the time of Cambyses on Elephantine Island and was subsequently destroyed in year fourteen of Darius by the criminal Vidranga. Give us permission to rebuild it on its original site (Ezra 6:1–5). Give us permission to offer meal and incense on its altar as they were in the past.

Text 36, AP 33, Cairo P. 3430—J. 43467

Text 36 notes the prohibition of animal sacrifices. There is no clear evidence that the Temple of Yahweh on Elephantine Island was rebuilt. Records from the military colony there end after 399 BCE and no archaeological evidence for the temple has come to light. This draft contains no addressee.

To:

From: Yedoniah son of Gemariah, Mauzi son of Natan, Shemaiah son of Haggai, Hoshea son of Yatom, Hoshea son of Nattum, who are all legal residents of Syene and own land on Elephantine Island.

If our lord will grant permission for the Temple of Yahweh, our divine patron, to be rebuilt on Elephantine Island, then we agree not to sacrifice sheep, oxen, or goats, but only incense and grain. If our lord will issue this decree, then we will make a donation to our lord's household of . . . silver, and one-thousand bushels [Aramaic: *ardab*] of barley.

JOB,
ECCLESIASTES

DECLARATIONS OF
INNOCENCE

Like the Pyramid Texts and the Coffin Texts, the Book of the Dead or the Book of the Coming Forth by Day was regularly carved or painted inside pyramids and tombs in Egypt after 2500 BCE. The Book of the Dead did not reach its final form until 500 BCE. The entire book has not been found on any one scroll. By 1500 BCE mass-produced excerpts from the Book of the Dead illustrated on papyrus were readily available to households that could afford them. Copies of the Book of the Dead are preserved today in the British Museum (Papyrus of Nu, #10477) in London and the Egyptian Museum in Cairo.

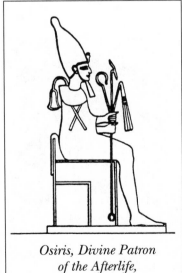

*Osiris, Divine Patron
of the Afterlife,
as a mummy*

Declarations of innocence or "negative confessions" were perhaps the most popular excerpts from the Book of the Dead. They consist of at least 192 chapters of varying lengths. Each is designed to bring about the resurrection of the dead and assure a blessed afterlife. There are also descriptions of the underworld [Egyptian: duat], the gates, the caverns, the day, the night, and a litany to Re.

Parallels to the declarations of innocence are found in the book of Job (Job 31).

Declaration 125

When you reach the Hall of Two Truths, confess your sins and say:
Hail to you, Osiris, divine patron of the Two Truths.
    I come to you so that you may show me your splendor.
I know your name and the forty-two members of the divine assembly
    Who dwell here with you in your Hall of Two Truths,
    Who punish evildoers in your presence.   (Job 31:3)
I now declare to you that I have put away evil,
    I will speak only the truth.

I have not sinned against anyone.
    I have not mistreated cattle.
I have not committed any sin within the temple.
    I have not sought restricted knowledge.
I have not done any harm.
    I have not given my laborers tasks too great for them.
My name has not been reported to Amun-Re.
    I have not blasphemed.
I have not deprived the orphans of their property.   (Job 31:18, 21)
    I have not done anything that the divine assembly prohibits.
I have not given false witness against slaves to their masters.
    I have not caused pain to others.   (Job 31:13)

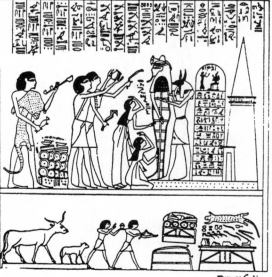

Preparation of a mummy and presentation of food as depicted in the Book of the Dead

I have not starved the hungry.   (Job 22:7)
    I have not caused others to weep.
I have not killed.
    I have not commanded to kill.
I have not failed to prepare food for the divine assembly.
    I have not eaten the bread of the divine assembly.
I have not stolen the food offerings of the dead.
    I have not committed adultery.   (Job 31:9)
I have not masturbated.
    I have not cut the bushel measure.
I have not moved boundary markers of another's fields.   (Deut 19:14)
    I have not used false weights for scales.   (Amos 8:5)
I have not taken the milk from the mouths of children.   (Job 31:16)
    I have not deprived herds of their pastures.
I have not trapped the birds of the divine assembly.
    I have not diverted irrigation water into my fields at the wrong time.
I have not built a dam across a river to irrigate my fields.
    I have not doused a cooking fire when it was needed.
I have not been late making meat offerings to the divine assembly.
    I have not offered less than my best cattle to the divine assembly.
I have not failed to step aside for a procession of the divine assembly.
    I solemnly declare that I am innocent!

Declaration of Innocence before the Divine Assembly

I have done nothing evil.
    I have not robbed.
I have not coveted.
    I have not stolen.
I have not murdered.   (Jer 7:9)
    I have not cut the grain ration.
I have not cheated.
    I have not stolen a sacrifice of the divine assembly.
I have not committed perjury.
    I have not stolen bread.
I have not sulked.
    I have not trespassed.
I have not slain the cattle of the divine assembly.
    I have not committed extortion. ·
I have not stolen the bread ration.
    I have not gossiped.
I have not allowed my mouth to betray me.
    I have not contended with another over property rights.

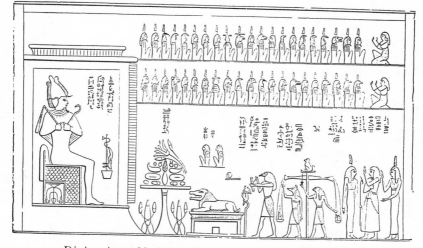

Divine Assembly before Osiris in the Hall of Judgment

I have not committed adultery.
  I have not defiled myself.
I have not instilled fear in another.
  I have not trespassed.
I have not been intemperate.
  I have not been blind to truth.
I have not been quarrelsome.
  I have not turned a blind eye to justice.
I have not sexually abused a young boy.
  I have not been abusive of another.
I have not been too hasty.
  I have not defaced an image of the divine assembly.
I have not said too much.
  I have not committed treason.
I have not bathed in water reserved for drinking.
  I have not raised my voice.
I have not cursed the divine assembly.   (Job 1:5)
  I have not been boastful.
I have not been arrogant.
  I have not desired more than I possess.   (Job 31:24–25)
I have not cursed the divine patron of my city....

A SUFFERER AND
A SOUL IN EGYPT

A Sufferer and a Soul in Egypt is a dispute over suicide composed in ancient Egypt between 2050 and 1800 BCE. It was written on papyrus sheets, the tops of which had already been destroyed when archaeologists recovered them shortly before 1900. They are now preserved in the Berlin Museum as Papyrus Berlin 3024.

Between 2258 and 2050 BCE, the social and political and economic structures of Egypt came apart. Consequently, teachers began to reevaluate Egypt's world view as well. A Sufferer and a Soul files a lawsuit against Egypt for its views on life and death. At the trial, the sufferer is the attorney for death and his ba-soul is the attorney for life. The sufferer proposes committing suicide as an antidote to pain and failure. The soul argues that

*Mourners in a painting at Beni Hasan
ride with the liver, lungs, stomach, and intestines of the dead in one boat
and the body in another*

it is the task of the living to get on with life, and that funerals are a waste of time for rich and poor alike. As an alternative to suicide, the soul proposes that the sufferer just stop conforming to society's expectations and start enjoying life. The soul closes its counter-argument with two parables to which the sufferer responds with four laments. The first lament equates the soul's advice with a series of putrid metaphors. The second lists all the reasons why death is preferable to life when things are bad. The third describes death as a friend who will free suffering human beings from their painful lives. The fourth promises that all those who die will live happily ever after with their divine patrons. The first lines in each stanza of each lament are the same.

A Sufferer and a Soul evaluates how to counsel people who conform to all of society's expectations, but who get sick of living when their efforts get them nowhere. Teachers in ancient Israel used similar trial genres in the books of Ecclesiastes and Job. These traditions do not present solutions to suffering; they simply study it.

1-39

Hear me out, my soul.

My life now is more than I can bear,
    Even you, my own soul, cannot understand me.
My life now is more terrible than anyone can imagine.
    I am alone.
So, come with me, my soul, to the grave.
    Stand beside me in death, like one who sings my eulogy....
If you cannot take away the misery of living,
    Do not withhold the mercy of dying from me.

Open the door of death for me.
    Is that too much to ask?
Life is only a transition.
    Even trees fall.
Crush out this evil life.
    Put an end to my misery.
Let Thoth, who resolves disputes, hear my case,
    Let Khonsu, who records the days of our lives, protect me.

Boaters in a painting at Beni Hasan recover a drowning victim

Let Ra, who sails the Ship of the Sun, judge me,
     Let Isdes, who judges the dead, defend me in the Hall of Justice.
My need presses upon me   (Job 3:17–19)
     What relief would come with release from life's burden.
My soul interrupts—

You are human, not divine.
     Your task is to live life to its fullest.   (Eccl 3:12)

lines 40–59

But, my soul—

I have not yet died, but death is a safe harbor.
     If you abandon me now, you will be left uncared for.
If you listen to me, we will prosper together.
     I will bring you to the land of the dead like a great man
     Who lies in a pyramid, an overseer beside his tomb.
I will take you with me to into the coolness of the grave,
     I will make other souls envy you.
I will shade you from the heat of the sun,
     I will make wandering souls envious of you....
If you continue to oppose my death,
     You will never find rest in the land of the dead.
Have patience, my soul, my companion,
     My heir will carry out my last wishes.
My heir will stand beside my tomb on the day of burial,
     My heir will carry my body to its grave.

lines 58–89

Now listen, my human friend—

There is no such thing as a happy funeral,
    and funerals always make people cry.
You just carry the body out of the house,
    You bury it on a sterile and sunless hillside.
Even granite chapels and pyramids decay,   (Eccl 2:11)
    Monuments are forgotten as soon as the builders die.
They are pitiful as paupers' graves on the banks of the Nile,
    They are no different than burials without funerals.
They have only the Nile as a pallbearer,
    The sun as an embalmer, and the fish as mourners.
So, listen to me,
    Take my advice.
Enjoy living.   (Eccl 3:12)
    Stop worrying.

You have heard the parable about death. . . .
Once, a man plowed a field,
    Loaded the harvest on a barge, and towed it to market.
At sunset, a terrible storm came up.
    The man, safe in town, survived,
But his wife and children at home perished,
    Lost when their houseboat capsized in the Lake of the
        Crocodiles.
The man sat down and mourned: "Should I weep for a wife, buried
without a funeral,
    And thus who cannot be raised to a new life?
Or should I weep for a child,
    Buried before it had even one life to live?"

You also know the parable about the stubborn man. . . .
Once a man ordered his wife to serve his meal early,
    But she refused: "This food is for our supper."
The man stormed out of the house,
    Arguing with himself as he went back to work.
When the man came home,
    He was still furious.
He would not listen to his wife's advice,
    He disturbed the peace of the household.

lines 90–110

My soul, do you really want me to go on living?
    When my life smells worse than...
      ...bird drop on a hot day,
      ...rotten fish in the full sun,
      ...the floor of a duck coop,
      ...the sweat of fishermen,
      ...a stagnant fish pond,
      ...the breath of a crocodile?

Do you really want me to go on living?
    When my reputation is worse than someone...
      ...accusing a faithful woman of adultery,
      ...calling a legitimate child a bastard,
      ...plotting to overthrow the government?

Can't you see?
    Everyone is a thief,
    There is no love among neighbors.   (Jer 9:4–5)
Can't you see?
    Hearts are covetous,
    People take what belongs to their neighbors.
Can't you see?
    The just have perished,
    Fools are everywhere.
Can't you see?
    Everyone chooses evil,   (Amos 5:14–15)
    Everyone rejects good.
Can't you see?
    Crimes outrage no one,
    Sins make everyone laugh....

Lines 130–60

Death stands before me today,
    Like health to the sick,
    Like freedom to the prisoner.
Death stands before me today,
    Like the smell of myrrh,   (Sir 24:15)
    Like a canopy on a windy day.

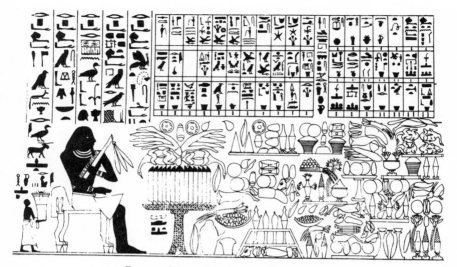

Deceased in a painting at Beni Hasan
seated with the food for the afterlife

Death stands before me today,
    Like the perfume of the lotus,
    Like sitting in the land of drunkenness.
Death stands before me today,
    Like a well-beaten path,   (Prov 5:5)
    Like a soldier returning home from war.
Death stands before me today,
    Like clear skies after a rain,
    Like suddenly recognizing the truth.
Death stands before me today,
    Like home to the traveler,
    Like his native land to an exile.

Surely, whoever goes to the land of the dead
    Will live with the divine assembly,
    Will judge the sins of the wicked.
Surely, whoever goes to the land of the dead
    Will ride in the Ship of the Sun,
    Will distribute rich gifts offered at temples.
Surely, whoever goes to the land of the dead
    Will be wise,
    Will have a hearing before Re the creator.   (Job 23:4–7)

My human friend—
>   Let us end our dispute as partners.

Throw your cares on the fire with your offerings,
>   Get on with your life.
Stay with me here,
>   Stop thinking about dying.
When it is time for you to die,
>   When your body returns to the earth,
Then I will travel with you to safe harbor,   (Ps 94:19)
>   Then we shall live together forever.

A FARMER AND
THE COURTS IN EGYPT

A Farmer and the Courts is part of the Berlin papyrus (#3023, 3025) recovered by German archaeologists before 1900. It contains the protests of an eloquent peasant who argues for his rights in the courts of Egypt during the first intermediate period (2134-2040 BCE). Narrative sections of prose introduce nine exchanges, which are composed in poetry, between the farmer and various judges. The teachers who composed A Farmer and the Courts during the Middle Kingdom (2040-1640 BCE) clearly felt that the events took place in a time of unrest caused by political and social instability in Egypt.

Parallels to A Farmer and the Courts appear in more than one tradition in ancient Israel. The books of Judges and Ruth

A painting at Beni Hasan depicting the harvesting of grapes (upper),
fishing, and bathing cattle (lower)

also reflect the prejudice of a later period that earlier times were lawless. The prophets champion human rights for the poor in much the same language as the farmer. The book of Job follows a structure similar to A Farmer and the Courts. In both, the petitioner is forced to make one plea after another, seemingly without hope of relief, until suddenly it is granted and his goods are restored. Finally, both the Wisdom of Solomon and A Farmer and the Courts stress that while individual human beings may die, the justice they do (Wis 8:13) and their good names last forever (Wis 1:15).

R:1–50

Once there was a farmer named Khun-Anup, who lived in the Field of Salt district near Thebes. One day he said to Meryt, his wife: "I am going down to the city for food. Go into the barn and see how much grain is left from last year's harvest." After determining that there were twenty-six measures of barley, the farmer instructed his wife to take six to make loaves and beer for his journey. The rest was left to feed his household.

The farmer loaded the asses with salt, reeds, leopard skins, wolf hides, and other goods from his district to trade. Then he set out for the city. He traveled south toward Herakleopolis through Per-fefi, north of Medenit. Nemty-nakht, son of Isri, who was an official of the chief steward Rensi, the son of Meru, was standing on the bank of the canal and saw the farmer coming. As he watched the farmer approach, Nemty-Nakht said to himself: "I think I have a scheme I can use to steal this farmer's goods." (1 Kgs 21:1–14)

At one point the public path along the embankment of the canal in front of Nemty-nakht's house was no wider than a loincloth. One side of the path was flooded with water, and the other side was overgrown with barley from Nemty-nakht's field. Nemty-nakht told one of his slaves: "Get me some clothes from my house!" When the slave brought them, Nemty-nakht laid the clothes down over the water, and stretched them across to the barley field.

B1:1–190

Just then, the farmer came down the public path. Nemty-nakht shouted to him: "Be careful, you farmer! You are about to step on my garments."

The farmer answered: "I am being careful! I do not wish to offend you, but your garments are right in my way. I cannot climb the steep embankment along the canal on one side of them, nor do I want to trample the grain in your field on the other. Please give me permission to pass." (Job 24:4)

As he stood there talking, one of the asses bit off a stalk of barley. Then Nemty-nakht said: "Now I am going to confiscate your ass for eating my grain. I will sentence it to the threshing floor for this offense."

But the farmer pleaded: "My intentions are good. Only one stalk has been damaged. If you do not let me pay for the damage done and buy back my donkey, I will appeal to Rensi, the son of Meru, who is the chief steward and governor of this district. Is it likely that he will allow me to be robbed in his own district?"

Nemty-nakht answered. "Why do the poor always want to speak to masters? You are speaking to me, not to the chief steward!" Then he took a stick and beat the farmer and confiscated his donkeys.

The farmer protested his painful sentence and the injustice done to him.

Nemty-nakht tried to cut off his complaints in the name of Osiris, the divine patron of silence.

The farmer protested the attempt to silence him and swore by Osiris that he would not keep quiet until his property was returned.

For ten days, the farmer appealed to Nemty-nakht without results. So, he went to Herakleopolis to appeal to Rensi, the son of Meru, who was the chief steward. As he was rushing off to board his barge, the official asked the farmer to file his protest with a lower court, which finally took his statement.

Eventually, Rensi and his council considered the case and decided that Nemty-nakht was guilty only of harassing a farmer who no longer worked for him and should be sentenced only to return the farmer's goods. However, Rensi did not announce the verdict. So the farmer went to see about his appeal in person.

The farmer's initial petition (B1: 52–71)

"You are the chief steward,
     You are my lord.
You are my last hope,
     You are my only judge.

When you sail the Lake of Justice,
     Fairness fills your sail...
Your boat will not be delayed,
     Your masts and yards will stand fast...

Spearing a crocodile in the Nile

You will not face the river's dangers,
    You will not see the face of the crocodile.
You father the orphan,
    You husband the widow.   (Exod 22:22; Deut 10:18)
You brother the divorced,
    You mother ["apron"] the motherless.
I will extol your name throughout the land,   (Ps 22:22–26)
    I will proclaim you a just judge.   (2 Sam 15:4)
... a ruler without greed,
    ... a great man without fault,
... a destroyer of lies,
    ... a just judge, who hears the cry of the poor.
Hear me when I speak, O worthy one,
    Give me justice, O celebrated one.
Relieve me of this burden of sorrow,   (Ps 25:17)
    And hear my case!"

The farmer appealed to Rensi in the name of Neb-kau-Ra, pharaoh of Upper and Lower Egypt.

So, Rensi went to the pharaoh and said: "My lord, I am hearing the case of a truly eloquent farmer. His goods have been stolen by a man in my service and he has come to me for justice."

Slaves in a painting at Beni Hasan carry food and goods

The pharaoh said: "I am ordering you to keep this man waiting without giving him any reply. Just keep him talking. You must write down each of his speeches and send them to me. Furthermore, without letting this farmer know, I want you to provide for his wife and children as well as for his own needs."

Each day, a friend of the chief steward delivered ten loaves of bread and two jars of beer to the farmer. Rensi also ordered the governor of the Field of Salt district to deliver three measures of grain to the farmer's wife every day.

The second time that the farmer comes to see about his appeal, the chief steward asks him whether these goods are really worth going to prison over.

The farmer's second petition (B1: 125–70)

Is it not wrong,
  When justice flees, banished from its seat,   (Eccl 3:16)
  When judges takes sides in a dispute,   (Lev 19:15; Deut 1:17; Prov 18:5)
  When magistrates are corrupt....   (Prov 24:23–26; 28:20–21)

It is now the case that
Those who distribute the grain put more in their own ration.
  Those authorized to give full measures short their people.   (Amos 8:5)

Lawmakers approve of robbery.
 Who is left to punish the wrongdoer?
The Inspector pushes aside the infirm.
 The respectable condone what is crooked.
One is publicly criminal,
 The other tolerates injustice.
 Do not learn from such as these.
Punishment lasts for a moment,
 Injustice goes on forever.
Good example is remembered forever.
 Follow this teaching:
'Do unto others,
 As you would have others do unto you.'   (Matt 7:12)
Thank others for their work,
 Parry blows before they strike,
 and give jobs to the most qualified . . . .

But you have become drunk with power,
 Content with your rich life.
Although the steersman faces forward,
 The barge is allowed to drift.
While the pharaoh remains in his palace,
 The steering oar is in your hand.
Yet evil exists on every side,
 Appeals remain as long as evil divides.

Now, lest it be said among the people,
 "What has become of him?"
Make your shoreline a shelter,
 Clear out the crocodiles that infest your landing.
Speak the truth,   (Zech 8:16)
 Do not allow your tongue to become
   your downfall.   (Mic 6:12)
Do not perjure yourself,   (Exod 20:16)
 Do not be like corrupt officials,
 Whose hearing is like a winnower's basket,
 Allowing truth to fall through without concern . . . . "
Wisest of men,
 Do not ignore only my difficulties.
You who must care for all upon the sea,
 See that I have begun my journey, but am shipwrecked.
Rescuer of the lost, see my plight,
 I stand here before you in agony!

Thoth, Divine Patron of Learning,
with the head of an ibis

The farmer's third petition: B1:175–205

"Do justice,   (Amos 5:14)
    And live.
Carry out sentences on convicts,
    And fulfill your duty beyond all others.
Does the hand-scale lie?   (Micah 6:11)
    Is the stand-scale tilted?   (Job 24:12)
    Is Thoth, divine patron of the scales, looking the other way?
Do not be tempted by corruption...   (2 Chr 19:6–7)
    Do not return evil for good,
    Do not substitute lesser for better goods,
    Or deceptive words will grow like weeds....
Do not speak falsely,
    Do not speak lightly, for you are the scales of justice
Do not waver from the true path,
    For if you tilt, so too will the scales of justice....

Do not steal,
    Do not make deals with thieves.
    Greed makes the powerful blind....   (Job 20:20; Prov 15:27)

See, you are a laundryman who neglects his friends,
    And washes clothes only for those who pay him.
See, you are the ferryman carrying only those who can pay,
    And thus your piety is tarnished.
See, you are the shopkeeper, who gives no credit to the poor....

B1:216–24

⌇ *When the farmer made this appeal before the chief steward at the gate court, Rensi had two guards arrest him and flog him.*

Nonetheless, the farmer said:
"The son of Meru continues to do evil.
    He sees, but does not see,   (Isa 6:10)
He hears, but does not hear,
    He ignores what he is told . . .
See, you are a town without a mayor,
    A generation without a hero,
    A boat without a steersman,
    A mob without a leader.
See, you are a grasping official,
    A mayor who takes bribes,
    A provincial overseer who should drive off the wicked,
    But who has become the portrait of evil himself."

⌇ *The farmer eventually makes nine appeals to Rensi. In each appeal, the farmer recites all the wrongs done to him, describes Egypt as a world turned upside down where lawgivers become lawbreakers, and he appeals to Rensi and others in authority to take their responsibilities seriously and give him justice. In one final burst of frustration, the farmer decides that his only hope for justice will be in the afterlife, where Anubis is the divine judge (Job 10:20-22; 14:7-14).*

B2:114–35

"Since you will not grant my appeal,
    I will take it before Anubis himself."   (Job 10:2; 19:25–26)

⌇ *Then Rensi, the son of Meru and the chief steward, sends two guards to arrest the farmer. The farmer is frightened. Thinking*

A painting at Beni Hasan depicts daily life and work in Egypt

that he is about to be sentenced to death, he makes a humble plea for death as an end to his troubles.

"Death long-desired arrives like water for the thirsty   (Job 5:26)
. . . like the first drop of milk on a baby's tongue."

Rensi reassures the farmer that no harm will come to him. Then he orders that the transcripts of the farmer's appeals, which he had sent to Pharaoh Neb-kau-Ra, be read aloud and the pharaoh's judgment announced. Nemty-nakht is summoned to the court and given an inventory of all the property that he is ordered to return to the farmer.

A SUFFERER AND A FRIEND IN BABYLON

A Sufferer and a Friend in Babylon is a theodicy or dialogue about human misery. The tradition developed in Babylon after 1000 BCE. The oldest copies, written in cuneiform, come from the library of Ashurbanipal (667–626 BCE) at Nineveh. The most recent copies come from the Persian period after 559 BCE. Archaeologists have reconstructed twenty-seven stanzas with eleven lines each of A Sufferer and a Friend in Babylon from tablets that Austen Henry Layard (1817–1894) recovered from Tell Nimrud in 1845. They are preserved today in the British Museum in London.

A Sufferer and a Friend in Babylon is acrostic. The first letters in each couplet spell out the name of the plaintiff: "I am Saggilk-kinam-ubbib, priest, cantor, and servant of the divine assembly and of the Great King." It is a parallel to the book of Job. Both are conversations, dialogues, or arguments. It is also parallel to the book of Ecclesiastes. Both argue that a world filled with suffering and evil proves that the divine assembly cannot be just.

Terra-cotta statue of a plaintiff from Island of Keos in the Aegean Sea

lines 1–20

The Sufferer

Come, my wise friend,
    Let me speak candidly with you.
Where can one find a teacher of your abilities?
    Where is there a scholar of your wisdom?
    Where is the counselor who will hear my grief?
I am without resources,
    I am lost in the depths of despair.
When I was a child, fate took my father from me,
    The mother who bore me went to the land of no return.
    My parents left me an orphan without a guardian.   (Job 29:12)

The Friend

Your story is too sad, my friend.
    Do not continue to dwell on these evils.
You have blinded yourself to common sense.
    Frowns have scarred your face.
Parents die, they cross the river.
    I too will take that passage.
If anyone could choose . . .
    Who would not choose to be rich?
Anyone who is faithful to our Godfather will be protected,   (Ps 34:9)
    Anyone who humbly fears our Godmother will prosper. (Mic 6:8)

lines 67–77

The Sufferer

Your thoughts soothe like the north wind,
    They bring relief.
My friend, theoretically your advice is sound,
    But let me raise one more issue.
Those who forget their divine patrons prosper.   (Job 21:7–16)
    Those who pray constantly are homeless and destitute.
As a young man, I sought the will of my divine patrons,   (Isa 58:2–3)
    I prayed and I fasted.

Prayer and fasting got me nowhere.
 The divine assembly decreed poverty for me, not wealth.
Cripples and fools outran me.
 Sinners prospered. I failed. (Jer 12:1)

lines 235–42

The Friend

Sinners will lose the position you covet.
 Soon they will vanish.
Sinners will lose the wealth earned without divine help.
 Thieves will steal such riches. (Job 18:5–21)
If you do not do the will of your divine patrons,
 What hope is there for success?
Those who submit to a divine yoke will never go hungry.
 They will eat even when food is scarce.
Seek the soothing wind of the divine assembly,
 And a year's losses will be restored in a moment. (Job 8:5–7)

*Babylonian carving of Lamashtu with a
lion's head as he holds a snake; miniatures above
are the seven plagues Lamashtu sends to earth*

lines 243–53

The Sufferer

I have searched the world for order,
> Everything is upside down.   (Eccl 3:16)
>> The divine assembly is powerless to restore order.
The father tows his boat through the canal,
> While his son lies idly in bed.
The elder son struts about like a lion,   (Gen 25:27)
> While the younger must work as a donkey driver.
The elder son walks the street without concern,
> While the younger son gives food to the poor.
What good has it done to bow down to the divine assembly,
> When now I bow before the dregs of society...?

lines 254–64

The Friend

You are wise and knowledgeable.
> Do not harden your heart.
> Do not falsely accuse your divine patrons.
The mind of the divine assembly is as unfathomable
> as the heavens,   (Job 11:7)
>> The way of your divine patrons is beyond human
>> understanding....
A cow's first calf may be a runt,
> While the second may be big and healthy.
A first child may be born a weakling,
> While the second may become a valiant warrior.
Though one may witness the will of one's divine patrons,
> No one can understand it.   (Job 15:2–4)

lines 265–75

The Sufferer

Listen, my friend, to my words,
> Hear my irrefutable arguments.   (Job 21:2)

People praise the powerful who commit murder,
    While they persecute the powerless, who are innocent.
People listen to the wicked, who despise their divine patrons,   (Jer 5:12)
    While they ignore the honest, who obey them.
People fill the storehouse of the wicked with gold,
    While they steal a beggar's bowl.
People support the schemes of the powerful,
    While they harass and impoverish the powerless. (Amos 2:7; 5:11)
Poor as I am, I am still oppressed,
    Despite my insignificance, I am persecuted.

lines 276–86

The Friend

When Enlil, ruler of the divine assembly, created humans,
    When Ea the glorious pinched them from the clay,
When Mami, mother and queen, shaped them,   (Job 15:5)
    The divine assembly endowed humans with twisted speech.
Their divine patrons empowered humans to lie,
    They gave them permission to speak falsely.
So people flatter the rich like royalty,
    Talk to them as if they were divine.
People treat the poor like thieves,
    Slander them like criminals.
People plot to kill the poor,
    Impose fines on them because they are powerless.   (Amos 2:8)
People terrorize the poor to death,
    Snuff out their lives like a flame.

lines 287–97

The Sufferer

You have been kind, my friend.
    Now look at how much I suffer.
Help me in my distress.
    Understand my suffering.
I am the humble slave of my divine patrons,
    Yet they do not help me.

I walk, without complaint, through the city square,
    I whisper, I do not cry out.
I keep my eyes down,
    I look only at the earth....
May my divine patrons, who abandoned me,
    Now have mercy on me.   (Ps 31:9)
May the divine assembly, who abandoned me,
    Now have mercy on me.   (Ps 69:17)
May Shamash, the good shepherd,   (Ps 28:9)
    Once again shepherd his people as he should.

Babylonian cylinder seal with members of the divine assembly
standing before Marduk, who is seated on his throne

PSALMS,
LAMENTATIONS

LAMENTS FOR UR

≋❙ *The Laments for Ur have been pieced together from over twenty tablets excavated at Nippur about ninety miles southeast of Baghdad in Iraq today. The Nippur excavations began in 1888 as the first American dig in the ancient Near East. John P. Peters, Herman V. Hilprecht, and John H. Haynes served as directors of the project for the University of Pennsylvania. The thirty thousand cuneiform tablets recovered are written in cuneiform Sumerian, a language like Hurrian and Eblaite that belongs to neither the Indo-European nor the Semitic family of languages. The tablets are preserved today in the University of Pennsylvania Museum in Philadelphia.*

Sumerian herders (bottom right)
commissioned this ceramic plaque to ask priests (top center)
to pray to the divine patrons of Nippur (seated) for them

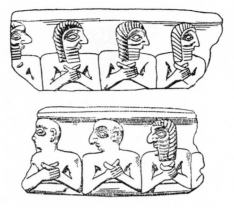

Sumerian worshipers on a bas relief at Lagash

Ur [Arabic: Tell al-Muqayyar] was initially settled by Ubaid peoples about 5000 BCE and developed into a major port city by the Sumerians after 3500 BCE in order to link Mesopotamia with the Persian Gulf and the Indus Valley. The Laments mourn the destruction of the city by the Elamites and the Amorites during the reign of Ibbi-Sin (2026-2004 BCE).

Rebuilding a temple was a dangerous undertaking. The Laments for Ur were sung at critical stages of the construction to remind Nanna, the divine patron of Ur, that, although the builders had to remove debris before restoring his temple, they were not destroying his temple, but rebuilding it.

Laments for Jerusalem, destroyed by the Babylonians in 587 BCE, in the books of Lamentations, Jeremiah, Ezekiel, and Psalms (Ps 137) are parallel to the Laments for Ur. A woman mourning for her husband or a mother weeping for her child [Sumerian: GALA; Akkadian: kalu], like the widow of Tekoa (2 Sam 14:1-20), is a common motif in laments. The mourner in the Laments for Ur is Ningal, the Godmother of the city. She uses the phrase "The Day of the Dust Storm" in the same way that the Bible uses the phrase "The Day of Yahweh" (Amos 5:18-20) or "That Day" (Isa 24:21; 26:1; Zech 13:1-4) to describe the day on which Ur was destroyed.

FIRST LAMENT

≋ *The first lament lists all the cities of Sumer that have been abandoned by their divine patrons and destroyed.*

1–36

Enlil, the shepherd of Sumer, has fled Nippur,   (Num 27:17)
    His sheep are without a shepherd.   (1 Kgs 22:17; Zech 13:7)
Enlil, divine patron of the Earth, has abandoned Nippur,
    His sheep are without a shepherd.   (Isa 32:14; Ezek 34:5)
Enlil has left Nippur,
    His sheep are without a shepherd.
Ninlil, wife of Enlil, has fled Nippur,
    Her sheep are without a shepherd.
Ninlil has abandoned her temple,
    Her sheep are without a shepherd....

SECOND LAMENT

≋ *The second lament calls on all the cities of Sumer to mourn for Ur.*

40–75

Cities of Sumer, weep bitter tears!   (Lam 2:9)
    Cities of Sumer, mourn!   (Ezek 27:32)
Weep bitter tears for Ur, the faithful city!
    Mourn with Nanna, the divine patron of the city!
Cities of Sumer, mourn!
    Weep bitter tears over the ruins of Ur.
Mourn with Nanna,
    Weep bitter tears as long as Nanna mourns!
Weep bitter tears over the walls of Ur!   (Jer 9:19)
    Mourn for Ekishnugal, the temple of Nanna....

THIRD LAMENT

≋ *In the third lament, Ningal, the Godmother of Ur, mourns for her city in the ruins of the Temple of Nanna, her husband.*

88–109

I mourn the Day of the Dust Storm, when Enlil destroyed Ur,
　　The Day of the Dust Storm that condemned my city to death.
My burden, the cause of my tears,
　　The Day of the Dust Storm that condemned my city to death.
My burden that condemned my city to death,
　　The cause of my tears as the Godmother of Ur.
I trembled as the Day of the Dust Storm drew near,
　　The Day of the Dust Storm that condemned my city to death.
My burden, the cause of my tears,
　　The merciless Day of the Dust Storm that condemned my city.
I could not flee the cruel violence of that Day,
　　Its fury was greater than all the joys of my life.
I trembled as that Night drew near,
　　—the Night of Tears that condemned my city to death.
I could not flee the cruel violence of that Night.
　　The Dust Storm filled me with fear and kept me from sleep.

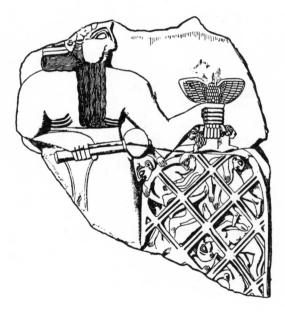

On the Stela of the Vultures Ningursu, divine patron of the Sumerian city of
Lagash, holds a net filled with his enemies and tied with his eagle seal

That Night, I could not go to bed,
    That Night, I could not fall asleep.
Night after night, I could not go to bed,
    Night after night, I could not fall asleep.   (Job 7:13–14)
The land of Ur is filled with sorrow,
    Sorrow fated for my land.
Although I screamed for the life of my calf, cried out for its release,
    I could not save my land from its misery.
My land was in distress,
    Distress that condemned my city to death.
Even if I could flap my wings like a bird,
    Even if I could fly to save my city,
Still my city would be destroyed,
    Still my city would be razed to its foundations,
    Still my Ur would be destroyed where it lays.

Fourth Lament

🏳 *The fourth lament petitions Anu, the divine patron of the sky,
and Enlil, the divine patron of the winds, to reverse their verdict
to destroy Ur.*

137–70

The Day of the Dust Storm struck Ur over and over,
    I watched the destruction of my city. . .,
The Day of the Dust Storm, the divine assembly condemned my city,
    Enlil commanded the total destruction of my city and its people,
The Day of the Dust Storm, I did not abandon my city,
    I did not forget my land.
I shed tears of sorrow before Anu,   (Jer 4:31)
        I uttered prayers of supplication before Enlil.   (Lam 1:17)
        I repeatedly cried, "Spare the city and its people!"   (Ps 74:19)

But Anu and Enlil did not relent;
    They gave no comfort to my heart.   (Lam 1:2)
Their command remained to destroy my city.
    Their decree was to kill my people. . . .

"Spare my city from destruction," I asked.
    "Spare Ur from destruction," I begged.
    "Spare its people from death," I pleaded with Anu and Enlil.

Anu would not listen to me,
>Enlil would not sooth my distress,
>He would not decree: "Grant her petition!"
Instead, Enlil and Anu ordered the city destroyed,
>They ordered Ur destroyed.   (Lam 2:2–3)
The fate of Ur was sealed,
>The people of Ur were sentenced to death.

FIFTH LAMENT

⌦ *The fifth lament describes the destruction of Ur as a dust storm,*
a drought, an earthquake, a flood, and lightning.

171–206

Enlil prepares the dust storm,
>And the people of Ur mourn.
He withholds the rain from the land;
>And the people of Ur mourn.
He delays the winds that water the crops of Sumer,
>And the people of Ur mourn.
He gives the winds that dry the land their orders,
>And the people of Ur mourn.
Enlil orders Kingaluda, the dust storm, to put the city to death,
>And the people of Ur mourn.   (Ps 57:1; Ezek 13:13)
He prepares the winds that dry the land,
>And the people of Ur mourn.
Enlil orders Gibil, the lightning, to prepare the dust storms.
>And the people of Ur mourn.
The winds that dry the land howl.
>And the people of Ur mourn.
The storm sweeps across the land,
>And the people of Ur mourn.   (Jer 49:36)
The winds that dry the land rush unrestrained to the sea,
>And the people of Ur mourn.
Great waves swallow the city's ships,
>And the people of Ur mourn.
Earthquakes rock the pillars of the earth,
>And the people of Ur mourn.
Lightning flashes and explodes in the dust storms.
>And the people of Ur mourn.

Lightning, searing as desert heat, escorts the storms,
　　Scorching as the noon sun.
Dust shrouds the sun,
　　Cuts off its life-giving light.

SIXTH LAMENT

▥ *The sixth lament describes the aftermath of the dust storm. Bod-*
ies are piled high at the gate and the walls and buildings of the
city are in ruins.

208–50

The dust storm leaves the city and the Temple of Nanna in ruins,
　　And the people of Ur mourn.
The dust storm scatters bodies everywhere like broken pots,
　　And the people of Ur mourn....
The walls are breached and corpses block the gates,   (Amos 4:3)
　　And the people of Ur mourn....   (Jer 8:2)

The main streets are choked with the dead.
　　Bodies fill the streets.   (Jer 9:21–22)
Where crowds once celebrated festivals, bodies lie in every street,
　　Corpses are piled on every road.   (Jer 16:4)
In the squares where people danced,
　　Heaps of corpses lie.   (Lam 5:15)
The blood of the dead fills every crevice,   (Ps 79:3)
　　Like molten metal in a worker's mold.
The bodies of the dead melt,
　　Their flesh is like the fat of sheep left in the sun.
Warriors wounded by an ax bleed to death.
　　Warriors wounded by a lance go untended.   (Lam 2:21)
Soldiers lie in the dust,
　　Fighters gasp like gazelles pierced by hunters' spears....

The elders of Ur are slaughtered,
　　And the people of Ur mourn.
The wise of Ur are scattered,
　　And the people of Ur mourn.
Mothers turn their backs on their daughters,
　　And the people of Ur mourn.   (Lam 4:4)

Fathers walk away from their sons,
    And the people of Ur mourn.
Women, children, and houses are abandoned and looted....

SEVENTH LAMENT

≋ *The seventh lament mourns the destruction of Ur by cataloging*
every person, place, and thing destroyed.

251–329

All the buildings outside the walls are destroyed.
    And the people of Ur say: "Our poor city!"
All the buildings inside the walls are destroyed.
    And the people of Ur say: "Our poor city!"   (Amos 5:16)
Ur, my fertile ewe, has been slaughtered.
    Its good shepherd is gone.
My strong ox no longer stands in its stable.
    Its oxherd is gone.
The daughters and sons of Ur have been carried away in ships.
    And the people of Ur say: "Our poor children!"   (Isa 5:13)

My poor city and temple are destroyed,   (Isa 1:7)
    The Temple of Nanna is destroyed, and the people of Ur are dead.
Poor me, I now have no place to sit or stand.
    Poor me, ruins I do not recognize stand in place of my city.

EIGHTH LAMENT

≋ *The eighth lament catalogs the disasters that have befallen Ur,*
and asks Anu and Enlil for permission to rebuild Ur.

330–84

May Anu, divine patron of the sky, decree: "Enough!"   (Lam 3:31–33)
    May Enlil, divine patron of the winds, grant Ningal a better fate.
May Anu rebuild Ur,
    May he restore the Temple of Ningal.
May Anu return your city to its former grandeur,
    May he make you, once again, its queen.

ELEVENTH LAMENT

🎐 *The eleventh lament asks Nanna for permission to rebuild Ur.*

415–35

Nanna, Divine Patron of Ur, answer those who pray to you for Ur,
    May you look with favor on those who stand before you.
Nanna, you know all things,
    Spare your faithful people....
Nanna, rebuild your city,   (Jer 31:38–40)
    Permit your people to praise you once again in your temple.

Hymn to Ninkasi

A hymn to Ninkasi is preserved on several clay tablets: AO 5385 in the Louvre in Paris, a Nippur tablet (Ni 5469) in the Archaeological Museum in Istanbul, and a text in the collection of cuneiform tablets in the Staatliche Museum in Berlin (VAT 6705).

The hymn describes how Sumerians brewed beer. They baked a bread [Akkadian: **bappir**] from barley or emmer wheat and sweetened it with date honey. The dried bread was crumbled, then cooked with water and sprouted barley. This mash was spread on a large mat to cool. The mash was seasoned with date honey and fermented. Finally, it was filtered through a strainer into a storage jar. Unfiltered beer was drunk from a common bowl through long reeds or metal straws.

Beer is mentioned frequently in the Bible (Deut 29:6, 1 Sam 1:15; Isa 29:9; 28:7; 24:9), and was offered to Yahweh as a sacrifice (Num 28:7; Deut 14:26). Wise rulers (Prov 31:4), Nazirites (Num 6:3; Judg 13:4-14), and priests on days they were scheduled to enter the sanctuary (Lev 10:9), did not drink beer. The poor drank beer to forget their suffering (Prov 31:6). Fools, who drank too much beer, became drunks (Ps 69:12; Isa 5:11+22; 56:12), started fights (Prov 20:1), and became false prophets (Micah 2:11).

You, Ninkasi, were born at the source of the rivers,
    You were nursed by Ninhursag....
She laid the foundations of your great city on the sacred lake,
    She finished its walls for you....
Your father was Enki-Nudimmud,
    Your mother was Ninti, Queen of the Underworld....

You, who soothe the mouth, knead the dough with a great paddle,
    You sweeten the bread bowl with dates.   (Exod 8:3)

Assyrians toasting at a banquet

You bake the bread in a great oven,   (Hos 7:4)
    You stack the barley in piles to sprout....

You, who slake thirst, dampen the piles of barley malt,
    While your great dogs guard them from thieves....
You ferment the bread and malt in a jar,
    Waves of foam rise and fall....

You, divine patron of brewers, spread the mash on great reed mats,
    You cool the wort....
You press the mash with both hands,
    You filter the honey-sweet brew....

Your strainer, Ninkasi, makes sweet music,   (Isa 25:6)
    As you skillfully drain the wort into a storage jar....
When you serve the filtered beer from the jar,
    It gushes out like the Tigris and Euphrates....

EBLA ARCHIVES

During their 1974 season, Giovanni Pettinato and Paolo Matthiae from the University of Rome recovered the royal archives of Ebla [Arabic: tell Mardikh] in Syria. These archives are preserved on clay tablets in the Eblaite language written in cuneiform script. The language of Ebla is Semitic. The tablets are terra-cotta. Most

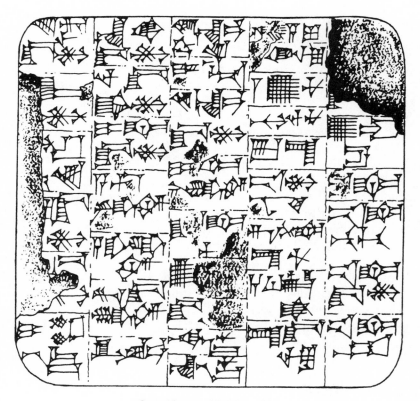

Cuneiform tablet from Ebla

258

are 6 x 6 inches square. There are also round tablets from 1 inch to 4 inches in diameter, and rectangular tablets from 10 x 9 inches square to 14 x 12 inches square. They are preserved today in the Aleppo Museum in Syria.

Between 3000 and 2275 BCE, Ebla engaged in trade and war with states throughout the world of the Bible, including Ur, Mari, Byblos, Hazor, Megiddo, Gaza, and Jaffa. Until the discovery of Ebla's massive temples and palaces, scholars had assumed that Egypt and Mesopotamia were the only great cultures during the Early Bronze period (3300-2300 BCE). Today, the thousands of tablets recovered at Ebla constitute the largest single find from the period. Eighty percent of the tablets found at Ebla are administrative. There are also word lists or dictionaries in which Eblaite nouns are translated into Sumerian and Akkadian. Some tablets contain letters, diplomatic records, hymns, and rubrics for rituals.

Initially, there was some excitement that the book of Genesis might have modeled the character of Abraham negotiating with Lot (Gen 13:5–14:24) on Ibrim, an official of Ebla, whose divine patron was Ya. "Abraham" and "Ibrim," "Ya" and "Yahweh" seemed identical. More careful study, however, showed there were more differences than similarities between these Ebla traditions and the Bible.

HYMN TO THE CREATOR OF
THE HEAVENS AND THE EARTH

Three exercise tablets contain almost the same text, which is translated here as a hymn celebrating the divine patron of Ebla as the creator of the heavens and the earth. The same text has also been translated as a list of Sumerian personal names beginning with LUGAL [Eblaite: "Great Man"] and two quotations. The hymn follows a pattern also found in the Enuma Elish Stories from Babylon, the Hymn to Ptah, and the Hymn to the Aten from Egypt as well as in the stories of the creation of the heavens and the earth in the book of Genesis (Gen 1:1–2:4).

TM.75.G.1682

You are the creator of the heavens and the earth
    There was no earth until you created it   (Ps 104:5–9)
There was no light until you created it.
    There was no sun until you created it.

You alone rule over all creation.   (Gen 1:1—2:4a)
    You alone feed us.

You alone protect us . . . .
    You alone never sleep.   (Ps 121:4)

You alone never die.
    You alone deliver us from our enemies.
    You alone give us peace.

MARRIAGE RITUAL

Two tablets in the archive of Palace G describe rituals to prepare a woman to marry the king of Ebla. She went to the Temple of Kura and to the cemetery at Binaš to honor the ancestors of her husband-to-be. The rituals were celebrated at the end of the dry season and lasted seven days.

To prepare for her wedding to the king of Ebla, Tabur-Damu hung the necklace of her old life around the neck of a goat and drove it into the hills. Parallel rituals appear in the book of Leviticus (Lev 16:1-34).

ARET XI 2:7–21

Next we purify the cemetery.

Put your silver necklace on the neck of a goat.
    Bring it to the gates of Kura and Barama.
Drive it into the hills of Alini   (Lev 16:7–10)
    Where it may stay forever.

RATIONS

Part of the administrative pattern in the Eblaite palace was the issuing of rations of bread, wine, garments, and tools to various officials, visiting dignitaries, and messengers.

TM.75.G.411

Issue . . . two *ninda* rations of bread to King Ibbi-Sipish.
Issue two *ninda* rations of bread to the queen.

Issue two *ninda* rations of bread to royal officials.
Issue three *ninda* rations of bread to the sons of royal officials.
Issue four *ninda* rations of bread to Dubuhu-Hada.
Issue two *ninda* rations of bread to Iptura
Issue two *ninda* rations of bread to the sons of the king.
Issue two *ninda* rations of bread to the daughters of the king.
Issue two *ninda* rations of bread...one ax,...to the elders
Issue four axes, ten *ninda* rations...to the ambassadors of foreign states

Annals of Enna-Dagan

*Enna-Dagan was the commanding officer of the soldiers who con-
quered Mari. The king of Ebla subsequently appointed him governor of Mari, although he calls himself the "King of Mari."
Parallels to the Annals of Enna-Dagan appear in the annals of the
rulers of Israel and Judah in the books of Samuel-Kings.*

TM.75.G.2367

From: Enna-Dagan, commanding officer at Mari
To:...king of Ebla

I laid siege to the cities of Aburu and Ilgi in the land of Belan. There, I
defeated the king of Mari. In the land of Lebanon I inflicted heavy casualties [Eblaite: "heaped up corpses"].
    I laid siege to the cities of Tibalat and Ilwi. There, I defeated the
king of Mari. In the land of Angai, I inflicted heavy casualties.... (2
Sam 8:1–12; 1 Kgs 15:16–22)
    I laid siege to the cities of Raeak, Irim, Asaltu, and Badul. There, I
defeated the king of Mari. Near the border of Nahal, I inflicted heavy
casualties.
    At Emar, Lalanium, and a trade colony of Ebla, I defeated the sol-
diers of Mari, under the command of Istup-sar. At Emar and Lalanium,
I inflicted heavy casualties.
    I liberated Galalabi...and a trade colony.
    At Zahiran, I defeated Iblul-Il, the king of Mari and Ashur. I in-
flicted extremely heavy casualties [Eblaite: "seven heaps of corpses"].
    At Sada, Addali, and Arisum in the land of Burman, I defeated
Iblul-Il, the king of Mari, and their Sukurrim allies. I inflicted heavy
casualties.
    At Saran and Dammium, I defeated Iblul-Il, the king of Mari. Twice
I inflicted heavy casualties. Iblul-Il, the king of Mari, fled toward Nerad

and took refuge in his fortress at Hasuwan. He sent the taxes that Mari owed Ebla to the city of Nema.

I defeated Emar, inflicting heavy casualties.

At Ganane, Nahal, and Sada in the land of Gasur, I defeated Iblul-Il, the king of Mari. I inflicted extremely heavy casualties.

I, Enna-Dagan, now king of Mari, defeated Iblul-Il, the former king of Mari, for the second time at the city of Barama. At Aburu and Tibalat in the land of Belan, I inflicted heavy casualties.

STORIES OF BAAL AND ANAT

The Stories of Baal and Anat are preserved on six broken clay tablets from Ugarit. They were written in the Ugaritic language in cuneiform script about 1400 BCE. The tablets were recovered at Ras Shamra, Syria (1930-1933) by a French team headed by Claude F. A. Schaeffer (1898-1982). Hans Bauer (1878-1937) pioneered the translation of Ugaritic, an alphabetic language with thirty-two letters.

Baal with his
lightning spear
and thunder club

The people of Ugarit told the Stories of Baal and Anat to mourn the death of Baal at the end of the rainless season and to celebrate his resurrection at the beginning of the rainy season (Ezek 8:14).

The Stories of Baal and Anat portray El and Baal in much the same way as the Bible portrays Yahweh. The divine patrons of both Ugarit and Israel share many of the same titles (Ps 68:5) and govern the cosmos with the help of a divine assembly (1 Kgs 22; Isa 6; Zech 3; Dan 7:10; Job 1—2; Ps 82:1); both battle with raging seas and with death itself (Ps 29); both build magnificent temples; and both are enthroned in the heavens (Isa 6:1; Dan 7:9). Likewise, Ahirat appears in the Bible as Asherah, as do Yamm, Mot, and Mt. Zaphon (Isa 14:13).

KTU I.3:ii, 1–42

 *Anat celebrates the grape harvest with a battle in which she wades in the blood of her enemies like farmers at Ugarit waded in the juice of their grapes. Slaves arm Anat for battle with cosmetics as if she were preparing to make love. The language and motifs for farming, for making war, and for making love are parallel in Semitic languages. Each is a passionate activity that arouses all five senses. Here Anat is a lover, a warrior, and a farmer—making love, making war and bringing in the harvest with equal passion.*

Seven slaves rub the skin of Anat with cream,   (2 Kgs 9:30; Esth 2:9)
    They tint her hands and feet with henna.   (Song 4:13–14)
Slaves scent the body of Anat with coriander perfume,
    They drape her in a purple robe.
Anat locks the doors of her sanctuary.
    She joins her warriors at the foot of the mountain.

Anat wages a fierce battle on the plain,
    She slaughters the armies of two cities.
She vanquishes soldiers from the seacoast in the west,
    She destroys soldiers from the east.
Their heads lie like clods of soil under her feet,   (Judg 7:12)
    Their hands mat like locusts in a swarm around her.
She strings their heads to make a necklace,
    She weaves their hands to make a belt.
She wades up to her knees in warriors' blood,   (Isa 63:3–6)
    She stands up to her thighs in their guts.   (Rev 14:18–20)

Inscribed ax head from Ugarit

With her arrows she routs seasoned warriors,
    With her bow she turns back veterans.

Anat returns to her sanctuary,
    The divine warrior returns to the House of Anat.
The fierce battle on the plain was not enough for her,
    With the slaughter of two armies, she was not content.
So, she stacks crates to be enemy soldiers,
    She sets up tables to be warriors, crushing vats to be heroes.
Once again, Anat fights with vigor,
    Once again, she slaughters every enemy in sight.
Anat's body trembles with gladness,
    Her heart fills with joy; she gloats with triumph,   (Ps 16:9)
Again, she wades knee-deep in warriors' blood,   (Rev 19:13)
    She stands up to her thighs in their guts.
Finally, these deadly games are enough for her,
    With the slaughter in her arena she is content.

The warriors' blood is washed from her house,   (Exod 19:10)
    The oil of peace is poured from a bowl.
Anat the young warrior washes her hands,
    Anat the valiant widow cleans her nails.
She washes the warriors' blood from her hands,
    She cleans their guts from her nails.
She takes down the crates,
    She puts the tables aside and stores the crushing vats.
She washes herself with dew from the sky,
    She anoints herself with oil from the earth,
She bathes with rain from the Rider of the Clouds   (Ps 104:3)
    She rinses with dew from the sky, and moisture from the stars.

KTU I:iv, 47-v, 4 (= CTA 3:iv, 94–99)

⊳ *Baal complains to Anat that he does not have a sanctuary of his own, but has to live in the House of El (2 Sam 7:1-17; 1 Kgs 5:3-6; 1 Chr 17:1-14).*

"I have no house like the other members of the divine assembly,
    No sanctuary like the other sons of Athirat.

The House of El is a place for wives and daughters:
      . . . for Athirat, mother of the sea

... for Pidray daughter of the sun
... for Tallay daughter of the rain
... for Arsay daughter of the land

Why must I work like a slave?
    Why must I make bricks?"

Anat swears to Baal: *(CTA 3: iv 99—v 4)*

"El will listen to me,
    I will make sure that the Bull answers me.
I shall lead him like a lamb to slaughter,   (Jer 11:19)
    I shall cover his old grey head with blood,   (1 Kgs 2:9)
    I will fill his old grey beard with guts...   (2 Sam 20:10)
If El does not give Baal a house like the others in the divine assembly,
    If he does not give Baal a sanctuary like the sons of El and Athirat."

KTU I.v, 5–39 (= CTA 3: v 4–39)

Anat stamps her foot and the earth trembles,
    She heads straight for El.
She journeys to the source of the twin rivers,   (Ps 29:10)
    She journeys to the fountain of the twin waters. (Job 38:16)
She walks right into the House of El,
    She bursts into the tent of the Father of Time....

Then Anat the young warrior speaks:

"El, how can you rejoice with your sons,
    How can you celebrate with your daughters?
How dare anyone in your house be happy....

I am going to smash your skull,
    Cover your old grey head with blood,
    and fill your old grey beard with guts.
I am going to drive you from the seven Halls of Wisdom,   (Prov 9:1)
    I am going to close the eight Halls of Judgment."   (Eccl 11:2)

El answers her:

"My daughter, you are a warrior,
    No one else is angrier than you.

Tell me, Anat, my young daughter,
>What do you want me to do?"

Anat the young warrior replies:

"El, your decrees are wise.
>Your wisdom endures forever. (Job 36:26)
>Happy the life that you command.
Mighty Baal is our leader, (Isa 33:22; Ps 96:4)
>Baal is a deliverer beyond all others. (Ps 95:3; 97:9)
All of us must bear his chalice,
>All of us must hand him the cup."

El the Bull cries out,
>El the King, who created Baal. (Deut 32:6)
Athirat and her children cry out,
>The Godmother pleads with the divine assembly:

"Baal has no house like the other members of the divine assembly.
>He has no sanctuary like the other children of Athirat."

≋ *By this combination of threats and flattery, Anat convinces El that Baal must have his own sanctuary. El orders Kothar-wa-hasis, the divine craftsman, to build the House of Baal.*

CTA 3.i, 11–38 = KTU 1.2 I

≋ *Yamm the Sea and Nahar the River question Baal's right to a sanctuary. Soon, a war begins between Baal, whose storms bring life-giving rain, and Yamm and Nahar, whose waves and floods destroy life.*

Yamm the Sea sends messengers to the divine assembly, (Ps 93:3–4)
>Nahar the River dispatches envoys to the Holy Ones....
They depart at once,
>They do not delay.
They head straight to the Mountain of El,
>They go directly to the divine assembly.
The members of the divine assembly are eating,
>The Holy Ones are right in the middle of a meal.
Baal stands beside El.

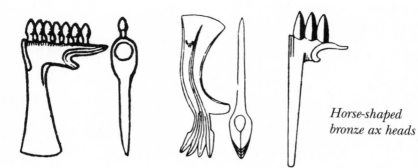

*Horse-shaped
bronze ax heads*

When the divine assembly see the messengers of Yamm coming,
    When they catch sight of the envoys of Nahar on their way,
They put their heads on their knees,   (1 Kgs 18:42)
    They bury their faces in the cushions on their couches.

Baal rebukes them:

"Why should you put your heads on your knees,
    Why should you bury your faces in the cushions on your couches?
Do not be afraid of the messengers of Yamm,
    Do not fear the envoys of Nahar.
Lift your heads up off your knees,
    Raise your heads from the cushions on your couches.   (Ps 24:9)
I will speak to the messengers of Yamm for you,
    I will deal with the envoys of Nahar."

The members of the divine assembly lift their heads from their knees,
    They raise their heads from the cushions on their couches.
When the messengers of Yamm arrive,
    When the envoys of Nahar enter,
They do not bow before El,
    They do not prostrate before the divine assembly.

They strike with tongues of fire,   (Ps 57:4; 64:3)
    They thunder at El the Bull, . . . :

"Hear the word of Yamm . . .
    This is the decree of Nahar . . .
El must give up this prisoner,
    The divine assembly must stop protecting Baal.

Surrender Baal and his followers,
> Give up the Heir of Dagan, so I may have his gold."

El the Bull . . . concedes:

"Baal is the slave of Yamm,
> The Heir of Dagan is in the power of Nahar.
Baal will pay you a ransom,
> He will make sacrifices to you fit for the Holy Ones."

To help Baal regain his throne, Kothar-wa-hasis forges powerful weapons for him.

CTA 3.iv,8–23 = KTU 1.2 IV

Kothar-wa-hasis says:

"Listen to me, Mighty Baal,
> Hear me out, Rider of the Clouds, (Ps 68:4)
Now is the time for you to strike,
> Slay your enemies, and eliminate your rivals. (Ps 92:9)
Now is the time to found an everlasting kingdom, (2 Sam 7:13)
> Establish your dominion throughout all generations." (Ps 145:13)

Then, Kothar-wa-hasis forges a battle-ax.
> He names it "Chaser."
"Chase Yamm away,
> Chase Yamm from his throne,
> Chase Nahar from his seat of power.
Fly from the hand of Baal,
> Fly like an eagle from his fingers.
Strike the shoulder of Yamm the Sea,
> Plunge into the chest of Nahar the River."
Yamm, however, is too strong,
> He does not fall.
Yamm does not even waver,
> He does not collapse.

So, Kothar-wa-hasis forges another battle-ax,
> He names it "Expeller."
"Expel Yamm,
> Expel him from his throne,
> Expel Nahar from his seat of power.

Fly from the hand of Baal,
    Fly like an eagle from his fingers.
Split the skull of Yamm the Sea,   (Ps 74:13–14)
    Divide the forehead of Nahar the River.
Now Yamm will fall,
    Now Nahar will collapse on the earth."   (Judg 5:27)

≋ *Baal defeats Yamm, and the Holy Ones proclaim him ruler of the divine assembly. Yamm, however, continues to attack the Mediterranean coast with fierce winter storms.*

CTA 4.vii, 37–50; 5.i, 15–35; 5.ii, 2–13

≋ *To celebrate his victory over Yamm, Kothar-wa-hasis builds the House of Baal on the clouds. Through a remarkable window in his house, Baal's thundering voice announces the rain he sends on the farms and pastures of Ugarit (1 Kgs 18:36–45).*

    Yamm is not Baal's only enemy. He also battles with Mot, ruler of the dead. Mot sends sirocco winds to dry up the mois-

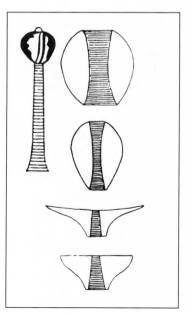

Egyptian club heads shaped like apples, pears, and saucers

*ture from Baal's rain so that the crops and pastures of Ugarit
wither (Hos 13:15). Baal sends messengers to Mot to save his land.*

Baal proclaims,

"From the House of Baal I rule over all the earth,
    Can I ignore this threat from the east? (Ps 68:16)
Shall I allow any other to establish a dominion?

"I will send a messenger to Mot...
    I will challenge the favorite of El.

"I alone rule the divine assembly, (Ps 95:3)
    Who but I can feed the Holy Ones? (Ps 145:15–16)
    Who but I can feed the peoples of the earth...?" (Gen 27:28)

Mot...responds,
    Death answers Baal:
"My throat is like that of a lion, (Isa 5:14)
    My hungry mouth is like the dolphin in the sea.
Death is a pool luring the wild oxen;
    Death is a spring baiting herds of deer. (Ps 42:1; 49:14)
The dust of the grave devours its prey, (Job 10:9; Eccl 3:20)
    Death eats whatever it wants with both hands....
I will drink the moisture of Baal.
    My throat will swallow his rain. (Prov 1:12)
    The mouth of Death will eat you alive...."

Mot stretches his lower lip to the earth.
    His upper lip to the sky,
    He licks the stars with his tongue.
Baal's rain runs off into Mot's mouth, (Ps 141:7)
    His moisture is swallowed by Mot's throat.
The olives shrivel,
    The produce of the earth wilts,
    The fruit of the trees drops off. (Hab 3:17)
Baal grows weak,
    The Rider of the Clouds begins to die.

"Go. Tell Mot...
    Deliver this message to Death.
Hear the word of Mighty Baal,
    Listen to the message of the greatest hero of all.
'Come to me, Death...
    I will be your slave forever.'" (Job 42:2; Ps 116:16)

Baal dies as his rain waters soak deep into the earth and the dry season begins. The divine assembly mourns the death of Baal. As a sign of mourning, they put dust in their hair and slash their bodies with knives (Job 2:12; Jer 16:6; Ezek 27:30). Anat sacrifices hundreds of animals to convince her godmother, Athirat, to replace the dead Baal (Gen 38; Deut 25:5-10; Ruth 4). Athirat gives her husband two sons: Yadi Yalhan and Athtar.

CTA 6.i, 48–65

Athirat says to El:
    "Make Yadi Yalhan king . . . ."

El the Merciful refuses.

"Yadi Yalhan is too feeble to take Baal's place,
    He cannot wield his lightning spear."

Then Athirat says,
    The Godmother speaks:
"Make Athtar the great king.
    Let Athtar the Great become king."
Athtar the Great climbs Mt. Zaphon,   (Isa 14:13)
    He ascends the throne of Mighty Baal
His feet do not even reach the footstool,   (Ps 132:7)
    His head does not even touch the headrest.
"I cannot serve as ruler of the divine assembly,
    I cannot dwell on the heights of Mt. Zaphon."
So Athtar the Great resigns,
    He steps down from the throne of Mighty Baal.
Athtar becomes the patron of farmland,
    The Awesome becomes the protector of pastures.

CTA 6.iii, 3–9

Using a legal gesture, Anat grabs the hem of Mot's tunic to demand the release of Baal from the dead (1 Sam 15:27). Mot refuses, so Anat cuts him to pieces and sows the pieces like seeds in a field. Then she goes to El and demands to know if Baal is dead or alive. El falls into a trance in order to witness Baal's resurrection from the dead.

*Godmother at Ugarit mates
with goats to bring the rain*

"Let me see if Mighty Baal lives,
　　Let me hear the Most High Ruler of the Earth breathe again,
Let El the Merciful dream;
　　Let the Creator of All lay his eyes on Baal.
Let me see the heavens rain olive oil,　　　　　　(Ezek 32:14; Joel 3:18)
　　Let me watch the dry stream beds flow with honey.　(Job 20:17)
Then I will know that Mighty Baal lives,　　　　　　(Job 19:25)
　　I will know that the Most High Lord breathes."

〰 *El sends Anat to Shapshu for help. Shapshu pours wine into the
dry furrows to soften the soil and raise Baal from the dead so
that the farmers of Ugarit can begin to plant.*

CTA 6.v, 9–24

After seven years of drought, Mot...speaks,
　　He complains to Mighty Baal:
"Because of you, Baal, I have lost face...　　　　　　(Ps 132:18)
　　Because of you...
I have been cut up with a sword,
　　I have been burnt with fire.

I have been ground with a millstone,
    I have been winnowed with a sieve.   (Jer 15:7; 51:2)
I have been scattered like seed in the fields,   (Ps 129:3)
    I have been sown in the sea...
Sacrifice one of your brothers for me to eat,
    Let us make peace....

CTA 6.vi, 16–40

In the face of Mot's threat to "consume" the multitudes of humanity, Baal tricks Death by feeding Mot his own brothers.

Mot plodded up Mt. Zaphon,
    He prostrated before Baal...
"Baal has fed me my own brothers;
    My own household has become my food!"

Mot marches up Mt. Zaphon,
    He confronts Baal...

Mot is strong, but so is Baal...   (1 Sam 18:7)
    They gore each other like wild bulls.   (Deut 33:17)
Mot is strong, but so is Baal.
    They strike out at each other like snakes.
Mot is strong, but so is Baal.
    They kick each other like stallions.
Mot is strong, but so is Baal....

Shapshu taunts Mot:
    "Listen to me, Death...
You can never defeat Mighty Baal,
    The Bull will tear the door frame from the House of the Dead,
He will overthrow your throne,
    He will break your scepter in two."   (Ps 125:3)

Fear seizes Mot....
    Death trembles at the words of Shapshu.
Finally, Mot yields: "Baal is 'Ruler of the Divine Assembly.'
    Let his majesty endure forever."

HYMN TO THE ATEN

A hymn to the Aten was inscribed in Egyptian hieroglyphics on the wall of the tomb of Ay, which Pharaoh Akhenaten (1353–1335 BCE) built for Queen Nefertiti's father at el-Amarna. This site stands on the east bank of the Nile River just north of the massif of Jebel Abu Feda, about one hundred miles south of today's Cairo. The royal tombs were cut into the walls of a ravine about four miles from the city in the Wadi Abu Hasah el-Bahari. The Egypt Exploration Fund excavated the site in 1891 and the German Orientgesellschaft continued the work from 1911 to 1914.

The Hymn to the Aten contains some lines from older hymns celebrating the sun disc and other members of Egypt's divine assembly, like Re as Har-of-the-horizon and Shu. Akhenaten designated the worship of the Aten as the state religion. Technically, the worship of Aten was not the monotheism of Judaism, Christianity, and Islam today. By elevating Aten as the sole divine patron of Egypt, by changing his name from Amenophis IV to Akhenaten, and by moving the royal palace from Thebes to el-Amarna, Akhenaten attempted to federalize the government of Egypt. He wanted to increase the authority of the pharaoh and decrease the authority of the priests and their divine patron, Amun-Re. The reform succeeded only until the coronation of Tutankhamen (1333–1323 BCE), when the priests once again resumed control.

The hymn celebrates the creator of Egypt shielded by the sun. From behind this solar screen, the warmth and light of the rays of Aten gently reach out to every corner of the land and bring Egypt to life. Close parallels to the Hymn to the Aten appear in the book of Psalms. Interestingly, both Aten and Yahweh are celebrated for doing everything that good midwives do for mothers and their children. Both give advice to expectant mothers on such things as proper nutrition, massaging the agitated *fetus during midterm traumas, clearing the airway of the new-born, and supplying everything else a newborn needs.*

2–4

As you, Aten, rise over the horizon,
    Your beauty, Giver of Life, is revealed.
You rise in the east,
    You fill the land with beauty.
Your glory shines high above the land,
    Your rays enrich the land you have created.
O Re, you reach to the ends of the earth,
    You bestow these lands on Akhenaten, your beloved son.
Although you are far away,
    Your rays touch the earth.
Although you shine on every human face,
    No one sees you go.

When you set upon the western horizon,
    The earth lies in darkness and death.   (Ps 104:20–3)
Sleepers lie beneath their covers,
    Seeing no one around them.
Their belongings under their pillows could vanish,
    They would not even notice.
The lion leaves his cave,
    The snake strikes,
When darkness blankets the land.
    The lands are quiet,
Their creator rests on the horizon.
    At daybreak, you rise again over the horizon,
You shine as the Aten bringing day.
    Your rays chase away the darkness,
The Two Lands of Egypt rejoice.
    Awake and erect,
You raise them up.

5–8

Bathed and dressed,
    They raise their hands in praise.
The whole land goes to work.   (Ps 104:23)

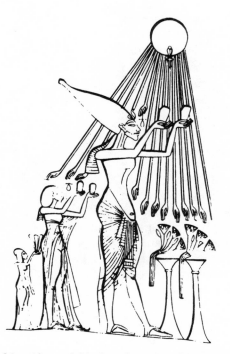

Akhenaten, his wife, and his daughters worship Aten, whose rays are hands

Cattle graze contented,
    Trees and plants turn green.
Birds fly to their nests, (Ps 104:12)
    They spread their wings to praise your *ka*.
All things that walk or fly come to life
    When you have risen.
Ships and barges sail up and down,
    Canals open at your rising.
Fish glide through the river,
    Your rays penetrate even dark waters. (Ps 104:25–26)

You join a woman and a man,
    You massage the fetus in its mother's womb, (Ps 139:13)
    You soothe the crying child unborn.
You nurse the hungry infant in the womb,
    You breathe into its nostrils the first breath of life.
You open the newborn's mouth on the day of its birth
    You meet every human need....

Innumerable are your unseen deeds,
    You have no equal!   (Ps 8:1; 104:24)
Alone, you fashioned the earth according to your plan,   (Col 1:15–20)
    All humans and animals, all that walk and fly.   (Ps 8:7–8)
In Syria-Palestine, Ethiopia and Egypt,
    You assign each a place.
You allot to each both needs and food,
    You count out to each the days of life.   (Job 14:5)
They have separate languages,
    And varied natures as well.   (Gen 11:9)
Their skins are different,
    For you have so distinguished the peoples.
You have made a Nile in the underworld,   (Gen 7:11)
    So it may be brought forth at your command
    To feed the people of the land.
Thus have you made them, wearying yourself
    On their behalf, you are lord of all.
In this way the Aten of the day arises,
    Majestic in its greatness....

10–11

You also give life to all distant lands,
    For you have placed a Nile in the heavens,
So that rain may fall upon the sea and make waves
    Upon the mountains like those in the sea, irrigating their fields.
How efficient are your designs, O lord of all time,   (Ps 104:24)
    With this Nile for the other lands and their creatures,
    With a Nile springing from the underworld for Egypt. (Ps 104:10)

Your rays give sustenance to every field,
    Your rising brings them life and growth.
You have established the seasons
    To nurture all that you have made,
The winter to cool them and the heat,
    So they may feel your touch.

You made the heavens in which to rise,
    That you might observe all things.
You alone are the Aten,
    Yet you alone rise.

You alone are the source of life.
  Appearing, glistening, departing and reappearing,
Your manifestations are without number.
  You are the Aten, the source of life.
Every village, harbor, field, road, and river sees your light,
  They feel your warmth.
You are the Aten,
  You are the light of the earth . . . .

12–13

You are my desire,
  No one knows you except Akhenaten, your son.   (Ps 104:29–30)
You have revealed yourself to me,
  You have shown me your plans and your power.
Your hand made Egypt,
  You created it.
When you rise,
  The earth lives.
When you set,
  The earth dies.
You are life itself,
  All live through you.
Every eye sees clearly until you set,
  All work must wait until you rise again.
At your rising, every arm works for your pharaoh,
  At your creation, every foot sets off to work.
You raise up the people for the son of your body,
  For the pharaoh of Upper and Lower Egypt.
Akhenaten rules with Ma'at, the divine patron of knowledge . . .
  Akhenaten and her royal highness, Nefertiti.

PROVERBS,
SIRACH,
WISDOM

TEACHINGS OF PTAH-HOTEP

Ptah-Hotep taught during the Old Kingdom in Egypt (2575–2134 BCE). The Teachings of Ptah-Hotep are preserved on papyrus sheets in hieratic or longhand Egyptian writing as well as on clay tablets. They were recovered in Egypt around 1900 by archaeologists from France and are at the Bibliothèque Nationale in Paris.

A teacher like Ptah-Hotep bore the title "Father" or "Mother" (Prov 1:8). A student was called "Child." Students came from powerful households, and teachers like Ptah-hotep prepared them to assume important positions in public life.

Teachers taught students to observe, to judge, and to act. They used the "saying" (Prov 1:17) to hand on their observations, and the "analogy" [Hebrew: masal] to hand on their judgments (Prov 9:17; 10:1). Analogies linked together form "teachings" [Egyptian: seba'it]. In the Teachings of Ptah-Hotep, introductory and concluding teachings that offer students general encouragement to excel in life sandwich teachings that provide advice on specific careers and professions into which the students will graduate. Students memorized the sayings and analogies of their teachers. Competent students, who could apply teachings and act accordingly, were "...like golden apples in silver settings" (Prov 25:11). The incompetent, who could not apply what they learned, were like "...a proverb which hangs limp in the mouth of a fool like crippled legs" (Prov 26:7).

Parallels to the Teachings of Ptah-Hotep appear in the books of Proverbs, Ecclesiastes, and Sirach. Both the Egyptian and biblical traditions teach students to avoid pride, get good advice (Prov 2:4), practice table manners (Prov 23:1; Sir 31:12), be reliable (Prov 25:13), make friends (Sir 6:7), and deal with women (Prov 6:24; Sir 9:1).

50–60

My students, in all things, be intelligent, not arrogant,
      Be wise, not over-confident.
Seek advice from the powerless,   (Prov 19:20)
      As well as from the powerful.
No one ever reaches one's full potential,
      There is always more to learn.
Wisdom hides like emeralds,   (Prov 2:1–5)
      But it can be found even in a young woman grinding grain.

85–95

If you become a ruler, do what is right,
      Stay above reproach.
Be just in your decisions,
      Never ignore the law.
Justice endures.
      Justice is as old as creation.
Injustice brings punishment,   (Prov 11:21)
      Injustice brings all your work to nothing.   (Prov 17:13)
Injustice brings success for a moment,
      Justice is an enduring inheritance.

120–42

If you serve a powerful patron,
      Take what your patron offers.
Do not look about with envy,
      Do not always hope for more ...   (Prov 23:1–3)
Stand humbly until your patron speaks to you,
      Speak only when spoken to.
      Laugh when your patron laughs ...
When the powerful are at the table,
      They may seem to dispense favors as they see fit,
Patrons may seem to bless only their clients,   (Prov 21:1)
      But their *ka*-souls are guided by the divine assembly,
      Therefore, do not complain about their choices.

Scribes in a painting at Beni Hasan record tax payments

147–60

If you become a trusted messenger for the powerful,
    Be completely reliable on every assignment.   (Prov 25:13)
Carry out your orders to the letter,
    Beware of causing a dispute between patrons.
    Withhold nothing,
    Forget nothing,
    Forge nothing,
    Repeat nothing,   (Sir 19:7, 10)
    Embellish nothing.
Do not make harsh language worse.
    Vulgarity turns the mighty into enemies.

175–85

If you work for the newly rich,
    Ignore their former lack of wealth and distinction.
Do not be prejudiced against them,
    Do not detest them for once being lower class.
Respect them for their accomplishments,
    Acknowledge them for their acquisition of land.
Land does not come of itself,
    Land must be earned.
It is their law for those who wish it.
    As for those who overstep, they are feared.
The divine assembly assigns the powerful their status.   (Ps 127:2)
    The divine assembly defends them, even when they sleep....

265–76

If you become a judge,
    Listen patiently to the plaintiff's suit.
Give plaintiffs time to air their cases.
    Plaintiffs want petitions heard more than granted.
If you interrupt plaintiffs, and are rude to petitioners,   (Sir 11:8)
    People will complain: "Why does the judge do that?"
To grant every petition is unnecessary,
    To hear every petition calms passions, prevents violence.

278–96

If you become the father of a household or are a houseguest,
    Stay away from the women of another's house.   (Prov 6:23–29)
Keep your mind on business, your eyes off pretty faces.
    Foolish dreamers become casualties of unwise actions.
Succumb to love sickness and lust,   (Prov 7:24–27)
    And nothing you do will succeed.

318–23

If you inherit land, take only your own portion of the land,
    Do not covet the land of others.   (Prov 15:27)
Those who respect the land of others earn respect,
    Those who defraud others lose their right to speak.
To covet even a small thing
    Transforms the peaceful into warriors.

328–34

If you become a landowner, establish a household,
    Be faithful to your wife.
Feed her, clothe her, make her happy,
    And she will provide you with an heir.   (Prov 31:10–12)
Do not sue her in court,
    But do not let her dominate you.

Students of Ptah-Hotep inspect villagers' work at his tomb

To judge a woman's moods
 Is to read a woman's eyes.
Keep your wife within the confines of your house.   (Prov 31:27–28)
 A wife without restraint flows like the rain,   (Prov 12:4)
 And is never to be found when bidden.

380–83

Happiness escapes those who spend their lives complaining.
Households are never founded by fools.   (Prov 15:19)

429–31

If you are promoted and are free from want,
 Be generous with the wealth the divine assembly gives you,
Take care of your village now that you can;
 You will stand among those who share their good fortune.

565–74

Finally, my students, remember, the wise follow their teachers' advice,
    Consequently, their projects do not fail.   (Prov 2:1–5)
The wise learn from these teachings and rise to positions of trust,
    Fools ignore these teachings and fall from favor.   (Prov 19:20)
The wise rise early to start to work,   (Hos 14:9)
    Fools rise early to worry about all there is to do.

TEACHINGS OF KHETY

More than six hundred copies of the *Teachings of Khety* have been recovered by archaeologists. They developed during the Middle Kingdom (2040-1640 BCE), and were copied by scribes throughout the New Kingdom (1550-1070 BCE) to practice writing. Two copies by the same Nineteenth Dynasty (1307-1196 BCE) scribe on the Papyrus Sallier II (10182) and on the Papyrus Anastasi VII (10222) and fragments on the Papyrus Chester Beatty (10699) are preserved in the British Museum in London. Fragments on an Eighteenth Dynasty (1550-1307 BCE) writing board are preserved in the Louvre Museum in Paris.

The *Teachings of Khety* are a satire creating an exaggerated and humorous contrast between the work of scribes and eighteen other trades. Parallels glorifying the work of scribes are found in

Scribes with reed pens behind their ears hold palettes of red and black ink and write on papyrus scrolls from cases beside them

the *Teachings of Ptah-hotep, the Teachings of Amen-em-ope, the book of Sirach (Sir 38:24–39:11), and elsewhere in the Bible (1 Chr 27:32; Ezra 7:6, 11; Matt 13:52; 1 Cor 1:20).*

Khety gave his son Pepy this advice as they sat together in the cabin on the deck of a ship sailing south to the palace of Pharaoh. He was en route to apprentice Pepy to the scribes who served the pharaoh.

"Learn to write, my son. I have seen how many other kinds of work destroy workers.... Learning to write can save you from all this suffering (Sir 38:24). As it says in the Book of Goals: 'No scribe anywhere in Egypt is poor....' No other profession can make such a claim."

"Love writing more than your mother. Writing is better than any other work in Egypt. Even as a young man, the scribe is treated with courtesy and sent on important errands. His career begins even before he wears the robe of an adult.

"I have never seen a sculptor or goldsmith serve as a messenger, but I have seen them at work, at the mouths of their furnaces, with their fingers like the scale-covered claws of a crocodile. Their sweat reeks like the odor of rotting fish.

Gardeners cutting down a tree

*Scribe with scroll
on his lap*

"The woodcutter is more wretched than a farmer. His field is the forest, his hoe an ax. He works until dark. His arms ache with heavy labor and he must still light his own fire.

"The jeweler shapes hard stones every day. To finish just one small piece of jewelry is a full day's work (Sir 38:27). When he lies down at dusk, his back aches and his thighs cramp.

"The barber shaves from dawn until dusk. . . . he is a slave to the chins of the world. Like bees in search of flowers, barbers flit from street to street in search of chins to shave. Only the persistent fill their bellies.

"The arrow maker must sail north to the delta swamps in search of reeds for shafts. When his days are done, he has been bitten by mosquitoes and stung by sand flies until his body is covered with bites.

"The potter is buried alive in clay (Sir 38:29–30). He wallows in mud like a pig to make his pots. His clothes are caked with clay, his loincloth is rotting. He breathes fire from the kiln. He works the clay with his feet, and is exhausted by its weight. He clomps along the streets and tracks mud into every courtyard. . . .

"The gardener bears a yoke. His shoulders slump with age and there is a festering sore on his neck (Sir 38:25–26). In the morning he waters his vegetables, in the evening he tends his herbs, and at noon he works in his orchard. . . . gardeners work themselves to death. . . .

"A weaver's work is worse than a woman's. With his knee against his chest, he can hardly breathe. If he stops before the day's end, he receives fifty lashes. He must bribe the doorkeeper with his food just to see the light of day. . . .

"The messenger treks into the desert, leaving his children to take care of his property. Faced with the threat of lions and nomads, he can be himself only when in Egypt. When he returns to his door, he is exhausted by his journey. Whether his house is a tent or built of bricks, he is never happy there. . . .

"The work of a fisherman is the worst of all because he shares the river with crocodiles, but he no longer even sees them. . . . Fear has blinded him to the death all around him.

"If you know how to write, you will do better than any of these other workers. You will be your own boss. You will not share their misery! It is my responsibility to make this journey with you to the palace. Your time as an apprentice is no more than a day. Your work as a scribe will last for an eternity, longer than the mountains. You will not be like these other workers, who must rise early to face another day of suffering."

THIRTY TEACHINGS OF AMEN-EM-OPE

Shortly after 1900, archaeologists recovered two versions of the teachings or "wise words" of Amen-em-ope. A twenty-seven page copy written in hieratic Egyptian longhand on papyrus sheets is preserved in the British Museum (#10474) in London.

Amen-em-ope taught in Egypt between 1250 and 1000 BCE. The Teachings of Ptah-Hotep (3000-2000 BCE) and the Teachings of Amen-em-ope demonstrate the consistency of Egypt's worldview over the two thousand years separating one tradition from the other. Both contrast the wise and the fool. The wise are soft-spoken or silent. Fools are hot-tempered or hot-headed. The wise know when to talk and when to listen. Fools let anger run or ruin their lives. There are, nonetheless, striking differences between one tradition and the other. The Teachings of Ptah-hotep promise material success. The Teachings of Amen-em-ope remind students that only the members of the divine assembly are perfect, and that few of the wise have material success.

Like most of the peoples of Syria-Palestine, the Hebrews hated Egypt as a house of slaves, but loved Egypt as a great teacher represented by Ptah-hotep and Amen-em-ope. The book of Proverbs (Prov 22:17—24:22) preserves portions of the Teachings of Amen-em-ope and imitates its structure. Both have a general introduction followed by thirty teachings of surprisingly similar advice on specific topics. "Have I not written for you thirty sayings of admonition and knowledge, to show you what is right and true, that you may give a true answer to those who sent you?" (Prov 22:20-21). The teachings of James in the New Testament (James 3:1-18) are also indebted to the Teachings of Amen-em-ope.

TEACHING ONE

iii:9–iv:1

Listen to what I say,
    Learn my words by heart.   (Prov 22:17–18)
Prosperity comes to those who keep my words in their hearts,
    Poverty comes to those who discard them.
Enshrine my words in your souls,
    Lock them away in your hearts.
When the words of fools blow like a storm,
    The words of the wise will hold your tongue like an anchor.
Live your lives with my words in your heart,
    And you will live your lives with success.
My words are a handbook for life on earth,
    My words will bring your body to life.

TEACHING TWO

iv:3–v:8

Do not steal from the poor,   (Prov 22:22)
    Do not cheat the cripple.
Do not abuse the elderly,
    Do not refuse to let the aged speak.
Do not conspire to defraud anyone yourself,
    Do not encourage anyone else's fraud.
Do not sue those who wrong you,
    Do not testify against them in court.

Scribes in a painting at Beni Hasan record tax payments

Injustice can turn on fools quicker than
>...floods eroding the bank of a canal,
>...north winds bearing down on a boat,
>...storms forming,
>...thunderbolts cracking,
>...crocodiles striking.

Fools cry out,
>Fools shout to the divine assembly for help.

Let Thoth, divine patron of the moon, judge their crimes.
>You must steer the boat to rescue them.

Do not treat fools the way fools treat you.
>Pull the fool up out of high water.

Give the fool your hand.
>Leave the punishment of the fool to the divine assembly.

Feed fools until they are full. (Prov 25:21–22)
>Give them your bread until they are ashamed.

Teaching Three

v:9–19

Stop and think before you speak.
>It is a quality pleasing to the divine assembly.

Never quarrel with fools,
>Nor cast barbed words at them.

Stay patient when confronted by enemies,
>Bend like the wind when attacked.
>Sleep before answering their accusations.

Anger explodes in fools,
>Like fire breaks out in straw.

Stay out of the way of angry fools,
>Let the divine assembly judge them.

Keep my words in your heart,
>Be a model for your children.

Teaching Four

vi:1–12

Fools talk out loud in the temple,
>They are like trees planted indoors. (Ps 1:4)

They bloom, but then wither.   (Jer 17:5–8)
    They are thrown into the canal,
They float far from home,
    They are burned as trash.   (Jer 11:16)

The wise are soft-spoken
    They are like trees planted in a garden.
They flourish, and double their yield ....   (Ps 1:3; Ezek 17:5–6)
    Their fruit is sweet,
Their shade is pleasant,
    They flourish in the garden forever.

TEACHING SIX

vii:11–ix:8

Do not move a surveyor's stone to steal a field,   (Prov 23:10)
    Do not move the surveyor's line to take a farm.
Do not covet another's land,
    Do not poach on the widow's field.
To forge a claim to a poorly marked field ...
    Cries out to Thoth, divine patron of the moon, for justice.
Those who steal the land of others,
        Oppress the poor ....
        Destroy the land
        Live only to put others to death.
Their homes will be vandalized,
        Their warehouses will be looted,
        Their heirs will be defrauded of their inheritance.
        Their property will be distributed to others.
Do not topple the markers on the boundaries of a field,
    Your conscience will destroy you.   (Prov 22:28; Hos 5:10)
To please Pharaoh ...
    Observe the borders of your neighbors' fields ...
To please Pharaoh ...
    Maintain the borders of your own field.
Do not plow across the boundary furrow of your neighbors,
    And your neighbors will not plow across yours.
Plow only your own fields,
    Eat only bread from your own threshing-floor ...

Better a single bushel from your divine patron,   (Prov 16:8; 19:1+22)
  Than five thousand stolen bushels.

Stolen grain does not make good bread in the bowl,
  Nor good feed in the barn,
  Nor good beer in the jar.
Stolen grain only spends the night in your granary.
  At dawn it vanishes.
Better is poverty from the hand of your divine patron   (Prov 15:16)
  Than wealth from a granary full of stolen grain.
Better is a single loaf and a happy heart   (Prov 15:17; 17:1)
  Than all the riches in the world and sorrow.

TEACHING SEVEN

ix:10–x:15

Do not spend tomorrow's riches,
  Today's wealth is all you own.   (Ps 52:7)
Do not set your heart on material goods,   (Eccl 5:10)
  Time makes beggars of us all.   (Ps 39:6)
Do not work to lay up a surplus,   (Prov 23:4–5)
  Toil only for what you need.

Stolen goods only spend the night,   (Ps 62:10)
  At dawn they vanish.
Dawn reveals where stolen goods spent the night,
  But they have vanished.
At night, the earth opens its mouth
  And renders its verdict on stolen goods.
At night, the earth consumes stolen goods
  And absorbs them into the underworld.
At night, stolen goods dig a hole into the underworld.
  They fly away like geese into the sky.

Do not boast over stolen wealth,   (Prov 21:6)
  Do not complain about your poverty.
Foolish soldiers outrun their brothers,
  Abandoned, they face the enemy alone.
Fools who are greedy strand their boats on sand bars,
  The wise who are patient sail freely with the wind...

TEACHING NINE

xi:12–xiii:9

Do not take counsel with fools,   (Prov 14:7)
    Do not seek their advice.
Do not speak back to superiors,
    Do not insult them.
Do not let superiors discuss their troubles with you,
    Do not give them free advice.
Seek advice from your peers,   (Prov 19:20)
    Do not ignore your equals.
More dangerous are the words of fools   (Prov 22:24–25)
    Than storm winds on open waters
Foolish words destroy...
    Foolish advice deserves a beating.
Fools dump their cargo on the whole world,
    But their shipments are weighed down with lies.
Fools deliver fraud;
    They ship quarrels....
Fools cause neighbors to quarrel,
    Fools are clouds blown by the winds of the moment...
The words of fools sound sweet,
    But they taste sour....

Therefore, do not rush after fools,
    The words of fools will drown you like a strong wind.

TEACHING ELEVEN

xiv:5–18

Do not covet the goods of the poor,
    Do not hunger for their bread.
The goods of the poor will stick in your throat,
    You cannot swallow them.

Those who perjure themselves for food
    Let their stomachs deceive their hearts.
Success obtained by fraud cannot last,
    The bad only spoils the good....
When you vomit a piece of bread too large to swallow,   (Prov 23:6–8)
    What you gained is lost....

TEACHING THIRTEEN

xv:19–xvi:14

Do not cheat your neighbor with false ledgers,
    It is an abomination for the divine assembly.
Do not bear false witness   (Prov 14:5)
    And destroy your neighbor with your words.
Do not over-assess the property of your neighbor,
    And inflate what you are owed.
If a poor neighbor owes you a great debt,   (Prov 22:26–27)
    Forgive two-thirds, collect one-third.   (Matt 18:27; Luke 7:41–42)
Make honesty your guide to life,
    And you will sleep soundly, and wake happily.
Better to be praised for loving your neighbor
    Than for a storehouse full of stolen wealth.
Better is bread eaten with a contented heart   (Prov 17:1)
    Than wealth spent with sorrow.

TEACHING EIGHTEEN

xix:10–xx:6

Do not go to bed worrying,   (Matt 6:34; James 4:13–15)
    Wondering: "What will tomorrow bring?"
No one knows what tomorrow brings,   (Prov 27:1)
    The divine assembly is perfect, but humans fail.
Human words are one thing,
    Divine actions are another.   (Prov 16:9; 19:21)
Do not say, "I am innocent,"   (Prov 20:9)
    And then file a lawsuit.

Butchers in a painting at Beni Hasan

Judgment belongs to the divine assembly,
      Verdicts are sealed by divine decree.
Before the divine assembly, no one is perfect,
      Before the divine assembly, everyone has failings.
Those who strive for perfection
      Can destroy it in a moment.

Control your temper....
      Do not let your tongue steer your life.
Your tongue may be the rudder of your boat,
      But Amun-Re, your divine patron, must be its pilot.

TEACHING NINETEEN

xx:8–19

Do not bear false witness against your neighbor,   (Exod 23:8)
      Do not defame the righteous.
Do not change your testimony,
      When witnesses challenge you....
Tell every judge the truth,
      Do not risk punishment for perjury.
If you perjure yourself before a judge
      Your false testimony will come back to haunt you....

TEACHING TWENTY

xx: 20–xxi:20

Do not bear false witness,
      Do not convict the innocent.
Do not court the favor of those dressed in linen,
      Do not ignore those in rags.
Do not take bribes from the powerful   (Ps 15:5)
      And oppress the poor for their sake.

Justice is a divine gift,
      Only the divine assembly decides right from wrong
Do not forge documents.
      They are a deadly trap,
      They will bring you before the royal inspector.

Painting at Beni Hasan depicts fishing in papyrus marshes

Do not alter the decrees of the divine assembly,
    Do not change the will of the divine assembly.
Do not claim for yourself the power of the divine assembly,
    Do not ignore divine providence.
Return stolen land to its legal owners,
    Choose life....

TEACHING TWENTY-FIVE

xxiv:8–20

Do not make fun of the blind,
    Do not tease the dwarf,   (Prov 17:5)
    Do not trip the lame.
Do not tease the insane,   (1 Sam 21:14)
    Do not lose patience with them when they make mistakes.

Humans are clay and straw,   (Ps 103:14; Isa 64:8)
    The divine assembly is their sculptor.   (Job 10:8–9; 33:6)
Every day the divine assembly tears down,
    And every day it builds up.
The divine assembly can make a time for thousands to be powerful,
    And a time for thousands to be powerless.   (Prov 29:13; Eccl 3:1–10)
Blessed are those who journey to the land of the dead.
    They will be safe in the hands of the divine assembly.

TEACHING TWENTY-EIGHT

xxvi:9–14

Do not arrest widows gleaning your fields,   (Ruth 2:2–9)
    Do not be impatient with their defense.
Give strangers olive oil from your jar,   (1 Kgs 17:12–16)
    And your household will have twice as much.
Blessed are those who respect the poor,
    More than those who honor the powerful.

TEACHING THIRTY

xxvii:6–26

To study these thirty teachings   (Prov 22:20)
    Is to become wise.   (Hos 14:9)
They are the book of books,
    They give wisdom to the simple.
Blessed are those who teach them to the simple.
    They will be cleansed of ignorance.
Fill your soul with these teachings,   (Deut 6:6)
    Put them in your heart.
Master these teachings,
    Hand them on to others.
The scribe, skilled in his tasks,   (Prov 22:29)
    Will become a client of the pharaoh.

TEACHINGS OF AHIQAR

⧉ *Ahiqar [Aramaic: 'hyqr] introduces himself as an advisor to Sen-nacherib (704-681 BCE) or to Esarhaddon (680-669 BCE), Great Kings of Assyria. In 1906, German archaeologists recovered an edition of his teachings on the island of Elephantine, which is today part of the city of Aswan in southern Egypt. This copy of Ahiqar's teachings was written in Aramaic about 500 BCE on re-cycled sheets of papyrus whose previous contents had been erased. They are preserved in the Staatliche Museum in Berlin.*

Ahiqar never had a child who could be his heir, so he adopted Nadin and trained him to take over his position in the Assyrian court. Once Nadin got into office, however, he betrayed Ahiqar by accusing him of treason. Ahiqar was sentenced to death, but the executioner had once been spared by Ahiqar, so he spared Ahiqar, who went into hiding. Ahiqar subsequently recovered his honor by helping the Great King of Assyria win a wager with the pharaoh of Egypt and exposing Nadin as a fool.

Some one hundred sayings, proverbs, adages, and stories in the Teachings of Ahiqar parallel the books of Proverbs and Judges (Judg 9:8-15; 2 Kgs 14:9). They teach how to speak diplomatically, how to avoid the anger of rulers and how to respect parents. They remind students that rulers are like members of the divine as-sembly and that fools are always punished. Like Joseph (Gen 37:2—50:26), Daniel (Dan 1:1—28), Mordecai (Esth 1—11), and Tobit (Tob 1:1—14:15)—where Ahiqar appears as Tobit's nephew (Tob 1:21-22; 4QTobarama)—Ahiqar is a wise man whose fortunes rise and fall, but, in the end, he prevails.

Saying 3. vi:81

Spare the rod,
    Spoil the child.   (Prov 13:24; 19:18; 23:13–14)

Saying 5. vi: 83

Beat the slave boy,
Rebuke the slave girl,   (Prov 26:3)
     Then they will obey.

Saying 9. vi:88

Lions ambush stags,
     Shed their blood,
     Eat their meat,
So it is when humans meet.

Saying 12. vi:92

Two kinds of people are a delight.
          A third pleases Shamash, the divine judge: (Prov 6:16–19)
Those who share their wine,
          Those who follow good advice,
          Those who can keep secrets....

Saying 14a. vi:96

Do not curse the day,
     If you have not seen the night.   (Job 3:1–3)

Saying 15. vii:98

Above all else, control your tongue.
          Do not repeat what you have heard.   (Sir 27:16–19)
A human word is a bird;   (Prov 26:2; Eccl 10:20)
          Once released, it can never be recaptured.

Saying 16. vii:99

Choose words carefully to teach another.   (Job 8:10; Eccl 5:2)
     The word is mightier than the sword.

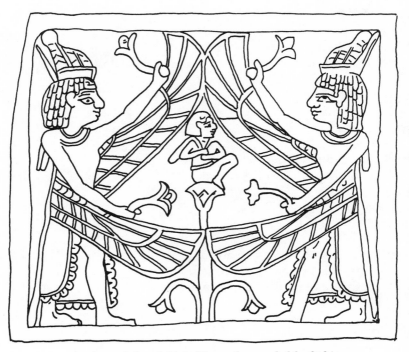

*An ivory inlay depicts Pharaoh guarded by Sphinx
and emerging as a fetus from a lotus*

Saying 18. vii:100

Rulers are often soft-spoken,
    But their words are two-edged swords.   (Wis 18:15–16; Heb 4:12)

Sayings 20 and 21. vii:103–4

A ruler's order is a consuming fire,   (Isa 10:16)
    Be swift to obey or it will burn your hands.

Make a ruler's order to be your heart's desire.
        Can kindling conquer the flame?   (Eccl 6:10; Isa 45:9)
        Can flesh conquer the knife?
        Can farmers conquer rulers?   (Isa 10:15)

Saying 23. vii:105

Gentle is the tongue of a ruler,
    But it can break a dragon's bones.   (Prov 25:15; Sir 28:17)
    Like death, it comes unexpected.

Saying 29. viii:111

I hauled sand and carried salt,   (Prov 27:3)
    But nothing is heavier than debt.   (Sir 22:15; 29:4–5)

Saying 32. viii:114–15

When the young speak mighty words that soar,   (Ps 8:2; Jer 1:6–9)
    Their words become prophecies.   (Matt 21:16)
    With divine help, they even make sense.   (Wis 10:21)

Saying 35. viii:118–120a

Once a leopard met a goat who was cold.

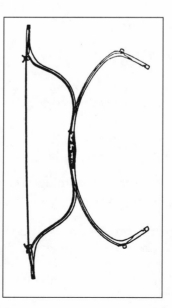

Composition bow,
strung (left) and
unstrung (right)

The leopard asked: "Would you like my coat,
    Would you like me to cover you?"
The goat answered: "What comfort is your coat?   (Job 30:2; Isa 1:11)
    You only want my hide."

A leopard does not approach a gazelle
    Unless it is looking for blood.

Saying 38. viii:124b–125

In the eyes of the divine assembly, a woodcutter working in the dark
    Is a thief burglarizing a house.   (Job 24:13–17)

Saying 39. ix:126

Do not draw your bow or shoot an arrow at the innocent. (Ps 11:2; 64:2, 7)
    Their divine patrons will turn your arrows back on you.

Saying 41. ix:127

Work your fields in season,
    Perform every task.
You will fill your belly,   (Prov 12:11; 28:19)
    You will feed your household.

Saying 43. ix:130

Do not borrow from the wicked.

When you borrow money,
    Work night and day to repay it.   (Prov 6:1–5)
Receiving a loan is sweet...
    Repaying a loan can cost all you possess.

Saying 47. ix:136

Do not be dissatisfied with your life.   (Ps 131:1)
    Do not covet honors which have been denied you. (Exod 20:17)

Saying 48. ix:137

Amassing wealth corrupts the heart.
                    (Ps 62:10; Ezek 28:5; Luke 12:13–21; 1 Tim 6:10)

Saying 49. ix:138

Those who do not honor their parents' name   (Exod 20:12; Prov 20:20)
    Are cursed for their evil by Shamash, the divine judge.

Sayings 54 and 55. x:142–44

Do not quarrel with those more powerful than you,
    Do not compete with those stronger than you.   (Sir 8:1)
    They will only add your power and strength to their own.

Saying 59. x:148

Do not be sweet enough to swallow,
    Do not be bitter enough to be spit out.

Saying 73. xi:165

A thorn bush asked a pomegranate tree: (Judg 9:8–15; 2 Kgs 14:9)
    "Why so many thorns to protect so little fruit?"
The pomegranate tree said:
    "Why so many thorns to protect no fruit at all?"

Saying 77. xi:171

If an unscrupulous creditor takes your cloak, let him have it.
    The divine judge will take his garments and give them to you.

Saying 94. xiii:192–93a

Guard your master's well carefully,   (Mt 25:14–30)
    Next time he may entrust you with his gold.

Saying 106. xiii:204

Someone said to a wild ass: "If you will let me ride you,
    I will let you live in my stable."
The wild ass replied: "Keep your stable!
    I want nothing to do with your riding me." (Job 39:5–8)

Saying 110. xiv:208

Do not send the Bedouin to sea, or the sailor into the desert.
    Everyone's work is unique. (Jer 13:23)

Saying 111. xiv:209

Let the one who treads the wine drink it. (Deut 25:4)
    Let the one who hates the taste of wine guard it.

A cylinder seal depicts four members of the divine assembly
standing before Shamash

TEACHINGS OF ANKHSHESHONQ

≋ *The Teachings of Ankhsheshonq are written in demotic script, a cursive style of Egyptian writing. The damaged papyrus on which they are written consists of twenty-eight columns and is preserved today in the British Museum in London (#10508).*

Ankhsheshonq, like Ahiqar, was charged with treason. He had tried to talk a friend out of assassinating the pharaoh, and did not report his friend. Ankhsheshonq wrote on broken pieces of pottery from jars in which his wine ration was delivered while he was in prison (4:18).

Like the Teachings of Amen-em-ope, the Teachings of Anhkhsheshonq developed in times of social chaos. Anhkhsheshonq teaches his students to fulfill their obligations to their divine patrons, even when their households do not prosper.

Parallels to the Teachings of Ankhsheshonq appear in the books of Proverbs and Sirach.

6:6

Honor your father and mother and you will prosper.   (Exod 20:12)

7:4–5

Do not instruct fools who hate you.   (Prov 23:9; Sir 22:9)
    Do not instruct those who do not learn from you.

7:18

Slaves who are not beaten become disobedient.   (Prov 29:19)

7:23–24

Speaking without thinking causes suffering.   (Sir 22:27)
    Do not say everything you think.

8:4–5

Do not begin tasks without counting the cost.
    Only well-thought-out plans lead to success.

8:7–8

Enjoy your body when you are young.
    Death comes to all.

8:12

Do not marry a woman whose husband is alive
    Unless you want to make an enemy.   (Prov 6:25–26)

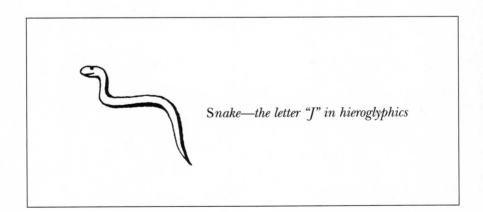

Snake—the letter "J" in hieroglyphics

8:17—9:4

Blessed is a city with a just ruler.
Blessed is a sanctuary with a wise priest.   (1 Sam 2:12—4:22)
Blessed is a field which is fertile.
Blessed is a silo which is full.
Blessed is a treasury which is well managed.
Blessed is a household managed by a wise woman.
Blessed is a man who thinks before he speaks....   (Prov 14:3; James 3:2)
Blessed is an army with a courageous commander.
Blessed is a village with impartial elders.
Blessed is a craftsman with good tools.

9:5–9

Do not ignore a legal claim.
Do not ignore a possible cure.
Do not ignore the pharaoh's command.
Do not ignore the needs of livestock.
     Those who ignore important matters will pay with their lives.
                                             (Prov 13:18;15:32)

9:12–13

Do not live in the same house with your in-laws.
     Do not live in the same neighborhood with your master.

9:16–17

Do not put off your work because "It is summer."   (Prov 6:6–11)
     Winter is coming.
Those who do not gather wood in summer,
     Shiver in the cold of winter.

9:24–25

Do not spend necessities to store a surplus.
     Spend only what you really need.

10:6

Only a fool tells a teacher: "Don't treat me like a fool!"

(Prov 23:9; Sir 22:9)

11:8–10

Do not kill a snake and then leave its tail.
Do not hurl a spear you cannot aim.
      Those who spit in the wind get wet.

11:11–14

Honor is based on one's household.
Honor is based on one's health.
Honor is based on an honest face.
Honor is based on what is done with one's hands.

11:19

Do not shame your son in front of his mother
      Unless you want to shame his father.

12:6

Do not do evil to someone
      Unless you want others to do evil to you.   (Matt 7:12)

12:21–22

Start only what you can finish.
      Do not pick fights you cannot win.

13:2

The wise seek friends,
      Fools seek enemies.

13:12

When you find your wife with a lover,
> It is time to look for a new bride.

14:9

Even a good deed acknowledged by only one in a hundred
> Is still a good deed that lives forever.　　　　(Luke 17:11–19)

14:14

Once bitten by a snake,
> Forever frightened by a rope.

15:6

Deeds are good
> Only when done for the truly needy.　　　　(Prov 14:21; 21:2)

15:9–12

Borrow money to expand a farm,
Borrow money to marry a wife,
Borrow money to celebrate your birthday.
> Do not borrow money to live an easy life.

18:11

The children of fools wander in the streets,　　　　(Deut 21:18–21)
> The children of the wise are at their parents' sides.

18:19–20

Blessed are those who warm their houses to the rafters.
> Cursed are those who build houses only to mortgage them.

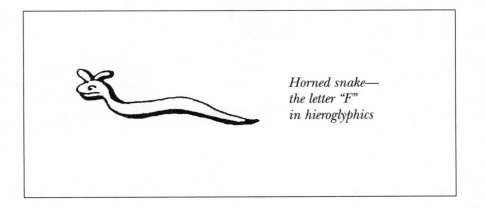

*Horned snake—
the letter "F"
in hieroglyphics*

19:10

Throw deeds into the river and they live forever,
    Keep track of deeds and they die.   (Eccl 11:1)

19:11–12

When two brothers quarrel,
    Do not come between them.
Anyone who comes between two brothers when they quarrel
    Becomes their enemy when they make peace.   (Prov 26:17)

20:4

Begin by planting a sycamore,
    End by planting any tree.

20:13

Snakes that are fed do not strike.

20:22–25

Waste is a vacant house.
Waste is an unmarried woman.

Waste is an ass that carries only bricks.
Waste is a boat that carries only straw.

21:14

Husbands who are ashamed of their wives will have no children.

22:3

Do not start fires you cannot extinguish.

22:19

Give one loaf to your laborer,
    Receive two loaves from the work of his shoulders.

23:6–7

A man who makes love to a married woman
    Will be executed on her threshold.   (Prov 6:25–26)

23:8

Better to dwell in your own house
    Than in someone else's mansion.   (Ps 37:16; Prov 16:8)

24:12

Yesterday's drunkenness does not slake today's thirst.

26:5–8

Those who save lives go to prison.
    Those who take lives go free.
Those who save go hungry.
    Inscrutable divine hands direct the fate of all.

26:14

Divine plans are one thing.
    Human desires are another.   (Prov 16:1, 9)

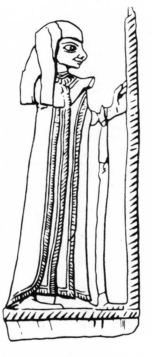

Royal woman at Megiddo

SONG OF SONGS

EGYPTIAN LOVE SONGS

Papyrus Harris 500 was recovered by British archaeologists at the beginning of the twentieth century from the rooms that Ramesses II (1290-1224 BCE) added to the Karnak Temple near the city of Luxor in central Egypt today. The scroll contains nineteen love songs divided into three separate groups. They are written in Egyptian hieroglyphics. The scroll is preserved today in the British Museum in London (P. British Museum 10060).

Love songs teach lovers how to make love and motivate them to make love well. In the world of the Bible, making love is a passionate work like farming, eating, fighting, learning, and offering sacrifice. The language and imagery describing one are often used to describe another. Erotica teaches lovers how to arouse each of the five senses. The songs are full of images of touching, tasting, smelling, hearing, and seeing.

Even though Egypt's love songs may be a thousand years older than those in the Song of Songs, the parallels are unmistakable.

Number 1

Her song:

I am still here with you,
    But your heart is no longer here with me.
Why have you stopped holding me?
    What have I done...?
You no longer seek to caress my thighs....

Would you leave me to get something to eat?
    Are you that much a slave to your belly? (3 Macc 7:11)

321

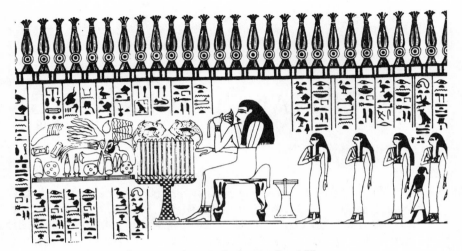

A woman in a painting at Beni Hasan
inhales scent of life-giving lotus

Would you leave me to look for something to wear?
     Would you leave me holding the sheet?

If you are thinking about something to eat,   (Song 7:9; Ezek 23:3)
     Then feast on my breasts, make my milk flow for you.
Better a day in the embrace of a lover...
     Than thousands of days elsewhere....

Number 2

Her song

Mix your body with mine...
     As honey mixes with water,   (Dan 2:43)
     As mandrake mixes with gum,
     As dough mixes with yeast....
Come to your lover,
     Like a horse charging onto the field of battle....
     Like a soldier....

Number 3

His song:

My lover is a marsh,
    My lover is lush with growth....
Her mouth is a lotus bud,
    Her breasts are mandrake blossoms.   (Song 7:13)
Her arms are vines,
    Her eyes are shaded like berries.
Her head is a trap built from branches...and I am the goose.
    Her hair is the bait in the trap...to ensnare me.   (Song 7:5)

Number 4

Her song:

My cup is still not full from making love with you.....
    My little jackal, you intoxicate me.   (Song 2:5)
I will not stop drinking your love,   (Song 4:10; 5:1; 8:2b)
    Even if they beat me with sticks into the marsh,
Even if they beat me north into Syria,
    Even if they flog me with palm branches south into Nubia,
Even if they scourge me with switches into the hills,
    Even if they force me with clubs into the plains,
I will not take their advice,
    I will not abandon the one I desire.   (Judg 15:1–8)

Fishing, as depicted in a painting at Beni Hasan

Number 5

His song:

I am sailing north with the current,
    Pulling the oar to the captain's command.
My bundle lies on my shoulder,
    I am headed for a holiday at Memphis.
I will pray to Ptah, the divine patron of truth,
    That a lover will sleep with me tonight.
The Nile makes me drunk with love.
    I see Ptah among the reeds,
    I see Sekhmet on the lotus leaves,
    I see Yadit sired in the lotus buds,
    I see Nefertem conceived in the lotus blossoms....   (Song 2:10–13)
The land reflects the joy of Hathor, daughter of the sun.
    Memphis is a jar of sweet mandrake wine,
    A gift for fair-faced Ptah.   (Gen 30:14–20; Song 7:13)

Number 6

His song:

I will lie down inside my house,
    I will pretend to be sick.
Then my neighbors will come in to see,
    And my lover will come with them.
She will put physicians to shame,
    She knows how to cure my illness.   (2 Sam 13:4–6; Song 2:5; 5:8)

Number 7

His song:

The woman, whom I love, is the lady of a great house.
    You enter her house in the center.
The doors are wide open, the bolt is unfastened,   (Song 5:2–6)
    Because she is angry with her lover....

Bird hunting, as depicted in a painting at Beni Hasan

If she hired me to guard her door,
    At least when I made her angry,
I would get to hear her voice,
    Even as I tremble like a child.

Number 8

Her song:

I am sailing north
    Sailing on the canal of Pharaoh.
I turn into the canal of Pre,
    I will pitch my tent overlooking the canal.

I have raced without rest,
    I have not stopped since I first thought of the Canal of Pre.
I can already see my lover...
    He is heading for the chamber of love....
I will stand with you at the entrance to the Canal of Ity,
    You will lead me to Heliopolis.
As we walk...into the trees around the chamber of love...
    I gather branches, and weave them into a fan.
We will see...,
    We will see if it fans me on my way to the garden of love.
My breasts are smothered with fruit,   (Song 7:8)
    My hair glistens with balm.   (Esth 2:12; Ruth 3:3)
When I am with you...
    I am a noble woman filled with pleasure,
    I am the queen of Egypt.

Isaiah,
Jeremiah,
Ezekiel,
Daniel,
Hosea,
Amos

STORIES OF ISHTAR AND TAMMUZ

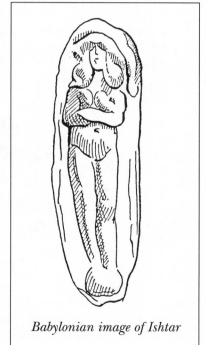

Austen Henry Layard (1817-1894) excavated Nimrud in 1845 for the British Museum, locating both the palace of Sennacherib (704-681 BCE) and the library of Ashurbanipal (667-626 BCE), where he recovered the Stories of Ishtar and Tammuz in Akkadian. Older versions of these stories in Sumerian were recovered at Nippur by J. P. Peters, J. H. Haynes and H. V. Hilprecht, who directed the excavations for the University of Pennsylvania (1889-1900). These were the first major excavations in Mesopotamia under American auspices. Four hundred and ten lines on thirteen tablets are preserved today at the Museum of the Ancient Orient in Istanbul, Turkey, and in the University of Pennsylvania Museum in Philadelphia.

Tammuz [Sumerian: Dumuzi] and Ishtar [Sumerian: Inanna] are lovers separated by death, but reunited by love. Tammuz descends into the land of the dead and Ishtar faithfully pursues and rescues him. The stories tell not only of two lovers, but also of the death of the earth during the long dry

Babylonian image of Ishtar

season and its rebirth at the beginning of the wet season during the celebration of the taklimtu *New Year in Assyria. Like the last drops of moisture that the parched soil sucked deep into the earth, Tammuz is drawn by stages into the land of the dead. Like the rain that moistens the soil at the end of the dry season so that farmers can plow and plant, the tears of Ishtar in the land of the dead bring Tammuz back to life. She raises him from the dead like the first leaves of the crops that sprout through the soil under a farmer's care at the beginning of the growing season.*

The book of Judges notes that "...for four days every year the daughters of Israel would go out to lament the daughter of Jephthah..." (Judg 11:39–40), which may describe the way the taklimtu *New Year was celebrated in Israel. The books of Kings caricature the name of Jezebel, the queen of Israel (2 Kgs 9:37). Her parents would have named her: "Where is my lord?" or "Where is Tammuz [Hebrew: 'izebul]?" no doubt because she was one of the first newborns at the end of the dry season and her birth offered a promise of the renewal of life in the land. In the Bible, however, Jezebel is referred to as "shameless" [Hebrew: izebul] or as "excrement" [Hebrew: zebel]. The book of Ezekiel (Ezek 8:1—11:25) indicts women for sitting at the north gate of the Temple and "...weeping for Tammuz" (Ezek 8:14). The book of Jeremiah contains a similar indictment of Jerusalem for celebrating Ishtar as "...the queen of heaven" (Jer 7:18).*

LOVE SONGS

PAPS 107.6:23–45 (UM 29-16-37; PRAK II B 46 obv. + PRAK II C 94 = ll. 26–38)

▰ *Ishtar and Tammuz, here as Inanna and Dumuzi, compare their lovemaking to stringing boundary stones into a necklace for Inanna.*

Inanna's song:

Let my lover bring boundary stones,
    Let him string boundary stones;
    Let Dumuzi plow between the boundary stones,

Let the small boundary stones adorn my neck,   (Song 4:9)
    Let the large boundary stones decorate my breasts.

Dumuzi's song:

Inanna is my devoted lover,
    For her I will plow.
Surely for her I will plow the boundary stones,
    For her Dumuzi will plow the boundary stones....

Inanna's song:

Dumuzi was created for me,
    Amaushumgalanna was made for me,
    With a beard as dark and rich as lapis lazuli.
Dumuzi was created for me by Anu, my godfather,
    Dumuzi was made for me with a beard as dark and rich
        as lapis lazuli
With a beard as dark and rich as lapis lazuli
    With a beard as dark and rich as lapis lazuli....

In the Sumerian stories, Ishtar tries to get Ereshkigal to release Tammuz from the underworld and fails. In the Akkadian stories, however, the mourning of Ishtar brings both Tammuz and the farmland back to life.

*Ashnan (right), divine patron of grain at Sumer, gives Tammuz,
the divine gardener, seedlings to plant*

ISHTAR'S DESCENT TO THE UNDERWORLD

Obverse Lines 1–20

Ishtar resolved to travel to the Land of No Return,   (Job 7:9–10)
    To the dark abode of Ereshkigal,
    To the house that none depart,
To the road to the Land of No Return,
    To the house where no light may enter,   (Job 17:12–13; 18:18)
Where dust and clay are their meal,
    Where they dwell in darkness,
Where, like birds, they exchange their clothes for feathers,
    Where dust covers every door and bolt.
When Ishtar reached the gate of the Land of No Return,
    She challenged the gatekeeper, saying:
"Open your gate so I may enter!
    If you fail to do this, I will smash the door,
I will shatter the bolt,
    I will uproot the doorpost, push aside the doors.   (Judg 16:3)
I will cause the dead to rise and consume the living,
    The dead will outnumber the living!"

≋▌ *The gatekeeper announces Ishtar's arrival to Ereshkigal, who tells*
    him to allow Ishtar to pass.

Lines 30–44

Why should Ishtar visit me? . . .

My bread is clay,
    My beer is water thick with silt,
I weep for separated lovers,
    I mourn miscarriages.

Unlock the gate for Ishtar,
    Extend to her the age-old custom of hospitality.

The gatekeeper opens the gate and bids her enter:

"Come, my lady, so that the underworld may give you proper welcome.
    Come, my lady, that rejoicing and celebration may begin."

He opens the first gate, and removes Ishtar's crown.

Ishtar asks, "Why have you removed my crown?"   (Isa 3:18–23)
    The gatekeeper replies: "...it is the law of Ereshkigal."

≋ *At each of the seven gates, the gatekeeper removes an item of Ishtar's clothing: earrings, necklaces, ornate breast plate, a belt containing birthstones that is suspended from her hips, bracelets from her arms and legs. Finally, Ishtar is as naked as the dead. When she passes through the last gate, she confronts Ereshkigal.*

Lines 64–79

The presence of Ishtar makes Ereshkigal furious.
    Ishtar rushes at her in a blind rage.
Ereshkigal...inflicts Ishtar with sixty diseases:
        Diseases of the eyes,
        Diseases of the arms,
        Diseases of the feet,
        Diseases of the heart,
        Diseases of the head,
        Diseases over her whole body!
        (Job 18:13)

While Ishtar is in the underworld,
    Bulls no longer mount their cows,
Asses no longer copulate with their jennies,
    Men and women sleep alone....

≋ *To bring the earth back to life, Ea commissions Asushunamir, who is as handsome as moonlight, to cast a spell on Ereshkigal to release Ishtar. When Ereshkigal realizes she has been tricked, she curses Asushunamir.*

Ishtar is escorted back through the gates of the underworld, her clothes are all returned, and Ereshkigal orders the release of Tammuz.

Lines 126–30

Release Tammuz, her lover,
        Wash him and anoint him with oil,   (Ruth 3:3; Mk 16:1)
        Clothe him in a purple garment,
        Allow him to play a flute of lapis lazuli,
        Let him make love...

⧉ *Ishtar returns to the earth immediately, but Tammuz is permit-*
ted to return only when it rains at the end of the dry season,
and when mourners weep at the graves of the dead.

Lines 136–38

Ishtar sings:

"When Tammuz rises from the dead,
     Then the lapis flute will play,
     Then the carnelian ring will appear.
When men and women weep for the dead,   (Ezek 8:14)
     Then the dead will return,
     Then the dead will smell incense once again...."

Ishtar as a nursing mother

VISIONS OF NEFERTI

◄ *The Visions of Neferti begin with Pharaoh Snefru (2680-2565 BCE) summoning Neferti to entertain him. Neferti announces the downfall of the Old Kingdom (2575-2134 BCE) and the establishment of the Twelfth Dynasty (1991-1783 BCE) by Amenemhet I (1991-1962 BCE), during whose reign the Visions of Neferti were composed. They extol the accomplishments of Amenemhet, and try to persuade him to extend his control eastward to prevent further invasions of Egypt from Syria-Palestine.*

One complete copy of the Visions of Neferti on the Papyrus Petersberg 1116B is preserved in the Hermitage Museum in St Petersberg, Russia. The copy was made during the Eighteenth Dynasty (1550-1307 BCE). Other fragments have also been recovered.

Like the Visions of Neferti, the books of Samuel-Kings (1 Kgs 13) and the book of Daniel (Dan 2—6) use the motif of entertaining a monarch with the prediction of his downfall.

10–14

"Your majesty, Neferti, a priest of Bastet, requests an audience. He is a self-made man, an accomplished scribe and very wealthy...."

Pharaoh Snefru—bless him with life, prosperity and health—ordered: "... Bring him to me...." (Dan 5:11–12)

Neferti prostrated before Pharaoh—bless him with life, prosperity and health—....

Pharaoh Snefru—bless him with life, prosperity and health—ordered:
"Speak, Neferti, my good man.
Entertain me with well chosen words and artful phrases."

15–19

Neferti asked: "Majesty,—bless him with life, prosperity and health—
    Do you wish to hear what-has-happened or what-is-to-come?"

Pharaoh Snefru—bless him with life, prosperity and health—answered:
    "Speak to me of what is to come. Today has passed."

Then Pharaoh motioned to a scribe to open his case, take out a scroll
and ink, and write down everything Neferti said . . . .

20–22

"Stir yourself, my heart" Neferti prayed.
    "Cry for this land where you were born . . . .
Do not be afraid to state the facts,
    Rise to the task before you."

22–24

"Officials no longer administer the land,
    What should be done is left undone.
Only Re can recreate cosmos   (Dan 9:16–19)
    From the chaos of Egypt today.
No order remains,
    No profit can be made.
No one cares about this land,   (Ezek 9:4)
    No one sheds a tear for Egypt,
No one cries out: 'What is happening to Egypt?'"

25–29

"The sun is shrouded,
    The sun never shines,
The people cannot see,
    There is no life,
The sun is covered in clouds,   (Ezek 30:3)
    Everyone is blind without it.
I can tell you what I see before me,
    I cannot tell what has not yet been decreed.

A painting at Beni Hasan depicts hunters trapping birds

The canals are dry,   (Isa 19:5–7; Ezek 30:12; 31:15)
    They can be crossed on foot.
Boatmen search for enough water to sail,
    The canals have turned into dry land....
The south wind blows against the north wind,
    There is now no wind at all."

29–38

"Strange birds from Syria-Palestine nest in the Delta marshes,
    They camp near the villages of Egypt.
The people of Egypt are helpless against them...,
    The goods of Egypt vanish.
Once thriving ponds filled with fish and fowl are dry.
    The goods of Egypt vanish.
Egypt is crushed by the weight of these starving herders,
    Enemies overrun Egypt from east...   (Gen 12:10–20; 47:1–11)
Desert herds drink from the Nile,
    Desert herders settle on the banks of the Nile without fear.
Fortresses are no longer secure,
    No guard hears or sees the enemy of the night...
    I alone stand watch through the night.   (Ezek 3:17)
Land is bought and sold,
    But no one knows by whom.
Legal transactions take place in secret,
    As the saying goes: 'The mute leads the blind and the deaf.'"

38–54

"I see a land of chaos.
    What is happening should never have happened.

A painting at Beni Hasan depicts Egyptians fighting warriors
from Syria-Palestine

Ordinary people are at war with one another...   (Jer 19:2)
      They make copper arrows like soldiers,
      They kill for bread.

"People laugh at the misfortune of others.
      No one weeps for the dying,
      No one mourns and fasts.   (Jer 16:6)

"People only look after their own welfare.   (Judg 21:25; Dan 11:14)
      No one mourns for another,
      No one cares.
People turn their backs on one another,   (Prov 6:16–17; Isa 1:21)
      They do not even notice one killing another.
      Sons kill their fathers,   (Prov 30:11)
      Brothers kill their brothers,
      and fathers kill their fathers.
Everyone says: 'I want.'
      The goods of Egypt vanish.
Egypt is full of corruption.
      Laws are ignored....
The property of Egyptians is seized,
      The property of Egyptians is given to strangers.
I see landowners in need,
      I see strangers prosper.
The once well-fed are now starving...,   (Prov 30:22; Eccl 10:5–6)

"Debts are paid only under threat,
      Witnesses are bribed.

Those who complain are beaten
    Those who are accused cry out: 'Kill them!'...   (Hos 5:10)

"Egypt's land is scarce,
    Its rulers are many.   (Eccl 5:8)
Farmers are poor,
    Tax collectors are rich.
Harvests are small,
    Taxes are high....
The sun is dark,
    No one knows the time,
    And no one can see his shadow.
    No one's face shines,
    No one's eyes sparkle like water.
The light of the sun is like the light of the moon,
    Night never ends...."

54–57

"I see a land of chaos.
The powerless are powerful.
    Masters bow to their slaves.
The living sleep with the dead...
    The rich beg,
    Beggars are rich,   (Eccl 10:7)
    Slaves are free....

Heliopolis has vanished,
    The birthplace of the divine assembly is no more."

58–62

"But a new pharaoh will come from the south,   (Isa 11:1; Jer 23:5)
    Amenemhet the Triumphant will be his name.
A son of southern Egypt will wear the white crown,
    A son of Nubia will wear the red crown.   (1 Kgs 13:2; Mic 5:2)
He will unite the two lands of Egypt,   (Dan 12:1)
    He will serve the divine patrons of both south and north.
At his coronation, he will have a firm grip on the oar,
    At the Heb-Sed festival he will put a steady hand on the tiller.

Happy are those who will live in his time,   (Isa 9:2–3; Zech 9:9)
    Their names will last forever.
He will execute conspirators,
    He will silence traitors.
He will destroy Syria-Palestine,   (Zech 9:10)
    He will set Libya on fire.
He will exile revolutionaries,
    He will imprison spies.
The winged serpent will guard his brow,
    The *uraeus* serpent will protect him from rebels.
He will rebuild the fortresses along the border,
    He will keep herders away.
They will beg for water,
    They will plead for their herds to drink.
Order will be restored to its rightful place,
    Chaos will be forced to flee.
Happy are those who serve this pharaoh.

"The wise will pour out an offering for me
    When they see that what I have said has happened..."

A painting at Beni Hasan
depicts an Egyptian
armed with a slingshot

MARI LETTERS

Mari [Arabic: Tell Hariri] was a state on the Euphrates in northern Syria that competed with Babylon for control of Mesopotamia until Hammurabi (1792-1750 BCE) conquered it in 1757 BCE. Artifacts recovered by a Bedouin digging a grave in 1933 launched an ongoing French expedition directed first by André Parrot, and then Jean Margueron. Some twenty-five thousand clay tablets, written in cuneiform, were recovered from the archives of Zimri-Lim, the last ruler of Mari. They are preserved today at the Louvre Museum in Paris and the Damascus Museum in Syria. Most of the tablets are about eight inches wide and ten inches high. Some are no larger than a postage stamp. Others are one to two feet high and one foot wide. There are economic records, diplomatic covenants, and some thirty letters that mention prophets.

At least three classes of male and female prophets advised Zimri-Lim. **Apilum** prophets spoke for the divine assembly (A.2925/A.2731). **Assinu** prophets were temple personnel (ARM 10.7). **Muhhu** prophets were ecstatics. The personal names of the prophets never appear in the letters, which could indicate that they were considered members of a sacred social class whose names could not be spoken (ARM 3.40). The more general term, nabî, appears only once (A.2209), but it is a cognate of nabî'—the Hebrew term for prophet.

Until the Mari archives were recovered, the only parallels to the prophets of ancient Israel were in the Story of Wen-Amun from Egypt. The letters contain messenger formulas like "arise, go...and say to..." similar to those found in the Bible. Although prophets in both Mari and Israel confront their monarchs in times of crisis, there are differences between them. Mari prophets never seem to speak to the people of Mari as a whole. They also use divination to interpret omens more regularly than the prophets of Israel.

A. 2731: 1–44

To: Zimri-Lim, king of Mari

From: Nur-Suen, official of Mari stationed at Kallassu

Repeatedly I have written to the king about the gift of livestock that he promised to the sanctuary of Addu, his divine patron. Addu, the divine patron of Kallassu, is still waiting for this livestock which you promised him....

An *apilu* prophet of Addu, divine patron of Kallassu, told me: "I am Addu, your divine patron. I am the divine patron of Kallassu...who helped you regain your father's throne and your father's house (Hos 11:1–9). What I gave, I can also take away! (1 Sam 12:14–15) If Zimri-Lim fulfills my request, I will give him greater power, more holdings, and command of lands and cities from the east to the west." (Gen 28:13–14; 1 Chr 12:15)

This is what was reported to me by the *apilu* prophet and it has been confirmed by additional oracles....When I served in Mari, I reported the words of the *apilu* prophets to you. There is no reason for me not to continue to send my lord, Zimri-Lim, such reports. If a disaster occurs at a future date, I would not want my lord to charge that I had not kept him informed about the words of the *apilu* prophets.

A. 2233

To: Zimri-Lim, ruler of Mari
From: Shibtu, queen of Mari

Qishti-Diritum, the *apilu* prophet of Diritum, came to the palace gate at Mari and spoke as following:

"No enemy will assail the throne of Mari. Zimri-Lim has sole title to the upper country. The ruler of Elam will be defeated!" (1 Sam 2:4; Ps 37:14–15)....

On another matter....

"...Ea said:...'Since the divine assembly is about to take a solemn oath, let us mix dirt from the threshold of the gate of Mari in water and drink it.' Then the divine assembly swore: 'We will not harm the walls of Mari, nor Dagan, its divine patron.'" (Num 5:17)

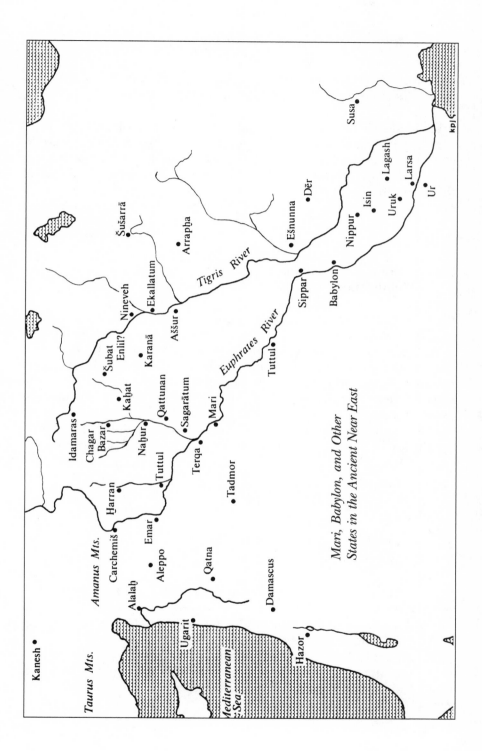

Mari, Babylon, and Other
States in the Ancient Near East

ARM 13.23:1–15

To: Zimri-Lim, ruler of Mari
From: Mukannisum, official of Mari stationed at Tuttul

After I offered the sacrifice to Dagan for the king's health, an *apilu* prophet of Dagan in Tuttul stood up and told me: "Babylon, what do you think you are doing? I will bring you down like a bird with a net (Hab 1:15–16). . . . I will give you, your seven covenant partners, and all their land to Zimri-Lim."

A.100

To: Zimri-Lim, king of Mari
From: Shibtu, queen of Mari

My lord, Zimri-Lim, the palace is in good order.

On the third day of the festival, Shelibum fell into ecstasy (1 Sam 10:6; 2 Kgs 3:15) in the sanctuary of Annunitum, your divine patron. Annunitum said: "You, Zimri-Lim, will be tested by a revolt. Take precautions. Surround yourself only with officials you trust. Let only officials who are faithful guard you. Do not go out of the palace without an escort. I will hand these rebels over to you."

To confirm the words of Shelibum, an *assinu* prophet, I am sending the king a lock of his hair and a piece of the hem from his tunic. (1 Sam 24:4–5)

A.2209

To: Zimri-Lim, king of Mari
From: Tebi-gerishu, an official of Mari

On the day after I arrived at Ashmad, I assembled the *nabî* prophets of the Hanu to divine the safety of my lord, Zimri-Lim. I asked them: "If my lord, Zimri-Lim, leaves the city for seven days to bathe at the Spring of Annitum, will he return in safety?" (2 Kgs 22:6)

They said: "When my lord, Zimri-Lim, makes the journey to worship Annunitum, he must be very careful. The army should be mobilized and a reinforced guard be placed over the city. My lord, Zimri-Lim, must protect himself."

ARM 3.40:1–23

To: Zimri-Lim, ruler of Mari
From: Kibri-Dagan, official of Mari stationed at Terqa

My lord, Zimri-Lim, you continue to enjoy the favor of your divine patrons, Dagan and Ikrub-El. The province of Terqa is peaceful.

The same day that I dispatched this report to the king, a *muhhu* prophet of Dagan, your divine patron, came and told me: "Dagan has sent me to you. Write to Zimri-Lim and remind the king to offer a funeral sacrifice for Yahdun-Lim, your father."

Therefore, I have written my lord, Zimri-Lim, this message so that he may take appropriate action.

A.994

To: Zimri-Lim, ruler of Mari
From: The Lady Adad-duri in Mari

My lord, Zimri-Lim, never since the time of your father's house have I had such a dream (Ezek 8). In my dream I entered the temple of Belet-ekallim, but the Lady of the House was not there (Ezek 10:18). Nor were the flanking statues which previously had stood before her. I searched, but, in my dream during the night watch, I could only weep.

I also had another dream. Dada, the priest of Ishtar Bishrian, stood in the gate of Belet-ekallim while a voice continually cried out, "Turn back, O Dagan. Turn back, O Dagan."

Dagan,
Divine Patron of Mari

On another matter...

   ...a *muhhutu* prophet rose in the temple of Annunitum and said, "Zimri-Lim, do not go on campaign. Stay in Mari and I will send you word when it safe to leave."

   Let my lord, Zimri-Lim, be cautious. I have sealed this letter with my hem and a lock of my hair.

Coronation of Zimri-Lim in his palace at Mari

STORY OF WEN-AMUN

Archaeologists recovered the Story of Wen-Amun at el-Hibeh, Egypt around 1899. It was written on papyrus in hieroglyphics as the 20th Dynasty (1196–1070 BCE) was collapsing. Today it is preserved in the Moscow Museum in Russia.

Pharaohs and priests regularly sent messengers to the mountains of Lebanon to harvest timber for architectural beams, for carving, and for constructing the hulls and masts of ships. The Story of Wen-Amun describes the experiences of one such messenger. Unlike Sinuhe, however, who travels in Syria-Palestine when Egypt is powerful, Wen-Amun travels at a time when Egypt is embroiled in a civil war. Herihor, priest of Thebes in southern Egypt, and Smendes, ruler of Tanis in northern Egypt, are both trying to overthrow Pharaoh Ramesses XI (1100–1070 BCE). The rulers of the Sea Peoples in Syria-Palestine and Cyprus take advantage of Egypt's weakness to drive hard bargains by bullying Wen-Amun. Wen-Amun is consumed with detail, and seems almost unaware of how much times have changed. He naively employs outdated techniques in his negotiations, techniques that are absolutely useless with rulers like Beder, Tjerker Baal, and Hatiba.

The Story of Wen-Amun describes the international power vacuum in the ancient Near East during which Israel emerged. It also describes some interesting manners and customs that appear in the Bible. The use of threats by Wen-Amun recalls those made by Rabshakeh, the messenger of Sennacherib, Great King of Assyria, to the officials of Hezekiah (2 Kgs 18:13–37). Wen-Amun carries a statue of Amun, his divine patron, along with him and uses it just as Rachel uses the statues of the divine patrons [Hebrew: teraphim] of her household (Gen 31:19–35). Ecstatic prophets appear in Byblos to advise their monarchs just as they do in Israel. The cedars of Lebanon are sacred property, just like the plunder from cities like Jericho (Josh 6:17–21), and their misappropriation demands

347

*the death penalty (Josh 7:10-25). Tjerker Baal harvests the cedars of
Lebanon for Wen-Amun, just as Hiram of Tyre does for Solomon
(1 Kgs 5:10-11). Tanetne heals Wen-Amun by singing, just as David
heals Saul by playing the lyre (1 Sam 16:14-23).*

i:1–50

I, Wen-Amun, priest at the gate of the temple of Amun, was dispatched
to buy timber for the sacred boat of Amun-Re, ruler of the divine assembly. When I docked at Tanis, I presented my letters of introduction from
Amun-Re to Smendes and his wife, Tanet-Amun. They ordered them
read aloud and agreed to do as Amun-Re had commanded. I remained
for the rest of that month in Tanis and then sailed in a ship under the
command of Mengebet.

When my ship docked at Dor, Beder, the ruler of the Tjerker, wel-
comed me with fifty loaves of bread, a jar of wine and a side of ox.

While we lay in port, one of the ship's crew stole the sixteen ounces
of gold and the ninety-eight ounces of silver bullion and vessels that I
was supposed to use to pay for the timber.

I went straight to Beder and reported: "I was robbed while at anchor in your harbor. As ruler of Dor it is your responsibility to investi-
gate the crime and recover this gold and silver."

*Amun wearing his crown
of twin feathers*

*Egyptian
harp player*

Beder replied: "Be careful whom you charge with a crime this serious. Do not bring your complaints to me. If the thief who boarded your ship and stole your gold and silver was my subject, I would reimburse you from my own treasury until the thief was apprehended. Since the thief was from your own ship's company, it is not my responsibility. Nevertheless, give me a few days and I will see if I can find him for you."

So I waited nine days in the harbor. Finally, I went back to Beder. "Since you cannot find my gold and silver, at least let my ship sail...."

He refused. "If you expect me to find your gold and silver, you must be patient and stay here...."

...Nonetheless, at dawn I sailed for Byblos. There was a Tjerker freighter from Dor in the harbor, and I confiscated one hundred and one ounces of silver bullion from the ship's master and told him I would keep it until Beder recovered my gold and silver or apprehended the thief who stole it. In the tent that I had pitched on the harbor shore, I celebrated my plan for replacing the gold and silver that I had lost and hid my treasure in a statue of Amun, protector of travelers (Gen 31:19) ....

As a reprisal for my actions, Tjerker Baal of Byblos ordered me out of his harbor. I responded: "How shall I go? Are you going to pay for a ship to take me back to Egypt?" I spent twenty-nine days camped at the harbor of Byblos and every day the harbor master sent the same message: "Get out of my harbor!"

One day, when Tjerker Baal was offering a sacrifice, a prophet went into a trance and became ecstatic (2 Kgs 3:15). The prophet announced: "Summon this Egyptian messenger and his statue of Amun, who dispatched him to Syria-Palestine." This prophecy occurred on the same night that I had booked passage on a freighter headed for Egypt. I had already loaded my possessions and was only waiting for it to get dark, so that I could smuggle my statue of Amun, protector of travelers, on board.

At that moment, the harbor master came to me and said: "Tjerker Baal orders you to stay until tomorrow."

I then replied: "Aren't you the same man who for the last twenty-nine days has ordered me to get out of your harbor? You are ordering me to stay only because you want me to miss my ship, which is sailing tonight; then you will come back in the morning and order me to get out."

The harbor master reported my objection to Tjerker Baal, who then ordered the captain of the freighter on which I had passage to remain at anchor until the next day.

The following morning Tjerker Baal sent for me. I left the statue in my tent at the harbor. As I entered, he was sitting in his upper room with his back to a window that overlooked the lapping waves of the Mediterranean Sea of Syria.

I greeted him with a blessing from Amun and he asked me: "When did you leave the temple of Amun in Egypt?"

I replied that I had been away from home five months.

Then he said: "May I see your letters of introduction from Amun-Re and his high priest?" I told him that I had given them to Smendes and his wife, Tanet-Amun.

Tjerker Baal became furious. "You have no papers? Where is the ship Smendes gave you to transport the timber, and where is its Syrian crew? Didn't Smendes conspire with the ship's captain to murder you and have your body thrown into the sea, so that there would be no trace of you or your statue of Amun?"

I objected: "Smendes outfitted me with an Egyptian, not a Syrian, ship and crew."

Tjerker Baal was not convinced. "Why would Smendes send an Egyptian ship to Syria, when right now there are twenty Syrian ships in my harbor and there are another fifty Syrian ships docked in the harbor at Sidon ruled by Werekter and under contract to him?"

ii: 2–83

When I kept silent he went on: "What are you really doing here?"

I answered: "I am here to buy timber for the great and noble ship of Amun-Re, ruler of the divine assembly. Therefore you should do what your father and grandfather before you have done."

Tjerker Baal replied: "Yes, my father and grandfather did supply timber for Amun-Re. All you need do is pay me and I will also supply it (1 Kgs 5:10–11). My predecessors did not carry out this commission until the pharaoh sent six freighters loaded with gifts from Egypt and these items had been placed in their storehouses. Tell me now, what have you brought me?"

At that point he sent for a scroll from the time of his father and grandfather and ordered it read aloud. It was a receipt for various items valued at 950,000 ounces of silver (Josh 7:20–25). Then he said: "If pharaoh were my lord and if I were his faithful client, he would not have to pay me a monarch's ransom in silver and gold, as he paid my father to carry out the commission of Amun. In any case, I am not your client, nor am I the client of the one who sent you. I need only say the word and the heavens over the mountains of Lebanon will open and wash their logs to the shore of the sea. But who will lash these logs in place and sail these freighters home to Egypt? Amun is the creator of every land that hears the thunder of Seth Baal. Egypt, your land, was his first born. Only a fool would leave the land that

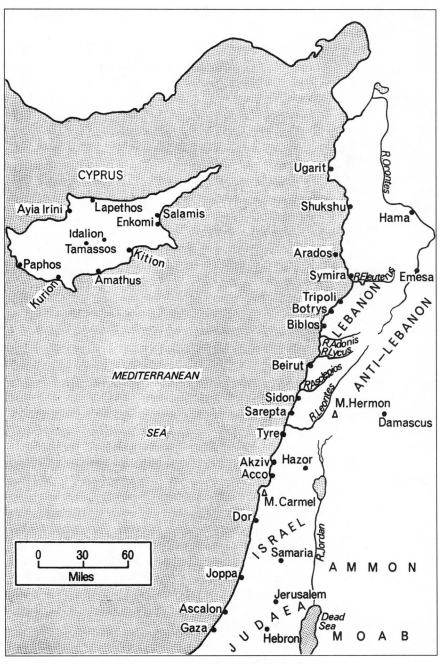

CYPRUS

Ayia Irini
Lapethos
Enkomi
Salamis
Idalion
Tamassos
Kition
Paphos
Amathus
Kurion

Ugarit
Shukshu
Hama
Arados
Symira
R.Eleuterus
Emesa
Tripoli
Botrys
Biblos
R.Adonis
R.Lycus
Beirut
R.Asclepios
MEDITERRANEAN
R.Leontes
Sidon
Sarepta
M.Hermon
Tyre
Damascus
SEA
Akziv
Hazor
Acco
M.Carmel
Dor
ISRAEL
R.Jordan
Samaria
AMMON
Joppa
Jerusalem
Ascalon
JUDAEA
Dead
Sea
Gaza
Hebron
MOAB

LEBANON
ANTI-LEBANON
R.Orontes

0   30   60
Miles

Cyprus and the Coast of Syria-Palestine
1000 BCE

invented ships and discovered how to navigate to come all the way here to me."

I replied: "You are wrong. My mission is not foolish. All of the ships on the Nile belong to Amun. The Mediterranean Sea and the mountains of Lebanon do not belong to Syria, but to Amun. He planted forests on the mountains of Lebanon as a source of timber to build the Amun-User-He, the most sacred ship on the face of the earth. It was Amun-Re, ruler of the divine assembly, who ordered the high priest, Herihor, to dispatch me on this mission with the statue of Amun. Now you have detained me and the statue of my divine patron for twenty-nine days in the harbor of Byblos. Surely, you knew Amun was there. Amun-Re is today what Amun-Re has always been. How dare you bargain with the ruler of the divine assembly over the cedars of Lebanon? As for your statement that previous pharaohs had sent gold and silver, that was because they lacked the ability to send life and health. It was in place of life and health that they sent these paltry gifts to your predecessors. Amun-Re is the giver of life and health, and it is he who was the lord of your predecessors (Acts 5:12–16). They made offerings to Amun throughout their reigns. You also are a client of Amun. If you agree to carry out the commands of Amun, then you and your entire land will be blessed with life and prosperity. If you refuse and withhold the timber that belongs to Amun-Re, ruler of the divine assembly, he will attack you and your land like a lion protecting its lair. Send for a scribe so that I may send a letter to Smendes and his wife, Tanet-Amun, whom Amun-Re appointed to care for northern Egypt. They will provide the ships and crews you need. I will tell the scribe: 'Write: When I return to southern Egypt, I will repay you for everything....'" A messenger took my letter to Egypt along with seven gifts: a keel, a bow-post, a stern-post, and four hewn timbers.

The messenger returned from Egypt to Syria in the first month of winter. With him, Smendes and his wife, Tanet-Amun, sent Tjerker Baal four priceless vases and one *kakmen*-vase, five silver vases, ten linen garments, ten bolts of linen fabric, five hundred linen mats, five hundred ox-hides, five hundred ropes, twenty sacks of lentils, and thirty baskets of fish. In addition, Tanet-Amun sent me personally: five linen garments, five bolts of linen fabric, a sack of lentils, and five baskets of fish.

Tjerker Baal was delighted and immediately dispatched three hundred loggers with three hundred oxen and their drivers to cut the timbers. The trees were felled and lay on the ground through the winter. During the third month of summer the logs were dragged to the seashore.

Tjerker Baal came out to inspect them and then said to me: "Come!"

When I stepped forward, the shadow of the Tjerker Baal's umbrella fell upon me and Pen-Amun the cupbearer shoved me aside, saying: "You are not worthy to bask in the shadow of Pharaoh's beloved son." Tjerker Baal became angry and ordered the cupbearer to leave me alone.

I was then officially presented to Tjerker Baal who announced: "I have carried out the commission which my father and grandfather previously carried out. You, however, have not done for me what your fathers previously did for them. The final consignment of timber has now arrived and has been stacked. Obey my command. Load it and leave. Face bad weather at sea before facing my bad temper another day in port. You are lucky that I have not done to you what I did to the messengers of Khaemwese whom I detained seventeen years here in Syria until they died." At that point he directed the cupbearer: "Take him to see their graves."

I pleaded: "Do not make me go see them. Khaemwese's messengers were merely humans, as was their patron. You do not have before you only a man, though you say: 'Go see your fellow humans.' You should now rejoice and erect a stele with the inscription: 'Amun-Re, ruler of the divine assembly, sent Amun, protector of travelers, his divine messenger, and Wen-Amun, his human messenger, to obtain timber for the great and noble ship of Amun-Re, ruler of the divine assembly. I felled the trees and loaded them on board my own ships worked by my own crews. I allowed them to return to Egypt so that they could request for me fifty more years of life from Amun.' Therefore, when another messenger comes from Egypt, who is skilled in writing and reads your name on the stele, you will drink from the fountain of life like the divine assembly who dwell in the west."

Tjerker Baal said: "That was quite a speech!"

I replied: "I can assure you that when I return to the temple of Amun, the high priest, upon seeing your accomplishments, will grant you merit for them."

I left Tjerker Baal of Byblos and went down to the seashore to supervise the loading of the logs. At just that moment, eleven ships belonging to the Tjerker of Dor dropped anchor. The commander of the fleet ordered his sailors: "Arrest him! Do not let his ship sail for Egypt." I sat down right there and wept.

The scribe of Tjerker Baal came to me and said: "What is it now?"

I told him: "Birds have migrated to Egypt twice since I arrived. Watch them as they fly toward the land of cool waters. These men have come to arrest me? How long must I remain here?"

He went and reported everything to Tjerker Baal and he wept also at this unfortunate turn of events. To comfort me he sent his scribe to me with two jars of wine and a sheep. He also sent Tanetne, an Egyptian singer, with this order: "Sing for him! Soothe his troubled spirit."

(1 Sam 16:14–23) He then sent word to me: "Eat, drink, and do not let your spirit be troubled. I will make a decision on this tomorrow."

The next morning, Tjerker Baal of Byblos convened an assembly to hear my case. He said to the Tjerker of Dor: "Why are you here?"

The Tjerker of Dor answered: "We have come in pursuit of the ships of our cursed enemy whom you are about to let escape to Egypt."

Tjerker Baal instructed the Tjerker of Dor: "I cannot arrest a messenger of Amun in my own country. I will send him away and you may then pursue and arrest him."

I was put on board my ship and sent away from that harbor. The winds carried me to Cyprus, the land of Alasiya, where a mob tried to murder me. I fought my way through the crowd toward the palace of Hatiba, ruler of Alasiya. As she walked from one building to another, I got her attention and then asked those crowding around me if anyone spoke Egyptian. One person said he did and I asked him: "Tell her majesty that even as far away as Thebes in the temple of Amun, Alasiya's reputation for justice is well known. Is she going to let an injustice like this ruin her country's reputation?"

Hatiba asked: "What is he saying?" I replied: "A raging sea and strong winds have driven me to your land. Will you allow me to be killed, despite the fact that I am a messenger of Amun? It is certain that a search will be made for me until the end of time. As for this crew of Tjerker Baal of Byblos, who are also in danger of being killed, surely Amun will find and kill ten crews of yours in revenge for their deaths."

Then she warned the people not to harm us and granted us sanctuary for the night....

YAVNE-YAM LETTER

≋ *Few scrolls written in Hebrew have been recovered because papyrus and parchment are biodegradable. Inscriptions in Hebrew, like the Yavne-Yam letter, on broken pieces of pottery or ostraca are virtually indestructible. During the reign of Josiah, ruler of Judah (640–609 BCE), a day laborer filed a plea with the governor of Yavne-Yam on the Mediterranean coast. It was written on a piece of pottery eight inches high and seven inches wide, and was one of seven ostraca recovered by J. Naveh, an Israeli archaeologist, in 1960. It was in the guardroom of the gate in a small fortress five miles northwest of Jamnia and two miles south of the Wadi Rubin [Hebrew: nahal soreq].*

The Yavne-Yam letter was probably dictated to a professional scribe. It is written in cursive style and contains a formal address in the first two lines, which was standard (1 Sam 26:19). The laborer is asking the governor to return his cloak, which was taken from him by his supervisor. The cloak was to serve as collateral until the laborer finished his work quota. Seemingly his supervisor is charging that the laborer still has work to do.

Parallels to the Yavne-Yam letter appear in the Farmer and the Courts in Egypt and in the books of Exodus (Exod 22:25-26) and Deuteronomy (Deut 24:12-17)

Let my lord the Governor pay heed to the words of his servant (1 Sam 26:19).

Several days ago, your servant was harvesting in Hasar-asam. The work went as usual and your servant completed the harvesting and storing of my quota of grain. . . . Despite the fact that your servant had completed his assigned work, Hoshaiahu, son of Shobai, kept your servant's cloak (Amos 2:8). He has held my cloak for days. All my fellow workers will testify—all those who work in the heat of the day will surely certify—that I am not guilty of any breach of contract.

Please order my supervisor to return my cloak either in fulfillment of the law (Exod 22:26–27) or as an act of mercy (Zech 7:9). Please do not remain silent and leave your servant without his cloak.... (Ps 35.22)

Water bird on Philistine pottery near Yavne-Yam

OUTLINE OF
MESOPOTAMIAN HISTORY

2600–2359   **Sumerian Period**—city states: Kish, Uruk, Ur, Lagash. Gilgamesh, cuneiform, ziggurat

2350–2150   **Akkadian Period**—Sargon of Agade (2334–2279 BCE), Naram-Sin (2254–2218 BCE); Ebla rivals Akkad

2150–2000   **Ur III Period**
Revival of Sumerian Culture
Code of Shulgi (2094–2047 BCE)

2000–1800   **Amorite Period**—struggle between Assyrians and new dynasties founded by Amorite leaders (Amurru) based at Larsa, Mari, and Babylon

1792–1750   **Hammurabi**
Code of Hammurabi

1600–1155   **Kassites** ruled southern Mesopotamia for 400 little known years; aided by the overthrow of Hammurabi's dynasty during the brief invasion of the Hittites

                   Hittites—centered in Asia Minor, they had two periods of prominence: the Old Hittite Kingdom (c. 1650–1420) and the New Hittite Kingdom (c. 1420–1200). Suppiluliumas I, Hattusilis III

                   Hurrians—kingdom of Mitanni dominated western Syria from c. 1400 to 1330; Nuzi; their defeat by the Hittites created a political vacuum filled by the Hittites and Assyrians (Tigris River area)

Ugarit—seacoast city in northern Syria, a trading center and nominal go-between for the Hittites and Egyptians between 1400 and 1200. Its alphabetic cuneiform literary texts closely parallel Old Testament poetic style: Aqhat, Baal, and Anat. This period of history was brought to an abrupt end with the invasion of the Sea Peoples (including the Philistines) who c. 1200 conquered the Hittites, destroyed Ugarit, and nearly conquered Egypt.

934–610   **Neo-Assyrian Period**—conquer Mesopotamia and Syria-Palestine in savage campaigns; Tiglath-pileser III, Shalmaneser III, Sargon II, Sennacherib, Ashurbanipal

626–539   **Neo-Babylonian (Chaldean) Period**—Nebuchadnezzar, Nabonidus, Belshazzar

550–330   **Persian Period**—Cyrus, Darius, Xerxes, Artaxerxes

332   **Alexander the Great** conquers Persians and Hellenistic Period begins; Ptolemies, Seleucids: Antiochus IV Epiphanes

OUTLINE OF EGYPTIAN HISTORY

2920–2575   **Early Dynastic Period—1st–2nd Dynasties**
Memphite royal culture, Nome provincial centers

2575–2134   **Old Kingdom—3rd–6th Dynasties**

3rd Dynasty (2649–2575):
Djoser and the step pyramid at Saqqara

4th Dynasty (2575–2465):
Pyramid Age, Giza pyramids of Khufu, Khephren, Menkaure

5th–6th Dynasties (2465–2150):
Pyramid Texts

2134–2040   **First Intermediate Period—7th–10th Dynasties**

2040–1640   **Middle Kingdom—11th–12th Dynasties**

1640–1532   **Second Intermediate Period—13th–17th Dynasties**

1550   **Hyksos expelled** from their capital, Avaris, in the Delta region by Ahmose I, founder of the 18th Dynasty

1550–1070   **New Kingdom**

18th Dynasty (1550–1307):
Tuthmosis III (1479–1425)

Akhenaten (1353–1335)
Tutankhamun (1333–1323)
Haremhab (1319–1307)

19th Dynasty (1307–1196)
Ramesses II (1290–1224)
Merneptah (1224–1214)

20th Dynasty (1196–1070)
Ramesses III (1194–1163)
Attack of the Sea Peoples

1070–712   **Third Intermediate Period—21st–26th Dynasties**
Egypt in decline
Shoshenq I (945–924 BCE)
Necho II (610–595 BCE)
Battle of Carchemish (605 BCE)

525   **Persian Period**
Conquest of Egypt by Cambyses

332   **Hellenistic Period**
Conquest of Egypt by Alexander the Great
Alexandria founded
Ptolemaic Pharaohs
Roman Emperors

OUTLINE OF
ISRAELITE HISTORY

A. **Premonarchic periods portrayed in the biblical text:**

1. Ancestral Period—Abraham/Sarah, Isaac/Rebekah, Jacob/Rachel and Leah (date uncertain)

2. Movement of Jacob/Israel's family into Goshen, Egypt; Joseph (perhaps dated to Hyksos Period, c. 1640–1550)

3. Exodus from Egypt—Moses and Aaron (perhaps in the reign of Ramesses II [1290–1224 BCE])

4. Settlement Period—Joshua, Merneptah Stela, incursions of the Sea Peoples, Philistines (c. 1250–1150)

5. Judges Period—Ehud, Deborah, Gideon, Jephthah, Samson (c. 1200–1020)

B. **Monarchy Period**

1. Early Monarchy—Samuel and Saul (c. 1020–1000)

2. United Kingdom—David and Solomon (c. 1000–922)

3. Divided Monarchy—Israel survives until 720 and Judah until 587

Names to remember in Israel: Jeroboam (first king), Ahab and Jezebel. Prophets—Elijah, Elisha, Amos, Hosea. Capital city—

Samaria. Conquered by Assyrian king Sargon II in 720—population deported

Names to remember in Judah: Rehoboam (first king), Jehoshaphat, Hezekiah, Josiah. Prophets—Isaiah, Micah, Jeremiah. Capital city—Jerusalem. Conquered by Nebuchadnezzar of Babylon in 597—Jehoiachin, Ezekiel and others taken into exile; final fall of Jerusalem in 587 with second deportation to Babylon

C. Exilic and Post-Exilic Period

1. Babylonian Exile (597–538): Ezekiel, Isaiah of Exile

2. Persian Period (538–332): Cyrus, Darius, Xerxes, Artaxerxes. Temple rebuilt (516), Zerubbabel, Haggai. Jerusalem's walls rebuilt (c. 445), Nehemiah. Renewal of covenant by Ezra (c. 400)

D. Hellenistic and Roman Period

1. Conquests of Alexander the Great (336–322) ended Persian control over Judah. All of Palestine became a part of the Hellenistic empire, ruled first by the Ptolemies and after 198 by the Seleucids. Maccabean revolt vs. Seleucid king Antiochus IV (Epiphanes) in 168 brought brief independence period (Hasmoneans)

2. Roman general Pompey captures Jerusalem in 63 BCE. Two unsuccessful revolts against Roman rule in 66–73 CE (when Herod's temple is destroyed) and the Bar-Kochba revolt in 132–135 CE. Jews were scattered throughout the Roman Empire in the Diaspora

BIBLIOGRAPHY FOR CRITICAL EDITIONS

Hymn to Ptah:

J. Junker, *Die Gotterlehre von Memphis* (1940), no. 23.

M. Lichtheim, *Ancient Egyptian Literature. A Book of Readings,* vol. 1 (1975), 51–57.

K. Sethe, *Das "Denkmal memphitishcher Theologie," der Schabakostein des Britischen Museums* (1928).

J. L. Foster, *Hymn Prayers, and Songs: An Anthology of Ancient Egyptian Lyric Poetry* (1995).

Stories of Atum:

E. A. W. Budge, *Egyptian Hieratic Papyri in the British Museum.* First Series (1910).

R. O. Faulkner, *The Papyrus Bremner-Rhind* (1933).

———, "The Bremner-Rhind Papyrus-III," *Journal of Egyptian Archaeology* 23 (1937), 166–85.

Enuma Elish Stories:

S. Dalley, *Myths from Mesopotamia* (1989), 228–77.

A. Deimel, *Enuma Elis* (2nd ed., 1936).

A. Heidel, *The Babylonian Genesis* (1942).

L. W. King, *The Seven Tablets of Creation* (2 vols., 1902).

R. Labat, *Le poeme babylonian de la creation* (1935).

W. G. Lambert and S. B. Parker, *Enuma elis: The Babylonian Epic of Creation* (1966).

B. Landsberger and J. K. Wilson, "The Fifth Tablet of 'Enuma Elish,'" *Journal of Near Eastern Studies* 20 (1961), 154–79.

S. Langdon, *The Babylonian Epic of Creation* (1923).

Stories of Gilgamesh:

S. Dalley, *Myths from Mesopotamia* (1989), 39–135.
A. Heidel, *The Gilgamesh Epic and Old Testament Parallels* (1946).
Peter Jensen, *Assyrisch-babylonische Mythen und Epen* (1900).
R. Campbell Thompson, *The Epic of Gilgamesh* (1930).
J. H. Tigay, *The Evolution of the Gilgamesh Epic* (1982).

Stories of Atrahasis:

S. Dalley, *Myths from Mesopotamia* (1989), 1–38.
W. G. Lambert, "A New Look at the Babylonian Background of Genesis," *Journal of Theological Studies* 16 (1965), 287–300.
W. G. Lambert and A. R. Millard, *Atra-Hasis: The Babylonian Story of the Flood* (1969).
A. R. Millard, "A New Babylonian Genesis Story," *Tyndale Bulletin* 18 (1967), 3–18.

Stories of Adapa:

F. M. Th. De Liagre Bohl, "Die Mythe vom weisen Adapa," *Die Welt des Orients* 2 (1959), 416–31.
S. Dalley, *Myths from Mesopotamia* (1989), 182–88.
A. Heidel, *Babylonian Genesis* (1942), 147–53.
S. Izre'el, "The Study of Oral Poetry: Reflections of a Neophyte," in M. E. Vogelzang and H. L. J. Vanstiphout, eds., *Mesopotamian Epic Literature: Oral or Aural?* (1992), 155–226.
J. A. Knudtzon, *Die El-Amarna-Tafeln* (1915), 965–69.
R. Campbell Thompson, *The Epic of Gilgamesh* (1930).

Nuzi Archives:

R. H. Pfeiffer and E. A. Speiser, eds., *One Hundred New Selected Nuzi Tablets. The Annual of the American Schools of Oriental Research* 16 (1935–36).
C. J. Gadd, "Tablets from Kirkuk," *Revue d'Assyriologie* 23 (1929), 49–161.
K. Grosz, "Dowry and Brideprice in Nuzi," in M. A. Morrison and D. I. Owen, eds., *Studies on the Civilization and Culture of Nuzi and the Hurrians* (1981), 161–82.
M. Morrison, "Urhi-kusuh DUMU LUGAL and the Family of Mus-apu: Texts from Group 19 (Part 1)," in *Nuzi and the Hurrians, IV: The Eastern Archives of Nuzi* (1993), 66–94.
E. A. Speiser, "A Significant New Will from Nuzi," *Journal of Cuneiform Studies* 17 (1963), 65–71.

Annals of Dedumose:

Josephus, *Against Apion* (i.14:73–89).
Manetho, *Aegyptiaca*, frag. 42, 1.75–89.

Annals of Kamose:

L. Habachi, *The Second Stela of Kamose and His Struggle Against the Hyksos Ruler and His Capital* (1972).

Annals of Hatshepsut:

J. Breasted, *Ancient Records of Egypt, II* (1906).
H. Brunner, *Die Geburt des Gottkonigs*, Agyptologische Abhandlungen 10 (1964).

Stories of Anubis and Bata:

A. H. Gardiner, *Late-Egyptian Stories* (1932), 9–29.
M. Lichtheim, *Ancient Egyptian Literature. A Book of Readings,* vol. 2 (1976), 203–11.
G. Moller, *Hieratische Lesestucke, II* (1927), 1–20.
Select Papyri in the Hieratic Character from the Collections of the British Museum, II (1860), Pls. ix–xix.

Stories of Aqhat:

A. Caquot, M. Sznycer, and A. Herdner, *Textes ougaritiques, I. Mythes et legendes* (1974).
M. D. Coogan, *Stories from Ancient Canaan* (1978), 27–47.
J. C. De Moor, *An Anthology of Religious Texts from Ugarit* (1987), 224–69.
J. C. De Moor and K. Spronk, *A Cuneiform Anthology of Religious Texts from Ugarit* (1987), 102–21.
J. Obermann, *How Daniel Was Blessed with a Son* (1946).
S. Parker, ed., *Ugaritic Narrative Poetry* (1997).
C. Virolleaud, *La legende phenicienne de Danel* (1936).
N. Wyatt, *Religious Texts from Ugarit: The Words of Ilimilku and His Colleagues* (1998)

Stories of Kirta

A. Caquot, M. Sznycer, and A. Herdner, *Textes ougaritiques, I. Mythes et legendes* (1974).

M. D. Coogan, *Stories from Ancient Canaan* (1978), 52–74.
J. C. De Moor, *An Anthology of Religious Texts from Ugarit* (1987), 191–223.
J. C. De Moor and K. Spronk, *A Cuneiform Anthology of Religious Texts from Ugarit* (1987), 78–101.
H. L. Ginsberg, *The Legend of King Keret* (1946).
S. Parker, ed., *Ugaritic Narrative Poetry* (1997).
N. Wyatt, *Religious Texts from Ugarit: The Words of Ilimilku and His Colleagues* (1998)

Story of Sargon of Agade:

B. R. Foster, *Before the Muses: An Anthology of Akkadian Literature,* vol. 2: *Mature, Late* (1993), 819–20.
L. W. King, *Chronicles Concerning Early Babylonian Kings, II* (1907), 87–96.
B. Lewis, *The Sargon Legend* (1980).

Treaty Between Ramesses II and Hattusilis III:

G. Beckman, *Hittite Diplomatic Texts* (1996), 90–95.
E. Edel, *Der agyptisch-hethitische Korrespondenz aus Boghazkoi in babylonischer und hethitischer Sprache* (1994).
E. F. Weidner, *Politische Dokumente aus Kleinasien* (1923), 112–23.

Annals of Merneptah:

P. Lacau, *Steles du nouvel empire, I* (1909), pp. 52–59, Pls. xvii–xix.
M. Lichtheim, *Ancient Egyptian Literature. A Book of Readings,* vol. 2 (1976), 73–78.
W. M. F. Petrie, *Six Temples at Thebes* (1897), Pls. xiii–xiv.

Code of Shulgi:

A. T. Clay, *Yale Oriental Series, Babylonian Texts,* Vol. I, no. 28.
J. J. Finkelstein, "Sex Offenses in Sumerian Laws," *JAOS* 86 (1966), 355–72.
———, "The Laws of Ur-Nammu," *JCS 22* (1968–69), 66–82.

Sumerian Code:

J. J. Finkelstein, "Sex Offenses in Sumerian Laws," *Journal of the American Oriental Society 86* (1966), 355–72.
M. Roth, *Law Collections from Mesopotamia and Asia Minor* (1995).

Code of Hammurabi:

E. Bergmann, *Codex Hammurabi: textus primigenius* (1953).
A. Deimel, *Codex Hammurabi, textus primigenius* (1930).
G. R. Driver and J. C. Miles, *The Babylonian Laws* (2 vols., 1952).
A. Finet, *Le Code de Hammurabi* (1973).
M. E. J. Richardson, *Hammurabi's Laws: Text, Translation and Glossary* (2000)
M. Roth, *Law Collections from Mesopotamia and Asia Minor* (1995).

Hittite Code:

J. Friedrich, *Die Hethitschen Gesetze* (1959).
H. A. Hoffner, Jr., *The Laws of the Hittites: a Critical Edition* (1997).
F. Hrozny, *Code Hittite provenant de l'Asie Mineure* (vers 1350 av. J.-C.), *1er partie, Transcription, traduction francaise* (1922).
E. Neufeld, *The Hittite Laws* (1951).
M. Roth, *Law Collections from Mesopotamia and Asia Minor* (1995).

Middle Assyrian Code:

G. R. Driver and J. C. Miles, *The Assyrian Laws, Edited with Translation and Commentary* (1935).
M. Roth, *Law Collections from Mesopotamia and Asia Minor* (1995).
R. Yaron, "Middle Assyrian Laws and the Bible," *Biblica* 51 (1970), 77–85.

Stories of Balaam:

J. A. Hackett, *The Balaam Text from Deir 'Alla* (1980).
J. Hoftijzer and G. van der Kooij, *Aramaic Texts from Deir 'Alla* (1976).
_____, *The Balaam Text from Deir 'Alla Re-Evaluated* (1991).

Stories of Sinuhe:
A. M. Blackman, *Middle Egyptian Stories, Part I*, Bibliotheca Aegyptiaca 2 (1932).
A. H. Gardiner, *Notes on the Story of Sinuhe* (1916).
R. Koch, *Die Erzählung des Sinuhe* (1990)
M. Lichtheim, *Ancient Egyptian Literature*, vol. 1 (1973), 222–35.
R. Parent, *L'affair Sinouhe* (1982).
R. B. Parkinson, *The Tale of Sinuhe and Other Ancient Egyptian Poems 1940–1640 BC* (1997).

Annals of Tuthmosis III:

M. S. Drower, "Inscriptions," in R. Mond and O. H. Myers, *Temples of Armant: A Preliminary Survey, The Text* (1940), 157–96.
R.O. Faulkner, "The Battle of Megiddo," *JEA* 28 (1942), 2–15.
H. Goedicke, *The Battle of Megiddo* (2000).
C. R. Lepsius, *Denkmaler aus Aegypten und Aethiopien, III* (1849–50).

El-Amarna Letters:

C. Bezold and E. A. W. Budge, *The Tell El-Amarna Tablets in the British Museum* (1892).
J. A. Knudtzon, *Die El-Amarna-Tafeln* (1907–1915).
W. L. Moran, *Les lettres d'el-Amarna* (1987).

Annals of Ramesses III:

J. A. Breasted, *Ancient Records of Egypt, IV* (1906).
W. F. Edgerton and J. A. Wilson, "Historical Records of Ramses III," *Studies in Ancient Oriental Civilization* 12 (1936).
Epigraphic Survey, *Medinet Habu, I. Earlier Historical Records of Ramses III* (1930).

Gezer Almanac:

W. F. Albright, "The Gezer Calendar," *Bulletin of the American Schools of Oriental Research* 82 (1943), 18–24.
J. C. L. Gibson, *Textbook of Syrian Semitic Inscriptions, I* (1971), 1–4.
W. H. Shea, "The Song of Seedtime and Harvest from Gezer," in J. C. de Moor and W. G. E. Watson, eds., *Verse in Ancient Near Eastern Prose* (1993), 243–50.
S. Talmon, "The Gezer Calendar and the Seasonal Cycle of Ancient Canaan," *Journal of the American Oriental Society* 83 (1963), 177–87.

Archives of Babatha:

H. Cotton, "The Guardianship of Jesus Son of Babatha: Roman and Local Law in the Province of Arabia," *Journal of Roman Studies* 83 (1993), 94–108.
Y. Yadin, *The Finds from the Bar-Kokhba Period in the Cave of Letters* (1963).
———, "The Life and Trials of Babata," in *Bar-Kokhba: the Rediscovery of the Legendary Hero of the Second Jewish Revolt against Rome* (1971), 22–53 + 265.

Y. Yadin, J. C. Greenfield, and A. Yardeni, "Babatha's Ketubba," *Israel Exploration Journal* 44 (1994), 75–101.

Y. Yadin, and B. A. Levine, eds., *The Documents from the Bar Kokhba Period in the Cave of Letters* (2002).

Annals of Tiglath-pileser I:

M. Cogan, "'Ripping Open Pregnant Women' in Light of an Assyrian Analogue," *Journal of the American Oriental Society* 103/4 (1983), 755–57.

E. Ebeling, *Literarische Keilschrifttexte aus Assur,* #62 (1953), 82–83.

———, "Ein Heidenlied auf Tiglatpileser I. und der Anfang einer neuen Version von 'Istars Hollenfahrt' nach einer Schulertafel aus Assur," *Orientalia* 18 (1949), 30–39.

Annals of Mesha:

R. Dussaud, *Les monuments palestiniens et judaiques* (1912), 4–22.

J. C. L. Gibson, *Textbook of Syrian Semitic Inscriptions, I* (1971), 71–84.

K. P. Jackson, "The Language of the Mesha' Inscription," in *Studies in the Mesha Inscription and Moab* (1989), 96–130.

Tell Dan Annals:

A. Biran and J. Naveh, "Aramaic Stele Fragment from Dan," *Israel Exploration Journal* 43 (1993), 81–98.

———, "The Tell Dan Inscription: A New Fragment," *Israel Exploration Journal* 45 (1995), 1–18.

J.-W. Wesselius, "The Road to Jezreel: Primary History and the Tel Dan Inscription," *Scandinavian Journal of the Old Testament* 15 (2001), 83–103.

Karatepe Annals of Azitawada:

H. T. Bossert and U. B. Alkim, *Karatepe II* (1947), Pls. xxix–xxxi, xl–xliv.

H. T. Bossert, et al., *Die Ausgrabungen auf dem Karatepe* (1950), Pl. xiv.

R. T. O'Callaghan, "The Phoenician Inscription on the King's Statue at Karatepe," *Catholic Biblical Quarterly* 11 (1949), 233–48.

J. Pedersen, "The Phoenician Inscription of Karatepe," *Acta Orientalia* 21 (1953), 33–56.

Annals of Shalmaneser III:

A. H. Layard, *Inscriptions in the Cuneiform Character* (1851).
————, *Monuments of Nineveh I* (1849), Pls. 53–56.
————, *Inscriptions in the Cuneiform Character from Assyrian Monuments* (1851), Pls. 87–98.

Annals of Tiglath-pileser III:

D. D. Luckenbill, *Ancient Records of Assyria and Babylonia, I* (1926).
P. Rost, *Die Keilschrifttexte Tiglat-Pilesers III nach den Papierabklatschen und Originalen des Britischen Museums* (1893).
H. Tadmor, *The Inscriptions of Tiglath-Pileser III King of Assyria* (1994).

Annals of Sargon II:

R. Borger, *Babylonisch-Assyrische Lesestucke* (1963), 54–58.
A. Fuchs, *Die Inschriften Sargons II. Aus Khorsabad* (1994).
H. Winckler, *Die Keilschrifttexte Sargons* (1889), Pl. 38.

Azekah Letter:

E. Frahm, *Einleitung in die Sanherib-Inschriften* (1997).
G. Galil, "A New Look at the 'Azekah Inscription,'" *RB* 102 (1995), 321–29.
N. Na'aman, "Sennacherib's 'Letter to God' on his Campaign to Judah," *BASOR* 214 (1974), 25–39.

Annals of Sennacherib:

R. Borger, *Babylonisch-assyrische Lesestucke* (1963), 67–69.
F. M. Fales, *Assyrian Royal Inscriptions* (1981).
D. D. Luckenbill, *The Annals of Sennacherib* (1924).

Siloam Dedication:

J. C. L. Gibson, *Textbook of Syrian Semitic Inscriptions, I* (1971), 21–23.
V. Sasson, "The Siloam Tunnel Inscription," *Palestine Exploration Quarterly* 114 (1982), 111–17.
K. A. D. Smelik, *Writings from Ancient Israel* (1991), 64–69.

Annals of Nebuchadnezzar:

J.-J. Glassner, *Chroniques mésopotamiennes* (1993).
A. K. Grayson, *Assyrian and Babylonian Chronicles, V* (1975).

D. J. Wiseman, *Chronicles of Chaldean Kings (626–556 B.C.) in the British Museum* (1956), 32–37, 73.

Arad Letters:

Y. Aharoni, *Arad Inscriptions* (1981).

J. C. L. Gibson, *Textbook of Syrian Semitic Inscriptions, I* (1971), 49–54.

J. M. Lindenberger, *Ancient Aramaic and Hebrew Letters* (1994), 103–10.

A. F. Rainey, "The Saga of Eliashib," *Biblical Archaeology Review* 13/2 (1987), 36–39.

K. A. D. Smelik, *Writings from Ancient Israel: A Handbook of Historical and Religious Documents* (1991), 101–15.

Lachish Letters:

A. Lemaire, *Inscriptions hebraiques, I: Les ostraca* (1977), 97–100.

J. M. Lindenberger, *Ancient Aramaic and Hebrew Letters* (1994), 110–16.

D. Pardee, *Handbook of Ancient Hebrew Letters* (1982), 78–81.

H. Torczyner, *Lachish I. The Lachish Letters* (1938), 33–43.

Decree of Cyrus:

R. Borger, *Handbuch der Keilschriftliteratur, I* (1967).

A. Kuhrt, "The Cyrus Cylinder and Achaemenid Imperial Policy," *Journal for the Study of the Old Testament* 25 (1983), 83–97.

F. H. Weissbach, *Die Keilinschriften der Achameniden* (1911), 2–9.

Elephantine Letters:

J. M. Lindenberger, *Ancient Aramaic and Hebrew Letters* (1994), 53–70.

B. Porten, *Archives from Elephantine* (1968), 278–98.

B. Porten and A. Yardeni, *Textbook of Aramaic Documents from Ancient Egypt: 1 Letters* (1986).

Y. Yadin, et al., eds., *The Documents from the Bar Kokhba Period in the Cave of Letters* (2002).

Declarations of Innocence:

T. G. Allen, *The Book of the Dead or Going Forth by Day* (1974).

E. A. W. Budge, *The Egyptian Book of the Dead: (The Papyrus of Ani) Egyptian Text: Transliteration and Translation* (1965).

L. H. Lesko, *The Ancient Egyptian Book of Two Ways* (1972).

M. Lichtheim, *Ancient Egyptian Literature,* vol. 2 (1976), 119–32.

A Sufferer and a Soul in Egypt:

W. Barta, *Das Gesprach eines Mannes mit seinem Ba* (1969).

A. Erman, *Gesprach eines Lebensmuden mit seiner Seele* (1896).

R. O. Faulkner, "The Man Who Was Tired of Life," *JEA* 42 (1956), 21–40.

H. Goedicke, *The Report about the Dispute of a Man with His Ba* (1970).

M. Lichtheim, *Ancient Egyptian Literature. A Book of Readings,* vol. 1 (1975), 163–69.

K. Sethe, *Aegyptische Lesestucke* (2nd ed., 1928), 43–46.

A Farmer and the Courts in Egypt:

M. Lichtheim, *Ancient Egyptian Literature. A Book of Readings,* vol. 1 (1975), 169–84.

R. B. Parkinson, *The Tale of the Eloquent Peasant* (1991).

F. Vogelsang and A. H. Gardiner, *Die Klagen des Bauern* (1908).

A Sufferer and a Friend in Babylon:

J. A. Craig, *Babylonian and Assyrian Religious Texts, I* (1895), Pls. 44–52.

W. G. Lambert, *Babylonian Wisdom Literature* (1960), 63–91.

Laments for Ur:

I. Bernhardt, *Sumerische literarische Texte aus Nippur II* (1967), 16, tablets 18–25.

M. E. Cohen, *The Canonical Lamentations of Ancient Mesopotamia, I* (1988).

T. Jacobsen, *The Harps That Once: Sumerian Poetry in Translation* (1987).

S. N. Kramer, *The Lament Over the Destruction of Ur* (1940).

Hymn to Ninkasi:

M. Civil, "A Hymn to the Beer Goddess and a Drinking Song," in *Studies Presented to A. Leo Oppenheim: From the Workshop of the Chicago Assyrian Dictionary* (1964), 67–89.

A. L. Oppenheim and L. F. Hartman, *On Beer and Brewing Techniques in Ancient Mesopotamia: According to the XXIIIrd Tablet of the Series HAR.ra=hubullu* (Supplement to the *Journal of the American Oriental Society* 10 (1950).

Ebla Archives:

G. Pettinato, *The Archives of Ebla: An Empire Inscribed in Clay* (1981).

J. Krecher, "The Ebla Tablets and Their Possible Significance for Biblical Studies," in A. Biran, ed., *Biblical Archaeology Today, 1990* (1993), 498–507.

I. Zatelli, "The Origin of the Biblical Scapegoat Ritual: The Evidence of Two Eblaite Texts," *Vetus Testamentum* 48 (1998), 254–63.

Stories of Baal and Anat:

A. Caquot, M. Sznycer, and A. Herdner, *Textes ougaritiques, I. Mythes et legendes* (1974).

M. D. Coogan, *Stories from Ancient Canaan* (1978), 75–115.

J. C. De Moor, *An Anthology of Religious Texts from Ugarit* (1987), 20–109.

J. C. De Moor and K. Spronk, *A Cuneiform Anthology of Religious Texts from Ugarit* (1987), 1–44.

C. H. Gordon, *Ugaritic Literature* (1949), 9–56.

S. B. Parker, ed., *Ugaritic Narrative Poetry* (1997).

N. H. Walls, *The Goddess Anat in Ugaritic Myth* (1992).

N. Wyatt, *Religious Texts from Ugarit* (1998).

Hymn to the Aten:

N. de G. Davies, *The Rock Tombs of El-Amarna, VI* (1908), Pl. xxvii.

M. Lichtheim, *Ancient Egyptian Literature. A Book of Readings, II: The New Kingdom* (1976), 90–92.

Teachings of Ptah-Hotep:

E. Devaud, *Les maximes de Ptah-hotep* (1916).

G. Jequier, *Le Papyrus Prisse et ses variantes* (1911).

M. Lichtheim, *Ancient Egyptian Literature. A Book of Readings, I: The Old and Middle Kingdoms* (1975), 61–80.

Z. Zaba, *Les Maximes de Ptah-hotep* (1956).

Teachings of Khety:

H. Brunner, *Die Lehre des Cheti, Sohnes des Duauf* (1944).

W. Helck, *Die Lehre des Dw3-Htjj* (1970).

M. Lichtheim, *Ancient Egyptian Literature, vol. 1* (1973), 184–92.

Thirty Teachings of Amen-em-ope:

E. A. W. Budge, *Facsimiles of Egyptian Hieratic Papyri in the British Museum, Second Series* (1923), Pls. i–xiv.

———, *The Teachings of Amen-em-apt, Son of Kanakht* (1924).

I. Grumach, *Untersuchungen zur Lebenslehre des Amenope* (1972).

M. Lichtheim, *Ancient Egyptian Literature. A Book of Readings,* vol. 2 (1976), 146–63.

Teachings of Ahiqar:

J. M. Lindenberger, *The Aramaic Proverbs of Ahiqar* (1983).

T. Noldeke, *Untersuchungen zum Achiqar-Roman* (1914).

F. Stummer, *Der Kritische Wert der altaramaischen Ahikartexte aus Elephantine* (1914).

Teachings of Ankhsheshonq:

S. R. K. Glanville, *The Instructions of 'Onchsheshonqy* (1955).

M. Lichtheim, *Ancient Egyptian Literature, III: The Late Period* (1980), 159–84.

Egyptian Love Songs:

E. A. W. Budge, *Facsimiles of Egyptian Hieratic Papyri in the British Museum, Second Series* (1923), Pl. xliii.

M. V. Fox, *The Song of Songs and the Ancient Egyptian Love Songs* (1985).

M. Lichtheim, *Ancient Egyptian Literature, A Book of Readings,* vol. 2: *The New Kingdom* (1976), 181–96.

Stories of Ishtar and Tammuz:

R. Borger, *Babylonisch-Assyrische Lesestucke, II* (1963), 86–93.

S. Dalley, *Myths from Mesopotamia* (1989), 154–62.

A. Heidel, *The Gilgamesh Epic and Old Testament Parallels* (1946), 121–28.

I. Sefati, *Love Songs in Sumerian Literature* (1998), 194–205.

Visions of Neferti:

H. Goedicke, *The Protocol of Neferyt* (1977).

W. Golenischeff, *Les papyrus hieratiques no. 1115, 1116A, et 1116B de l'Ermitage Imperial a St. Petersbourg* (1913), Pls. 23–25.

W. Helck, *Die Prophezeiung des Nfr.tj* (1970).

M. Lichtheim, *Ancient Egyptian Literature. A Book of Readings,* vol. 1 (1975), 139–45.

Mari Letters:

B. Batto, *Studies on Women at Mari* (1974).

F. Ellermeier, *Prophetie in Mari und Israel* (1968).

H. B. Huffmon, "Prophecy in the Mari Letters," *Biblical Archaeologist* 31/4 (1968), 101–24.

W. L. Moran, "New Evidence from Mari on the History of Prophecy," *Biblica* 50 (1969), 15–56.

M. Nissinen, with contributions by C. L. Seow and R. K. Ritner, *Prophets and Prophecy in the Ancient Near East* (2003).

J. J. M. Roberts, "The Mari Prophetic Texts in Transliteration and English Translation," in *The Bible and the Ancient Near East: Collected Essays* (2002), 157–253.

Story of Wen-Amun:

A. H. Gardiner, *Late-Egyptian Stories* (1932), 61–76.

H. Goedicke, *The Report of Wenamun* (1975).

G. Moller, *Hieratische Lesestucke, II* (1927), 29.

Yavne-Yam Letter:

J. C. L. Gibson, *Textbook of Syrian Semitic Inscriptions, I* (1971), 26–30.

J. M. Lindenberger, *Ancient Aramaic and Hebrew Letters* (1994), 96–98.

J. Naveh, "A Hebrew Letter from the Seventh Century B.C.," *Israel Exploration Journal* 10 (1960), 129–39.

K. A. D. Smelik, "The Literary Structure of the Yavneh-Yam Ostracon," *IEJ* 42 (1992), 55–61.

BIBLIOGRAPHY FOR
PICTURES

Biran, A. and J. Naveh. "The Tell Dan Inscription: A New Fragment." *Israel Exploration Journal* 45/1 (1995): 1–18.

Castel, F. *The History of Israel and Judah in Old Testament Times* (Mahwah, NJ: Paulist Press, 1985).

Contenau, G. *Everyday Life in Babylon and Assyria* (London: Edward Arnold Ltd., 1954).

Crawford, H. *Sumer and the Sumerians* (Cambridge: Cambridge University Press, 1991).

Erman, A. *Life in Ancient Egypt* (London: Macmillan and Co., 1894).

Fiore, S. *Voices from the Clay* (Norman, OK.: University of Oklahoma Press, 1965).

Frankfort, H. *Cylinder Seals* (London: Gregg Press, 1939).

Gardiner, A. *Egypt of the Pharaohs* (New York: Oxford University Press, 1966).

Habachi, L. *The Second Stela of Kamose and His Struggle Against the Hyksos Ruler and His Capital* (1972).

Janssen, R. and J. *Egyptian Household Animals* (Aylesbury, UK: Shire Publications, 1989).

Jastrow, M. *The Civilization of Babylonia and Assyria* (Philadelphia: J. B. Lippincott Company, 1915).

Manning, S. *The Land of the Pharaohs* (New York: Fleming H. Revell Company, 1924).

Maspero, G. *Manual of Egyptian Archaeology*, 6th ed. (New York: G. P. Putnam's Sons, 1926).

Michalowski, K. *Art of Ancient Egypt* (New York: Harry N. Abrams Inc., 1969).

Montet, P. *Lives of the Pharaohs* (Cleveland: The World Publishing Company, 1968).

Moortgat, A. *The Art of Ancient Mesopotamia* (London: Phaidon, 1969).

Murray, M. A. and J. C. Ellis. *A Street in Petra* (London: British School of Egyptian Archaeology, 1940).

Nelson, H. H. and U. Holshcher. *Work in Western Thebes 1931–33* (Chicago: University of Chicago Press, 1934).

Newsome, J. D., Jr. *By the Waters of Babylon* (Atlanta: John Knox Press, 1979).

Perrot, G. and C. Chipiez. *History of Art in Phoenicia and Its Dependencies* (London: Chapman and Hall Ltd., 1885).

Pettinato, G. *The Archives of Ebla: An Empire Inscribed in Clay* (Garden City, NY: Doubleday, 1981).

Quirke, S. *Who Were the Pharaohs?* (London: British Museum Publications, 1990).

Rawlinson, F. *History of Ancient Egypt, Vol. II* (New York: John B. Alden, 1886).

———. *Ancient Egypt* (London: G. P. Putnam's Sons, 1904).

Saggs, H. W. F. *Everyday Life in Babylonia and Assyria* (London: B. T. Batsford Ltd., 1965).

Tadmor, M. *Inscriptions Reveal,* 2nd ed. (Jerusalem: Israel Museum, 1973).

Woldering, I. *The Art of Egypt: The Time of the Pharaohs* (New York: Crown Publishers, 1963).

ABBREVIATIONS

AA	Agyptologische Abhandlungen, Wiesbaden
AASOR	The Annual of the American Schools of Oriental Research
AO	tablets in the collections of the Louvre Museum
AP	Aramaic Papyri
ARET	Archivi reali di Ebla
ARI	Assyrian Royal Inscriptions. Grayson (1972–76)
ARM	Archives royales de Mari, Textes cuneiformes
BASOR	*Bulletin of the American Schools of Oriental Research*
BM	tablets in the collections of the British Museum
Cowley	A. Cowley, ed., *Aramaic Papyri of the Fifth Century B.C.* (Oxford, 1923)
CT	Cuneiform Texts from Babylonian Tablets in the British Museum (London, 1896)
CTA	A. Herdner, *Corpus des tablettes en cuneiformes alphabetiques decouvertes a Ras-Shamra-Ugarit de 1929–1939* (Paris, 1963)
EA	J. A. Knudtzon, Die El-Amarna-Tafeln
Gadd	C. J. Gadd, "Tablets from Kirkuk," *Revue d'Assyriologie* 23 (1929), 49–161
HSS	Harvard Semitic Series
IEJ	*Israel Exploration Journal*

JAOS	*Journal of the American Oriental Society*
JCS	*Journal of Cuneiform Studies*
JEA	*Journal of Egyptian Archaeology*
JNES	*Journal of Near Eastern Studies*
KTU	*Die keilalphabetischen Text aus Ugarit. Dietrich, Loretz and Sanmartin* (1976)
KV	Valley of the Kings
Ni	tablets excavated at Nippur, in the collections of the Archaeological Museum of Istanbul
PAPS	Proceedings of the American Philosophical Society
PRAK	H. de Genouillac, Premières recherches archéologique à Kich
TM	Siglum for tablets from Tell Mardikh (Ebla)
UM	tablets in the collection of the University Museum of the University of Pennsylvania, Philadelphia
VAT	tablets in the collections of the Staatliche Museum, Berlin
WO	Die Welt des Orients
YOS	Yale Oriental Series, Babylonian Texts
ZA	Zeitschrift fur Assyriologie

TEXT ABBREVIATIONS

Adapa	Stories of Adapa
Ahiqar	Teachings of Ahiqar
Amarna	el-Amarna Letters
Amen-em-ope	Teachings of Amen-em-ope
Ankhsheshonq	Teachings of Ankhsheshonq
Anubis	Stories of Anubis and Bata

Aqhat	Stories of Aqhat
Arad	Arad Letters
Aten	Hymn to the Aten
Atrahasis	Stories of Atrahasis
Atum	Hymn to Atum
Azekah	Azekah Letter
Baal	Stories of Baal and Anat
Babatha	Archives of Babatha
Balaam	Stories of Balaam
CH	Code of Hammurabi
Cyrus	A Decree of Cyrus
Declarations	Declarations of Innocence
Dedumose	Annals of Dedumose
Ebla	Ebla Archives
Elephantine	Elephantine Letters
Enuma	Enuma Elish Stories
Farmer	A Farmer and the Courts
Friend	A Sufferer and a Friend
Gezer	Gezer Almanac
Gilgamesh	Stories of Gilgamesh
Hatshepsut	Annals of Hatshepsut
Hittite	Hittite Code
Ishtar	Stories of Ishtar and Tammuz
Kamose	Annals of Kamose
Karatepe	Karatepe Annals of Azitawada
Khety	Teachings of Khety
Kirta	Stories of Kirta
Lachish	Lachish Letters
Love Songs	Egyptian Love Songs

MAL	Middle Assyrian Code
Mari	Mari Letters
Merneptah	Annals of Merneptah
Mesha	Annals of Mesha
Nebuchadnezzar	Annals of Nebuchadnezzar
Neferti	Visions of Neferti
Ninkasi	Hymn to Ninkasi
Nuzi	Nuzi Archives
Ptah	Hymn to Ptah
Ptah-Hotep	Teachings of Ptah-Hotep
Ramesses II	A Treaty Between Ramesses II and Hattusilis III
Ramesses III	Medinet Habu Annals of Ramesses III
Sargon	Story of Sargon of Agade
Sargon II	Annals of Sargon II
Sennacherib	Annals of Sennacherib
Shalmaneser	Annals of Shalmaneser III
Shulgi	Code of Shulgi
Siloam	Dedication of the Siloam Channel
Sinuhe	Stories of Sinuhe
Soul	A Sufferer and a Soul
Sumer	Sumerian Code
Tell Dan	Tell Dan Annals
TP I	Annals of Tiglath-pileser I
TP III	Nimrud Annals of Tiglath-pileser III
Tuthmosis III	Annals of Tuthmosis III
Ur	Laments for Ur
Wen-Amun	Memoirs of Wen-Amun
Yavne-Yam	Yavne-Yam Letter

BIBLICAL CITATION/TEXT AND PARALLELS INDEX

The following index provides a page and biblical citation index in conjunction with a text and parallel index. The scheme used for the parallels is as follows:

1 = genre: creation story, flood story, law, teaching
2 = verbal parallel: direct word or phrase parallels
3 = motif: barren wife, greed, widows and orphans, divine war
4 = social/scientific: anthropomorphism, taboo, propaganda
5 = plot parallel: similar action in both texts
6 = historical parallel: name, event, place

CITATION	PAGE	TEXT	PARALLEL

GENESIS

CITATION	PAGE	TEXT	PARALLEL
1:1—2:4a	34	Atrahasis	1 · creation story
	3	Ptah	1 · creation story
	8	Atum	1 · creation story
	259, 260	Ebla	1 · creation story
1:1–2	12	Enuma	1 · creation story
	12	Enuma	2 · Tehom
1:2	8	Atum	2 · primordial chaos
1:3	5	Ptah	2 · naming
1:6–7	17	Enuma	2 · firmament
1:15–16	17	Enuma	2 · moon
1:26–27	17	Enuma	2 · humans

CITATION	PAGE	TEXT	PARALLEL
1:31—2:1	6	Ptah	2 · rest
2:4b—4:2	21	Gilgamesh	1 · Eden story
2:6–7	8	Atum	1 · creation story
	8	Atum	2 · moisture/man
2:7	36	Atrahasis	1 · creation story
	36	Atrahasis	4 · anthropomorphism
	17	Enuma	5 · shaping human
	78	Aqhat	2 · breath
2:7–15	18	Enuma	5 · humans
	18	Enuma	4 · anthropomorphism
2:16–17	46	Adapa	5 · prohibited food
3:5	23	Gilgamesh	5 · gaining knowledge
3:7	23	Gilgamesh	5 · making clothing
3:20	35	Atrahasis	2 · mother of living
3:21	23	Gilgamesh	5 · making clothing
3:22	46	Adapa	3 · divine food
3:23–24	46	Adapa	5 · dismissed from divine realm
4:3–16	65	Anubis	3 · sibling rivalry
4:10–12	78	Aqhat	1 · curse
4:17	174	Karatepe	5 · building/naming city
4:23–24	79	Aqhat	1 · boast
6:1—11:26	21	Gilgamesh	1 · flood story
	34	Atrahasis	1 · flood story
	132	Balaam	3 · divine warning
6:14	28	Gilgamesh	2 · pitch
	40	Atrahasis	2 · pitch
6:15–16	28	Gilgamesh	5 · construction of ark
6:19—7:9	27	Gilgamesh	2 · animals
7:4–10	40	Atrahasis	2 · seven days
7:11	278	Aten	2 · fountains of deep
	40	Atrahasis	2 · fountains of deep
7:11–12	28	Gilgamesh	2 · fountains of deep
7:21–23	41	Atrahasis	5 · all life destroyed
7:23–24	29	Gilgamesh	5 · all humanity dies
8:3–4	29	Gilgamesh	5 · landing
8:6–12	29	Gilgamesh	5 · birds released
8:17–19	29	Gilgamesh	5 · release
8:20	29	Gilgamesh	5 · sacrifice
8:21	42	Atrahasis	2 · smell
	29	Gilgamesh	5 · deity smells sacrifice
9:20–21	79	Aqhat	2 · drunk

CITATION	PAGE	TEXT	PARALLEL
25:19—33:20	65	Anubis	3 · sibling rivalry
25:20—37:2	137	Sinuhe	1 · biography
	137	Sinuhe	5 · herder
	47	Nuzi	4 · social customs
25:21	71	Aqhat	5 · prayer for child
25:27	242	Friend	3 · older vs. younger
26:18–25	160	Babatha	2 · water rights
27:1–45	71	Aqhat	3 · rival twins
	71	Aqhat	4 · inheritance
27:27–29	50	Nuzi	1 · blessing
27:28	271	Baal	2 · deity's largesse
27:29	78	Aqhat	1 · blessing
28:10–17	81	Kirta	1 · dream theophany
	82	Kirta	5 · dream
28:13–14	342	Mari	3 · covenant
29:31—30:24	49	Nuzi	4 · surrogate
30:1–24	71	Aqhat	3 · barren wife
30:14–20	324	Love Songs	2 · mandrake
30:27–34	52	Nuzi	5 · herding contract
30:40–43	66	Anubis	5 · breeding
31:1–21	48	Nuzi	2 · idols
	48	Nuzi	4 · inheritance rights
31:19	349	Wen-Amun	2 · idol
31:19–35	347	Wen-Amun	2 · idol
31:39	114	CH	1 · contract
	114	CH	2 · mangled animals
31:44–54	92	Ramesses II	1 · covenant
	92	Ramesses II	2 · "If you"
31:50–54	96	Ramesses II	3 · curse
31:51–53	95	Ramesses II	1 · covenant
	95	Ramesses II	2 · gods witness
34	104	Sumer	5 · rape
34:1–12	104	Sumer	2 · rape
35:17	36	Atrahasis	2 · midwife
	36	Atrahasis	3 · birthing
37:2—50:26	303	Ahiqar	1 · wisdom
	303	Ahiqar	3 · restored fortune
38	118	Hittite	5 · levir
	272	Baal	1 · law (levir)
	272	Baal	3 · heir
	272	Baal	4 · mourning ritual

CITATION	PAGE	TEXT	PARALLEL
13:5	139	Sinuhe	2 · abundant land
15:1–10	11	Enuma	3 · divine warrior
15:3	166	TP I	3 · divine warrior
15:20	140	Sinuhe	2 · female singers
19:10	265	Baal	5 · washing
	265	Baal	4 · ritual cleansing
20:12	308	Ahiqar	2 · honor parents
	310	Ankhsheshonq	2 · honor parents
20:13	102	Shulgi	2 · murder
20:15	107	CH	2 · theft
20:16	235	Farmer	1 · law
	235	Farmer	2 · false witness
20:17	307	Ahiqar	2 · coveting
21:2–11	109	CH	2 · slavery
21:15	111	CH	2 · striking parents
21:16	107	CH	2 · kidnapping
21:18–19	116	Hittite	2 · injury
	116	Hittite	4 · compensation
	113	CH	2 · injury
	113	CH	4 · compensation
21:22	124	MAL	2 · miscarriage
	103	Sumer	2 · miscarriage
21:22–23	117	Hittite	2 · miscarriage
	113	CH	2 · miscarriage
21:22–25	128	MAL	2 · miscarriage
21:24	112	CH	2 · Talion
21:26	112	CH	2 · Talion/slave
21:28–36	113	CH	2 · goring ox
22:1–4	117	Hittite	2 · theft
22:2–3	108	CH	2 · burglary
22:2–3, 7	117	Hittite	2 · burglary
22:5	108	CH	2 · illegal grazing
22:6	117	Hittite	2 · fire
22:7–8	109	CH	2 · stolen goods
22:10–13	114	CH	2 · mangled animal
	114	CH	5 · body as evidence
22:14–15	113	CH	2 · hired animal
22:16	104	Sumer	2 · seduction of virgin
22:16–17	130	MAL	2 · seduction of virgin
	130	MAL	4 · marriage law
22:18	128	MAL	2 · sorcery

CITATION	PAGE	TEXT	PARALLEL
	117	Hittite	2 · sorcery
22:22	233	Farmer	3 · widow/orphan
22:26–27	355, 356	Yavne-Yam	1 · law
	355, 356	Yavne-Yam	2 · pledge garment
23:1–3	106	CH	2 · false witness
23:6–8	107	CH	2 · bribe
23:8	300	Amen-em-ope	2 · bribe
23:26	42	Atrahasis	2 · barren women
29:4	82	Kirta	2 · washing
	82	Kirta	4 · ritual cleansing
34:29–30	72	Aqhat	2 · shining face

LEVITICUS

CITATION	PAGE	TEXT	PARALLEL
10:6	44	Adapa	2 · hair
	44	Adapa	4 · mourning ritual
10:9	256	Ninkasi	2 · beer
16:1–34	260	Ebla	4 · scapegoat ritual
16:7–10	260	Ebla	4 · scapegoat ritual
18:6–18	111	CH	2 · incest
	111	CH	1 · decalogue
	117	Hittite	4 · marriage taboos
18:8	111	CH	2 · incest with mother
	111	CH	4 · marriage taboos
18:15	111	CH	2 · incest
	111	CH	2 · daughter-in-law
	111	CH	4 · marriage taboos
18:22	123	MAL	2 · homosexuality
19:11, 13	107	CH	2 · theft
19:15	107	CH	2 · unjust judge
	234	Farmer	2 · unjust judge
19:20–21	102	Shulgi	2 · slave woman
19:20–22	111	CH	2 · slave woman
20:10–21	111	CH	3 · illicit sex
	124	MAL	2 · adultery
20:11	111	CH	2 · incest with mother
	111	CH	4 · marriage taboos
20:12	111	CH	2 · daughter-in-law
	111	CH	2 · incest
	111	CH	4 · marriage taboos

CITATION	PAGE	TEXT	PARALLEL
20:13	123	MAL	2 · homosexuality
20:27	128	MAL	2 · sorcery
23:5–8	212	Elephantine	5 · festival—Passover
	212	Elephantine	2 · unleavened bread
24:16	120	MAL	2 · blasphemy
24:19–20	112	CH	2 · talion
24:20	112	CH	2 · talion

NUMBERS

5:11–31	110	CH	2 · adultery
	110	CH	4 · ordeal
	123	MAL	4 · ordeal
5:12–22	110	CH	2 · adultery
	110	CH	5 · oath taken
5:17	342	Mari	5 · ritual drink
	342	Mari	4 · trial by ordeal
6:3	256	Ninkasi	2 · beer
22:1—24:25	132	Balaam	1 · prophecy
	132	Balaam	6 · Balaam
22:28–30	65	Anubis	1 · fable
	68	Anubis	5 · talking animal
24:2–4	132	Balaam	6 · Balaam
25:4	184	TP III	2 · impalement
27:1–11	49	Nuzi	4 · daughters inherit
27:17	249	Ur	2 · no shepherd
28:7	256	Ninkasi	2 · beer
30:2	69	Anubis	4 · oath before divine patron
31:3–6	179	Shalmaneser	3 · campaign annals
36:1–12	49	Nuzi	4 · inheritance
	49	Nuzi	5 · marriage contract

DEUTERONOMY

1:17	234	Farmer	2 · unjust judge
4:34	148	Amarna	2 · mighty arm of deity
5:19	107	CH	2 · theft
6:6	302	Amen-em-ope	1 · admonition
	302	Amen-em-ope	2 · fill

Citation	Page	Text	Parallel
23:15–16	93	Ramesses II	2 · fugitive slaves
	102	Shulgi	2 · fugitive slaves
	108	CH	2 · fugitive slaves
24:1	126	MAL	2 · divorce
24:1–4	110	CH	2 · divorce
24:7	107	CH	2 · kidnapping
24:12–17	355	Yavne-Yam	1 · law
	355	Yavne-Yam	2 · pledge garment
24:16	120	MAL	2 · sentencing
24:20	156	Gezer	2 · olive harvest
25:4	309	Ahiqar	2 · worker's wages
25:5–10	115	Hittite	1 · law (will)
	118	Hittite	5 · levir
	125	MAL	5 · levir
	272	Baal	1 · law (levir)
25:11–12	121	MAL	2 · genitalia
	121	MAL	4 · female taboo
26:12	156	Gezer	2 · harvest
	156	Gezer	5 · distribution
25:13–15	109	CH	2 · false scales
27:20	111	CH	4 · incest
27:20, 22–23	111	CH	4 · incest
29:6	256	Ninkasi	2 · beer
31:8	171	Tell Dan	2 · deity processes before
32:6	267	Baal	2 · creator
32:11	76	Aqhat	2 · soaring bird
32:14	199	Arad	2 · new wine
32:38	72	Aqhat	1 · sacrifice
	72	Aqhat	5 · feast
33:17	274	Baal	2 · goring bull

JOSHUA

2:6	156	Gezer	2 · flax
6:1–16	83	Kirta	5 · seven day siege
6:17–24	347	Wen-Amun	4 · sacred property
6:26	86	Kirta	1 · curse
	86	Kirta	2 · rebuilding
	175	Karatepe	1 · curse
	175	Karatepe	2 · rebuilding gate

CITATION	PAGE	TEXT	PARALLEL
11:39–40	330	Ishtar	4 · mourning ritual
13:1–23	61	Hatshepsut	1 · annunciation
13:1—16:31	151	Ramesses III	1 · annals
13:2–3	71	Aqhat	3 · barren wife
13:4, 14	256	Ninkasi	2 · beer
15:1–8	333	Love Songs	5 · determined lover
15:11–13	148	Amarna	5 · handing over rebel
16:3	332	Ishtar	5 · gate posts removed
19:22	174	Karatepe	2 · evil men
20:38	203	Lachish	2 · signal fire
21:25	338	Neferti	2 · selfishness
	338	Neferti	3 · anarchy

RUTH

CITATION	PAGE	TEXT	PARALLEL
1:1—4:22	159	Babatha	5 · widow's rights
2:2–9	302	Amen-em-ope	1 · law
	302	Amen-em-ope	3 · widows and orphans
	302	Amen-em-ope	5 · widow gleaning
2:14	199	Arad	2 · sour wine
2:23	156	Gezer	2 · harvest
3:3	326	Love Songs	2 · anointing hair
	333	Ishtar	2 · anointing with oil
	333	Ishtar	5 · washing and anointing
3:13	84	Kirta	1 · oath
4	118	Hittite	1 · law
	118	Hittite	5 · levir
	272	Baal	1 · law (levir)
4:11–12	85	Kirta	1 · blessing

1 SAMUEL

CITATION	PAGE	TEXT	PARALLEL
1:1—4:1 + 7:3—8:13	151	Ramesses III	1 · annals
1:2–17	71	Aqhat	3 · barren wife
1:4	72	Aqhat	2 · sacrificial portion
1:9–18	61	Hatshepsut	1 · annunciation
1:11	82	Kirta	1 · plea
	82	Kirta	2 · son
1:15	256	Ninkasi	2 · beer

CITATION	PAGE	TEXT	PARALLEL
28:3	117	Hittite	5 · witch
	128	MAL	5 · witch
30:27	198	Arad	6 · Ramoth-Negev
31:10	191	Sennacherib	2 · impalement

2 SAMUEL

1:2	69	Anubis	4 · mourning ritual
1:27	78	Aqhat	1 · eulogy
	78	Aqhat	2 · mighty fallen
2:18–23	16	Enuma	1 · taunt
	16	Enuma	5 · single combat
3:31	76	Aqhat	5 · tearing of robe
5:6–8	15	Enuma	1 · taunt
7:1–17	265	Baal	4 · propaganda
	265	Baal	5 · house for divine patron
7:13	269	Baal	1 · covenant
	269	Baal	4 · divine right rule
7:14	82	Kirta	4 · father role
8:1–12	261	Ebla	1 · royal annals
	261	Ebla	5 · conquest list
8:2	169	Mesha	5 · sacrifice of captives
8:9	179	Shalmaneser	6 · Hamath
8:15	106	CH	3 · just king
10:4	123	MAL	5 · beard shaved
10:6	179	Shalmaneser	1 · annal
	179	Shalmaneser	5 · alliance
12:16	132	Balaam	2 · fasting
13:4–6	324	Love Songs	5 · fake illness
13:19	69	Anubis	4 · mourning ritual
14:1–20	248	Ur	1 · petition
	248	Ur	3 · widows and orphans
15:1–6	81	Kirta	5 · son's revolt
15:1–14	86	Kirta	5 · king's flight
15:2	73	Aqhat	2 · gate
	73	Aqhat	4 · place of justice
15:4	233	Farmer	1 · law
	233	Farmer	2 · petitioners
15:21	150	Amarna	1 · oath

CITATION	PAGE	TEXT	PARALLEL
16:21–28	168	Mesha	1 · annal
16:23–24	169	Mesha	6 · Omri/Samaria
16:24	174	Karatepe	5 · building/naming of city
16:29—22:40	178	Shalmaneser	1 · annals
17:1	39	Atrahasis	2 · drought
	133	Balaam	2 · drought
17:12–16	302	Amen-em-ope	2 · oil
	302	Amen-em-ope	4 · hospitality
18:36–45	270	Baal	2 · rain
	270	Baal	5 · divine patron brings rain
18:42	268	Baal	3 · subjection
	268	Baal	5 · face in knees
20:1–11	15	Enuma	1 · taunt
21:1–14	231	Farmer	5 · plot to steal
21:23–24, 27	213	Elephantine	1 · curse
	213	Elephantine	2 · eaten by dogs
22	263	Baal	2 · divine assembly
22:17	249	Ur	2 · no shepherd

2 KINGS

3:4	168	Mesha	6 · Mesha
3:8	198	Arad	6 · "Way of Edom"
3:15	349	Wen-Amun	1 · prophecy
	349	Wen-Amun	5 · ecstasy
	344	Mari	1 · prophecy
	344	Mari	5 · ecstasy
3:22	184	TP III	2 · blood-red water
4:8–17	71	Aqhat	3 · barren wife
4:34–37	85	Kirta	1 · miracle story
	85	Kirta	5 · cure
5:7	74	Aqhat	5 · granting life
5:10–14	85	Kirta	1 · miracle story
	85	Kirta	5 · cure
6:9	203	Lachish	1 · prophetic warning
8:11–12	166	TP I	2 · pregnant women
	166	TP I	5 · pillaging
9:1—10:28	170	Tell Dan	6 · Jehu
9:1—10:33	178	Shalmaneser	1 · annals
9:1—10:36	181	Shalmaneser	6 · Jehu

CITATION	PAGE	TEXT	PARALLEL

1 CHRONICLES

11:2	106	CH	2 · shepherd
12:15	342	Mari	2 · east and west
17:1–14	265	Baal	5 · house for god
27:32	290	Khety	2 · scribes

2 CHRONICLES

6:22–23	69	Anubis	4 · oath before divine patron
9:8	106	CH	2 · justice
11:5–10	188	Azekah	6 · Azekah
19:6–7	236	Farmer	1 · law
	236	Farmer	2 · bribes
29:1—32:33	193	Siloam	1 · annal
32:30	194	Siloam	6 · tunnel
36:10	197	Nebuchadnezzar	6 · new king chosen

EZRA

1:1–4	208	Cyrus	6 · temple funds
2:44	199	Arad	2 · Keros
6:1–5	214	Elephantine	1 · decree
	214	Elephantine	5 · rebuilding temple
6:1–15	208	Cyrus	6 · temple
6:3–5	208	Cyrus	1 · decree
	208	Cyrus	5 · rebuilding temple
6:15	196	Nebuchadnezzar	2 · month
6:20	210	Elephantine	2 · Passover
7:6, 11	290	Khety	2 · scribes
8:23	213	Elephantine	5 · fasting
	213	Elephantine	4 · mourning ritual
8:33	198	Arad	6 · Meremoth

NEHEMIAH

| 1:1 | 196 | Nebuchadnezzar | 2 · month |
| 1:2 | 210 | Elephantine | 6 · Hanani |

CITATION	PAGE	TEXT	PARALLEL
2:5	213	Elephantine	1 · petition
4:1	214	Elephantine	6 · Sanballat
7:2	210	Elephantine	6 · Hanani
7:47	199	Arad	2 · Keros
8:18	71	Aqhat	5 · seven-day ritual
9:1	213	Elephantine	5 · sackcloth and fast
	213	Elephantine	4 · mourning ritual
13:4	200	Arad	5 · housed in temple

ESTHER

2:9	264	Baal	2 · cosmetics
2:12	326	Love Songs	2 · anoint hair
3:2	147	Amarna	5 · obeisance
3:7	196	Nebuchadnezzar	2 · month

JOB

1—2	263	Baal	2 · divine assembly
1:5	222	Declarations	1 · curse
1:13–19	81	Kirta	5 · death of family
1:20	76	Aqhat	4 · mourning ritual
	76	Aqhat	5 · tearing robe
2:12	272	Baal	4 · mourning ritual
3:1–3	304	Ahiqar	1 · curse
3:16	42	Atrahasis	2 · stillborn child
3:17–19	225	Soul	2 · death's release
5:26	238	Farmer	1 · analogy
	238	Farmer	3 · stages of life
7:9–10	332	Ishtar	2 · no return
7:13–14	251	Ur	2 · bed's comforts
7:16	25	Gilgamesh	3 · shortness of life
8:5–7	241	Friend	2 · good to come
8:10	304	Ahiqar	2 · danger of teaching
10:2	237	Farmer	1 · appeal to deity
10:8–9	302	Amen-em-ope	1 · creation story
	302	Amen-em-ope	2 · potter's clay
10:9	271	Baal	2 · dust of grave
10:20–22	237	Farmer	2 · afterlife
	237	Farmer	4 · concept of death

CITATION	PAGE	TEXT	PARALLEL
11:7	242	Friend	2 · depths of god
14:5	25	Gilgamesh	3 · shortness of life
	278	Aten	2 · days numbered
14:7–14	237	Farmer	2 · afterlife
	237	Farmer	4 · concept of death
15:2–4	242	Friend	2 · unwise words
15:5	243	Friend	2 · lying mouth
17:12–13	332	Ishtar	2 · darkness
18:5–21	241	Friend	2 · wicked perish
18:13	333	Ishtar	2 · consuming disease
18:18	332	Ishtar	2 · darkness
19:25	273	Baal	1 · assurance
	273	Baal	2 · life
19:25–26	237	Farmer	1 · appeal to deity
20:17	273	Baal	2 · streams of honey
20:20	236	Farmer	2 · eyes
21:2	242	Friend	1 · address mode
21:7–16	240	Friend	2 · wicked prosper
21:23	81	Kirta	3 · unexpected death
22:7	221	Declarations	2 · hungry
23:4–7	228	Soul	2 · fair hearing
24:4	232	Farmer	5 · thrust poor off path
24:12	236	Farmer	2 · refuse to hear
24:13–17	307	Ahiqar	2 · darkness/crime
24:20	26	Gilgamesh	2 · worm
29:12	240	Friend	2 · orphan
30:2	307	Ahiqar	2 · what good?
31	219	Declarations	3 · oath of clearance
31:3	220	Declarations	2 · just deserts
31:9	221	Declarations	2 · adultery
31:13	220	Declarations	2 · false witness
31:16	221	Declarations	2 · feeding poor
31:18, 21	220	Declarations	3 · orphan
31:24–25	222	Declarations	2 · greed
33:6	302	Amen-em-ope	1 · creation story
	302	Amen-em-ope	2 · potter's clay
33:15	82	Kirta	1 · dream theophany
34:15	26	Gilgamesh	5 · dead return to dust
36:26	267	Baal	1 · title
	267	Baal	2 · untold years
38:16	266	Baal	2 · springs of sea

CITATION	PAGE	TEXT	PARALLEL
39:5–8	309	Ahiqar	2 · wild ass
39:26	76	Aqhat	2 · soaring birds
42:2	271	Baal	3 · submission
	271	Baal	5 · hero surrenders
42:10–15	85	Kirta	5 · new family
42:10–17	81	Kirta	5 · reversed fortunes

PSALMS

1:3	296	Amen-em-ope	2 · tree
1:4	295	Amen-em-ope	3 · contrast
2:12	35	Atrahasis	5 · kissing feet
	209	Cyrus	5 · kissing feet
7:10–11	69	Anubis	2 · divine judge
8	11	Enuma	1 · creation story
8:1	278	Aten	1 · hymn of praise
	278	Aten	2 · how majestic
8:2	306	Ahiqar	2 · child
	306	Ahiqar	3 · unexpected wisdom
8:7–8	278	Aten	2 · all creatures
10:6	75	Aqhat	3 · false pride
11:2	307	Ahiqar	2 · shooting bow
15	106	CH	3 · just king
15:5	300	Amen-em-ope	2 · bribe
16:9	265	Baal	2 · glad heart
19	11	Enuma	1 · creation story
21:4	74	Aqhat	2 · asking for life
22:22–26	233	Farmer	1 · hymn of praise
22:29	26	Gilgamesh	5 · dead return to dust
24:8	166	TP I	3 · divine warrior
24:9	268	Baal	1 · exhortation
	268	Baal	2 · lifting up heads
25:17	233	Farmer	1 · legal petition
28:9	244	Friend	2 · shepherd
29	263	Baal	1 · cosmic battle
29:10	266	Baal	2 · source of flood
29:11	175	Karatepe	1 · blessing
31:9	244	Friend	2 · help in distress
34:9	240	Friend	2 · fearing God
35:11	148	Amarna	1 · plea

CITATION	PAGE	TEXT	PARALLEL
	148	Amarna	2 · accusers
35:22	356	Yavne-Yam	1 · plea for justice
37:14–15	342	Mari	5 · weapons broken
37:16	316	Ankhsheshonq	1 · "Better" proverb
	316	Ankhsheshonq	3 · being satisfied
39:6	297	Amen-em-ope	3 · greed
41:3	86	Kirta	2 · sickbed
42:1	271	Baal	2 · spring/deer
49:14	271	Baal	2 · lure of death
50	11	Enuma	1 · creation story
52:7	297	Amen-em-ope	3 · greed
57:1	252	Ur	2 · storms
57:4	268	Baal	2 · tongues like swords
59:5	213	Elephantine	2 · evil plotters
61:6–7	175	Karatepe	1 · blessing
62:10	297	Amen-em-ope	2 · riches
	297	Amen-em-ope	3 · greed
	308	Ahiqar	3 · greed
63:11	72	Aqhat	2 · mouths
64:2, 7	307	Ahiqar	2 · shooting bow
64:3	268	Baal	2 · tongues like swords
68:4	269	Baal	2 · cloud rider
	77	Aqhat	2 · cloud rider
68:5	86	Kirta	3 · widows and orphans
	263	Baal	3 · widows and orphans
68:16	271	Baal	2 · envy of ruler
69:12	256	Ninkasi	3 · drunken fools
69:17	244	Friend	2 · distress
69:21	199	Arad	2 · sour wine
72:17	175	Karatepe	1 · blessing
	175	Karatepe	2 · name enduring
74:13–14	270	Baal	5 · slaying leviathan
	270	Baal	5 · parting waters
	15	Enuma	2 · sea serpent
74:19	251	Ur	1 · deliverance prayer
79:3	253	Ur	2 · blood
82:1	84	Kirta	2 · divine assembly
	263	Baal	2 · divine assembly
82:2	86	Kirta	5 · judge unjustly
82:7	75	Aqhat	2 · mortality
83:15	188	Azekah	2 · hurricane

CITATION	PAGE	TEXT	PARALLEL
22:17–18	294	Amen-em-ope	1 · admonition
	294	Amen-em-ope	2 · heart
22:20	302	Amen-em-ope	1 · admonition
	302	Amen-em-ope	2 · study
22:20–21	293	Amen-em-ope	2 · thirty
22:22	294	Amen-em-ope	2 · robbing poor
22:24–25	298	Amen-em-ope	2 · bad company
22:26–27	299	Amen-em-ope	1 · admonition
	299	Amen-em-ope	2 · forgiving debt
22:28	296	Amen-em-ope	2 · landmark
	296	Amen-em-ope	4 · property taboo
22:29	302	Amen-em-ope	2 · skill
23:1	283	Ptah-Hotep	2 · table manners
23:1–3	284	Ptah-Hotep	2 · table manners
23:4–5	297	Amen-em-ope	2 · striving/greed
	297	Amen-em-ope	2 · riches/wings
23:6–8	298	Amen-em-ope	2 · vomit
	298	Amen-em-ope	3 · waste
23:9	310, 313	Ankhsheshonq	2 · fools
23:10	296	Amen-em-ope	2 · landmark
	296	Amen-em-ope	4 · property taboo
23:13–14	303	Ahiqar	2 · discipline
24:23–26	234	Farmer	2 · corrupt judge
25:11	283	Ptah-Hotep	1 · analogy
25:13	283, 285	Ptah-Hotep	2 · reliability
25:15	306	Ahiqar	2 · king's tongue
25:21–22	295	Amen-em-ope	2 · feeding hungry
26:2	304	Ahiqar	2 · word
26:3	304	Ahiqar	5 · beating servants
26:7	283	Ptah-Hotep	1 · analogy
26:17	315	Ankhsheshonq	2 · quarrel
27:1	299	Amen-em-ope	2 · worry
27:3	306	Ahiqar	3 · comparison
28:19	307	Ahiqar	2 · work and eat
28:20–21	234	Farmer	2 · corrupt judge
29:13	302	Amen-em-ope	2 · poor and rich
	302	Amen-em-ope	3 · fate
29:14–16	86	Kirta	1 · law
	86	Kirta	3 · widows and orphans
	86	Kirta	5 · king's justice
29:19	311	Ankhsheshonq	2 · disciplining servant

CITATION	PAGE	TEXT	PARALLEL
4:9	331	Ishtar	2 · jeweled necklace
4:10	323	Love Songs	2 · love/wine
4:13–14	264	Baal	2 · henna
5:1	323	Love Songs	2 · intoxication
5:2–6	324	Love Songs	2 · door/latch
	324	Love Songs	3 · double entendre
5:8	324	Love Songs	5 · lovesickness
7:5	323	Love Songs	2 · hair snare
	323	Love Songs	3 · trap
7:8	326	Love Songs	2 · breasts
7:9	322	Love Songs	2 · breasts
7:13	323, 324	Love Songs	2 · mandrake
	323	Love Songs	3 · love garden
8:2b	323	Love Songs	2 · drink

ISAIAH

CITATION	PAGE	TEXT	PARALLEL
1:5	202	Lachish	2 · being sick at heart
1:7	254	Ur	5 · devastated land
1:11	307	Ahiqar	2 · what good?
1:17	73	Aqhat	3 · widows and orphans
	86	Kirta	3 · widows and orphans
1:21	338	Neferti	2 · murder
3:18–23	333	Ishtar	5 · finery removed
5:6	156	Gezer	2 · pruning vines
	39	Atrahasis	2 · witholding rain
5:11+22	256	Ninkasi	2 · beer
5:13	254	Ur	1 · prophecy
	254	Ur	2 · Woe!
5:14	271	Baal	2 · death's mouth
5:29	153	Ramesses III	2 · roaring lions
6	263	Baal	2 · divine assembly
6:1	263	Baal	2 · deity enthroned
6:10	237	Farmer	2 · see/not see
9:2–3	340	Neferti	2 · people rejoice
9:6	72	Aqhat	5 · birth of son
10:2	86	Kirta	1 · law
	86	Kirta	3 · widows and orphans
10:13	106	CH	2 · raging bull
10:15	305	Ahiqar	2 · obey authority

CITATION	PAGE	TEXT	PARALLEL
	173	Karatepe	4 · universal rule
45:9	305	Ahiqar	2 · challenge
45:13	209	Cyrus	2 · god's chosen
	209	Cyrus	5 · exiles freed
45:23	148	Amarna	2 · bowed knee
46:11	76	Aqhat	2 · bird of prey
51:17–18	72	Aqhat	5 · solace a drunk
51:8	26	Gilgamesh	2 · worm
	26	Gilgamesh	5 · worm eats dead
54:1	42	Atrahasis	2 · barren women
56:12	256	Ninkasi	2 · beer
58:2–3	240	Friend	2 · prayer
60:14	148, 149	Amarna	2 · obeisance
63:3–6	264	Baal	3 · divine war
	264	Baal	5 · wading in blood
64:8	62	Hatshepsut	2 · divine potter
	302	Amen-em-ope	1 · creation story
	302	Amen-em-ope	2 · potter's clay
	302	Amen-em-ope	4 · anthropomorphism

JEREMIAH

CITATION	PAGE	TEXT	PARALLEL
1:6–9	306	Ahiqar	2 · good sense
	306	Ahiqar	3 · unexpected event
1:10	15	Enuma	1 · investiture
	15	Enuma	2 · power
4:31	251	Ur	1 · plea
5:12	243	Friend	1 · false teaching
5:17	58	Kamose	2 · loss of produce
6:1	203	Lachish	2 · signal fire
7:9	221	Declarations	1 · list
	221	Declarations	3 · legal restrictions
7:18	330	Ishtar	2 · Queen of Heaven
7:33	180	Shalmaneser	5 · unburied bodies
8:2	253	Ur	5 · unburied corpses
8:18	202	Lachish	2 · sick at heart
9:4–5	227	Soul	2 · neighbor
	227	Soul	3 · anarchy
9:19	249	Ur	2 · city walls
9:21–22	253	Ur	5 · dead in squares

CITATION	PAGE	TEXT	PARALLEL
11:16	296	Amen-em-ope	2 · tree
11:19	266	Baal	2 · lamb/slaughter
12:1	241	Friend	2 · wicked prosper
13:23	309	Ahiqar	2 · professions
	309	Ahiqar	3 · order in life
15:7	274	Baal	2 · winnowing
16:4	253	Ur	5 · unburied bodies
16:6	272	Baal	4 · destruction ritual
	272	Baal	5 · mourning
	338	Neferti	2 · no mourners
17:5–8	296	Amen-em-ope	2 · tree
18:2–6	35	Atrahasis	1 · creation story
	35	Atrahasis	2 · potter's clay
	35	Atrahasis	4 · anthropomorphism
19:2	338	Neferti	5 · civil strife
20:1	198	Arad	6 · Pashur
21:1–10	153	Ramesses III	3 · divine warrior
21:5	148	Amarna	2 · mighty arm of deity
23:5	339	Neferti	3 · redeemer king
25:34	133	Balaam	5 · flocks in disarray
26:22	203	Lachish	6 · Elnathan
28:3, 6	169	Mesha	5 · sacred vessels seized
29:1–2	197	Nebuchadnezzar	6 · exiles and loot taken
31:38–40	255	Ur	1 · petition
	255	Ur	2 · restoration
34:1–7	208	Cyrus	6 · Jerusalem
34:6–7	203	Lachish	6 · Azekah/Lachish
34:7	188	Azekah	6 · Azekah
37:7–10	196	Nebuchadnezzar	6 · Egypt
37:21	198	Arad	2 · bread ration
40:10	156	Gezer	2 · reaping fruit
49:36	252	Ur	2 · winds
51:2	274	Baal	2 · winnowing
	274	Baal	4 · divine justice

LAMENTATIONS

1:2	251	Ur	2 · no comfort
1:17	251	Ur	1 · supplication
2:2–3	251	Ur	5 · divine destruction

CITATION	PAGE	TEXT	PARALLEL
2:8	132	Balaam	5 · divine destruction
2:9	249	Ur	2 · gate
	249	Ur	4 · site of justice
2:10	132	Balaam	2 · garment
	132	Balaam	3 · reversal
	132	Balaam	4 · mourning ritual
	213	Elephantine	2 · sackcloth
	213	Elephantine	4 · mourning ritual
2:11	76	Aqhat	2 · weeping
2:21	253	Ur	2 · scattered bodies
3:2	133	Balaam	2 · darkness
3:31–33	254	Ur	2 · restoration
4:4	253	Ur	2 · daughter
	253	Ur	3 · anarchy
4:22	200	Arad	6 · Edomite invasion
5:15	253	Ur	5 · joy turns to sorrow

EZEKIEL

CITATION	PAGE	TEXT	PARALLEL
3:17	337	Neferti	2 · sentry
8	345	Mari	5 · desecrated temple
8:1—11:25	330	Ishtar	2 · Tammuz
8:14	263	Baal	4 · mourning ritual
	334	Ishtar	2 · Tammuz
	334	Ishtar	4 · mourning ritual
9:4	336	Neferti	2 · regret
10:18	345	Mari	5 · deity abandons temple
10:18–19	208	Cyrus	5 · deity's departure
13:13	252	Ur	2 · stormy winds
17:5–6	296	Amen-em-ope	2 · tree
17:15	203	Lachish	5 · ambassadors to Egypt
22:7	86	Kirta	1 · law
	86	Kirta	3 · widows and orphans
23:3	322	Love Songs	2 · breasts
26:11	153	Ramesses III	2 · trampling hoofs
27:8	180	Shalmaneser	6 · Arvad
27:30	272	Baal	4 · destruction ritual
	272	Baal	5 · mourning
27:32	249	Ur	1 · wail

CITATION	PAGE	TEXT	PARALLEL
	173	Karatepe	2 · rising sun
	173	Karatepe	4 · universal rule

TOBIT

1:1—14:15	303	Ahiqar	1 · wisdom
	303	Ahiqar	3 · restored fortune
1:21–22	303	Ahiqar	2 · Ahiqar

JUDITH

13:2–9	79	Aqhat	3 · revenge
	79	Aqhat	5 · murder

THE WISDOM OF SOLOMON

1:15	231	Farmer	1 · teaching
	231	Farmer	2 · justice
	231	Farmer	3 · eternal things
8:13	231	Farmer	1 · teaching
	231	Farmer	2 · justice
	231	Farmer	3 · eternal things
10:21	306	Ahiqar	2 · child
	306	Ahiqar	3 · unexpected wisdom
18:15–16	305	Ahiqar	2 · word like sword

SIRACH

6:7	283	Ptah-Hotep	2 · friend
8:1	308	Ahiqar	2 · contend/powerful
9:1	283	Ptah-Hotep	2 · wife
11:8	286	Ptah-Hotep	2 · interrupting
19:7, 10	285	Ptah-Hotep	2 · repeating nothing
22:9	310, 313	Ankhsheshonq	2 · fool
22:15	306	Ahiqar	2 · sand and salt
22:27	311	Ankhsheshonq	2 · guard your words
24:15	227	Soul	2 · myrrh
27:16–19	304	Ahiqar	2 · word

SUBJECT INDEX

More Praise for *Old Testament Parallels: Laws and Stories from the Ancient Near East*

"The book's most distinctive didactic tool...is its "Parallels Chart"...a carefully compiled list of over four hundred parallels to biblical passages in the nonbiblical literature.... It should help beginning students bridge the gap in a responsible way between the contemporary world of Western post-modernism and the premodern world reflected in the literature of Israel and her neighbors.... Old Testament Parallels deserves a wide reading."

—Michael S. Moore, *Restoration Quarterly*

"...this material never fails to be stimulating.... Matthews and Benjamin are active contributing scholars.... They are diligent and personable. We are even more in their debt."

—Dan Gentry Kent, *Southwestern Journal of Theology*

"...the book has an attractive format with many line drawings. Useful appendices include a bibliography which directs readers to in-depth treatments of the selected texts, several brief outlines of ancient Near Eastern history, and a parallels chart which lists in its four columns: chapter and verse citations from the Bible, the page of this book which contains a parallel, the name of the ancient work, and the way in which it parallels the biblical text."

—John F. Brug, *Wisconsin Lutheran Quarterly*

"...the texts are presented in a 'reader-centered translation.' Short introductions and commentaries are provided, and references to Old Testament passages are noted. The comments are balanced and the authors avoid jumping to rapid conclusions.... There is also a bibliography for the extra-biblical texts and a very clear chart paralleling the biblical and extra-biblical texts.... this very useful and affordable book can be highly recommended to students."

—Walter Vogels, *Eglise et Theologie*

"The book concludes with history outlines for Mesopotamia, Egypt, and the Israelites, a bibliography of the cited texts and picture sources, and a useful index of biblical passages which not only gives the page where the biblical text is cited, but also the name of the parallel text and the nature of the parallel offered. The index itself has thus become a useful reference tool."

—David Baker, *Ashland Theological Journal*